COLD

STORAGE

Wendell Rawls, Jr.

SIMON AND SCHUSTER NEW YORK

Copyright © 1980 by Wendell Rawls, Jr.
All rights reserved
including the right of reproduction
in whole or in part in any form
Published by Simon and Schuster
A Division of Gulf & Western Corporation
Simon & Schuster Building
Rockefeller Center
1230 Avenue of the Americas
New York, New York 10020
Designed by Irving Perkins
Manufactured in the United States of America
Printed and bound by The Book Press, Inc.
1 2 3 4 5 6 7 8 9 10

Library of Congress Cataloging in Publication Data

Rawls, Wendell, Jr.
    Cold storage.

    1. Farview State Hospital.   2. Psychiatric
hospital care—Pennsylvania—Biography.
3. Rehabilitation of criminals—Pennsylvania—Biography.
I. Title.
RC445.P4F34   365'.9748'36   79-21926

ISBN 0-671-24287-3

For my good friends

Acel Moore
  Who had the source
John Carroll
  Who listened to him
Steve Lovelady
  Who had the touch
Gene Roberts
  Who had the vision

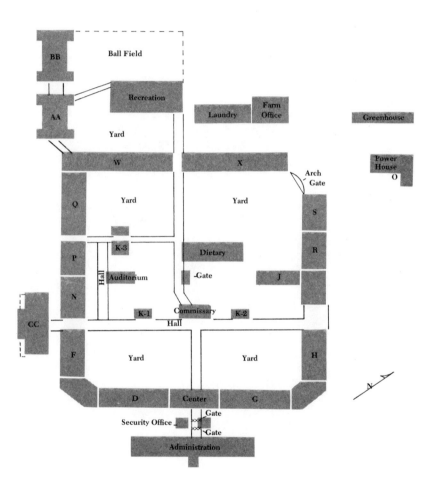

Z

BB

Ball Field

Recreation

Laundry

Farm Office

Greenhouse

AA

Yard

Power House

O

W

X

Arch Gate

Q

Yard

Yard

S

K-3

R

P

Dietary

J

Auditorium

Hall

Gate

N

Commissary

CC

K-1

K-2

E

Hall

F

Yard

Yard

H

D

Center

G

N

Security Office

Gate

Gate

Administration

Prologue

Of all the creatures that were made, he [man] is the most detest-
able. Of the entire brood he is the only one—the solitary one—
that possesses malice. That is the basest of all instinct, passions,
vices—the most hateful. . . . He is the only creature that inflicts
pain for sport, knowing it to be pain. . . . Also in all the list, he
is the only creature that has a nasty mind.

—MARK TWAIN

IT WAS an hour or two past deadline for the first edition of the
Philadelphia Inquirer one evening in the early spring of 1976. I
was sitting at a typewriter, but was looking through the windows
to the traffic on Broad Street when Gene Roberts, the executive
editor, ambled up and lowered into a chair in front of me.

"Whatchu know?" he asked, scratching at the blue oxford cloth
of the button-down-collar shirt that covered the stomach of one
of the two or three best newspaper editors in the United States,
at least.

I don't remember what banality I uttered in response, but he
didn't seem to be listening anyway. He had something on his

9

mind, and after what seemed like an hour but was really only a couple of minutes of his staring through me, his mind returned to the newsroom, perhaps from some place that sells Chinese porcelain. He grinned his half-sheepish, half-mischievous grin and asked, "Are you married to coverin' politics?"

I was scheduled to finish the piece in my typewriter—something about a super-rich couple from Pittsburgh who had kidnapped their children from each other as part of a mean custody fight—then pick up Jimmy Carter's presidential campaign as it left the New York primary and entered the Pennsylvania primary. Then I was to stay with the campaign for the duration, whatever that would mean. I looked at Roberts, but he continued before I answered.

"I mean, if you thought there was a better story would you like to do *it?*"

He knew the answer without my affirming, and he started telling me about a man who had called Acel Moore, another reporter, and how Acel had met with him two or three times outside the newspaper office before the man could be persuaded to come inside and tell his story to an editor. The man did not like or trust white people and he did not want to come inside and talk to any. Roberts told about how John Carroll, the metropolitan editor, had agreed to give the former mental patient ten or fifteen minutes and ended up listening to him for two hours.

As the newspaper described the incident in the nomination letter to the Pulitzer Prize curator:

"Weeping, he told of horrors witnessed a decade earlier—of bloody human cockfights staged to amuse the guards, of men being beaten again and again by guards until they died, of murdered men being certified as heart attack victims.

"He also told of his long search for someone who would listen to him. For more than two years, he had been telling his story to the state police, the F.B.I., the state attorney general's office and other agencies—but no one took him seriously.

"It all seemed farfetched. But months of investigation by Moore and Rawls proved it to be true. What the patient had seen, it turned out, was merely a glimpse of the whole picture.

"For decades, Farview had been a place of murder, brutality, falsified medical records and corruption."

The next evening, Acel and I talked to the former patient for more than three hours with a tape recorder running throughout. For every incident he described, we asked for corroboration, names, whereabouts, places, dates, times. He had some of the answers, but as we later saw with virtually every other former Farview patient we interviewed, he could identify guards only by nickname. The reason for that, we learned, was that the guards almost never wore name tags or any other form of identification. As recently as the spring of 1978, that continued to be the practice at the hospital.

After the interview, Roberts decided that Acel and I should take two or three weeks to see if any of the former patient's allegations could be verified. Then, if we thought it was worth pursuing, we would start our investigation in earnest and see what we could come up with in a couple of months' reporting.

The reporting required about three months in all, during which time the original source was shadowed by plainclothes policemen, often arrested on spurious charges while he was on errands for his employer, and detained for hours. Policemen would interrupt him with "interrogations" at his work and would park their cars near his employer's front and rear entrances. He received telephone calls late at night from state police investigators, and when he met Acel and me for lunch, policemen would sit at an adjacent table and pull back their suit coats to expose a pistol.

At the same time, Acel received telephone threats against his former wife and his young son.

During the three months of the investigation, we interviewed about 200 people. We went to Colorado Springs, Mobile, Chicago, Los Angeles, Missouri, New York, New Jersey and throughout Pennsylvania to talk to witnesses and gather information. We talked to everyone we could find who knew anything about Farview. Everyone except Pennsylvania Governor Milton J. Shapp. He refused to talk to us.

The investigation disclosed that Farview State Hospital was not a hospital at all. Officially, it was Pennsylvania's institution for the criminally insane. But in fact, it had been a warehouse where an odd assortment of inmates—some criminal, some insane, some neither—were kept out of society's sight. It was not a pleasant place. Troublemakers, or those who looked as if they might be troublemakers, paid a high price. Sometimes it was a beating, or two beatings, or years of beatings. Sometimes it was death.

Farview, we discovered, was a place where a commitment could become a life sentence, where some men were put away forever.

The initial series of newspaper articles was published in June and July, 1976. Not a single fact in it was ever challenged. Some in the present hospital administration, about whom this book is not written, claimed that the institution had made significant recent improvements, but conceded past abuses. Their most common complaint was voiced in a single question: "Why are you writing about what went on in the past?"

The answer was simple then and is now. A society well-informed about abuses that have occurred is better prepared, if it cares, to prevent abuses from occurring in the future.

I left the *Philadelphia Inquirer* in 1977 and joined the Washington Bureau of *The New York Times*. But Farview victims and their families continued to emerge with stories to tell about what had happened inside the Farview they knew.

Their stories and those reported in the newspaper have led, some three years later, to this book. Like the newspaper articles, *Cold Storage* is based on scores of interviews and thousands of pages of documents, some of which were obtained long after the series was published, for use specifically in this book.

Those interviewed include former and present guards, hospital administrators, physicians, state officials, state policemen, attorneys, social workers, psychiatrists, university researchers, special prosecutors, politicians, judges and, of course, former patients in the hospital. The documents include numerous previously suppressed state police reports, grand jury findings, coroner's jury hearings, investigations by a special Pennsylvania State Senate committee, academic research studies and federal government reviews. In addition, there are things I witnessed firsthand in visits to the hospital.

To the best of my knowledge, everything in *Cold Storage* is true. All the names, except for Acel Moore's, have been changed, along with identifying features of the people involved. Many of the patients are still alive and have a right to privacy. The families of those who died at Farview have the same right. The guards, doctors and some of the patients are composites of two or more people who were in the hospital in the past.

I have made selections from some two decades of events and compressed them into little more than a typical year inside Farview. I have re-created some scenes and have written about people's thoughts and feelings. The scenes are based on factual accounts of what actually occurred, and the thoughts and feelings were expressed or described by former guards, patients and relatives of murdered patients.

Some of the dialogue has been re-created in order to maintain the narrative and tempo of the book, but much of it was taken from interviews or directly from documents, letters, memoranda, reports and sworn testimony.

For me this format was necessary in order to take the reader behind the brick walls and barred windows and into the minds of those who lived and died inside Farview, a place where man's inhumanity to man was limitless and where everyone, staff members and patients alike, had to live every day in a system based on hustles, extortions, thefts, brutality and fear.

When the cornerstone was laid for the construction of the hospital on July 24, 1909, Dr. Charles G. Wagner, superintendent of the State Hospital for the Insane at Binghamton, New York, had this comment:

"If there were places of this kind available, there would be no longer any excuse for the deplorable practice of placing the insane even temporarily in common jails where, often, regardless of sex or mental disturbance they are grossly ill-treated. . . . Concentrated effort on behalf of the individual patient will be the watchword of the future.

"Your wards will be well-ventilated apartments, lighted by electricity, heated by steam and comfortably furnished, with carpetings on the floors, pictures on the walls and draperies at the windows; for all of these things help to banish the idea of prison bars and to make an environment that tends to aid the recovery of the patient."

That isn't quite the way it worked out at Farview.

PART I

The vilest deeds like poison weeds
Bloom well in prison air:
It is only what is good in man
That wastes and withers there:
Pale Anguish keeps the heavy gate
And the warder is Despair.
                    —OSCAR WILDE

1

THE CAR moved steadily up the long, winding grade, the wiper blades slinging water aside in the monotonous slap, slap, slap of synchronized metronomes, the tires hissing like angry vipers as they slid through the thin sheen on the narrow, curving highway. The man alone in the back seat peered through the rain-streaked window on his left and watched God urinate on the world.

He had always felt that way about rain. Snow was different. It was quiet and soft and slow and fun when he was a boy. Not rain. Rain, he thought, was a pain in the ass. He remembered his mother explaining that rain was God's way of giving the world a bath. He remembered that baths were a pain in the ass, too, when he was a boy.

His father never saw rain the same way his mother had. For him, rain was the difference between making a crop and not. Sometimes it would rain for days and days at the wrong time, making it impossible to put plow or seed in the soggy ground in the spring or get the straggling results out of the field in late summer. At other crucial times God would deny the world a bath for a month or more. To the day he died, his father read the skies and cursed them as regularly and as devotedly as his mother read the Bible and praised it.

"It's God's will," his mother had repeatedly insisted.

"Well, why does He sucker me into planting something He ain't going to let grow anyway?" his father had always asked.

Garth agreed with his father. Rain was just God's way of relieving Himself when it did Him the most good, not when it helped the poor bastards below.

The car slowed when it reached the top of Moosic Mountain, and turned right. He lifted his meaty hands to swipe again at the steamed right rear window, and the short, shiny chain clinked against the glass. He could make out a blurred dark mass of thick, dripping woods that had bordered the highway all the way up the mountain. Glancing quickly back to the left, he saw a sign on what seemed to be a low gray stone wall or a grave marker. As the car rolled along he could get a quick focus on only two words: *Farview* and *Hospital.*

He looked through the windshield but could not see the hospital immediately. Then suddenly it loomed through the mist as the car curved around the trees. It was an immense sort of Victorian-style red-brick and granite structure. Viewed from afar, it could have passed for a monastery or military school. There were some small buildings ranged about the main structure, and one of them, the first one the car reached as it passed through the open, unattended gate in the high chain-link fence, resembled a college dormitory. Garth slid his muscular bulk across the back seat and wiped at the left rear window.

The mountainside dropped gradually away from the hospital in gently rolling hillocks over which the eye could travel for miles on clearer days. Small white barns and farmhouses dotted the distance. Earlier in the fall the changing leaves had turned the hills into piles of gold and rubies and emeralds. But now, in late November, the hospital stood like an ominous fortress over dreary, rugged mounds of hard, ugly browns and grays.

Garth didn't know what, exactly, he had expected this place to look like, though he had mused about it off and on during the long trip. Actually he had thought more about what the inside would look like than the outside. He didn't figure on seeing the outside but twice—coming and going. It was the inside that worried him. He had been stunned earlier that morning when told his destination. Even so, when he read the words on the sign just now, he was jolted anew.

Farview . . . Farview . . . Farview. The word caromed through his brain like a billiard ball in a fresh break. To him Farview was a concept. An image. A bewilderment. The prison grapevine was like a four-party line in a rural telephone system and Farview was as talked-about as a knocked-up preacher's daughter. What he had heard about Farview was considerable, and he had seen the mere threat of being sent there set a hardened inmate to apologizing for all real or imagined transgressions, and to promising to keep his feet on the path of righteousness for all future time.

It never took long for a man behind The Walls to learn that Farview was more than an asylum for the criminally insane. In prison, when inmates and guards referred to it they described it as a place to do hard time, a place where the uncontrollable were controlled, the unbreakable broken. Or else they never came away.

He thought the reputation was probably exaggerated, because prisoners, like soldiers and drugstore Casanovas, tended to hyperbole. But he was apprehensive nonetheless. It was supposed to be a hospital, but why had he always heard it referred to by so many ominous names—the Place of No Return, Hell, the Animal Farm, Auschwitz, the Last Stop?

He lifted his iron-cuffed hands to his eyes and rubbed them. His mind raced back to the events of the previous day, trying to sort out what had happened to bring him to this place. He knew he had made a mistake, but he had not expected it to come to this.

*

The morning before, he had dipped the mop into the bucket and lifted it without pulling the dingy strands through the wringer attachment. Gray water splashed onto the concrete floor and he pushed it in slow, quarter-moon strokes from the wall on one side to the bars at the front of the cells on the other. For six years it had been the same thing every morning and he had not understood why from the second day.

"Don't these handles fit anybody else's hand?" he asked the tall skinny guard, who stood mute, arms folded across his ribs, as he had stood every morning for six years. The guard had stopped answering the questions years before.

"Why don't you fake an injury, Wade?" he asked the hulking inmate. "Them headaches don't seem to be getting you out of much mopping." The mop stopped its slow arc from wall to bars and the inmate straightened.

Garth was scarcely more than six feet tall, but at thirty-two he was thick and square and hard. He looked like two or three stacks of cinder blocks mortared together, with a block placed on top for a head. But the head was not solid cinder. Questions came out of it, and most of them began with the word *Why*, as in "Why do I have to mop every morning while the rest of these birds sit on their asses?" The questions were always challenging and rarely answered.

He looked menacingly at the guard, but he resumed his mopping and became more conscious of the two-month-old throbbing behind his right eye. The headaches were not contrived, and a prison doctor had prescribed medication. The pain was not constant but it was occasionally intense and the medication helped. Four times a day a guard brought him a capsule from the dispensary. At least twice a day, when a behemoth guard named Johnson brought the pre-breakfast and pre-lunch capsules, Garth swallowed a snide remark with the pill. Johnson had not brought a pill before breakfast today and Garth's request to visit the dispensary had been met with "You just start mopping, they'll be around in a while."

When he saw Johnson come through the doorway and into the cellblock, relief and resentment alternately flipped through his cinder-block head.

"Where you been?" he asked, too eagerly and almost belligerently.

"What do you think I am, your fucking servant?" Johnson shot back. "You want this pill or do you want to bitch?"

Garth glowered but he extended his arm slowly toward Johnson, palm turned up. "The pill," he said.

Johnson held out the capsule but dropped it deliberately short of Garth's hand. It whirled end over end like a placekicked football and hit the wet floor between them. Garth stood motionless, arm still extended. He stared at Johnson. His eyes turned smoky and the muscles below his prominent cheekbones tightened spasmodically. He sensed rather than saw the guard's leg move slightly, and he dropped his eyes to search the floor for the pill. The guard's boot blocked his view of it but he heard the shell snap as the capsule was crushed underfoot.

A series of millisecond sensations made bobsled runs behind his eyes. He sensed that all eyes on the cellblock were riveted to him and Johnson. He knew that the other inmates expected him to do something and in the periphery of his vision he saw the tall, skinny guard unfold his arms and begin to move toward them. He knew that his brother, behind him at the end of the cellblock, would want to help him but would stand agonized and do nothing. He knew he was about to extend an already too-long prison term.

His thick plumber's fingers, chapped and scaly with thin purple cracks at the knuckles, tightened around the mop handle. The cracks turned faded lavender as his fingers whitened on the worn wood. He took a slow step backward and dropped the extended hand to join the one on the handle. Almost in the same motion the mop became a pugil stick and the knot of wet cords smacked hard into Johnson's face just above his gleaming white bicuspids. The guard's head jerked back and his body followed it. Garth turned the mop into a thin, five-foot bat and as the huge guard raised his hands to protect his face Garth moved forward and redirected the sweep of the bat, the hard, wet knot end digging into Johnson's ribs. The black guard doubled over, stumbled backward, and fell. Discarding the mop, Garth sprawled atop the groaning guard and cocked his fist for delivery from above his right shoulder.

The guard saw the fist coming and brought his hands before his face. The fist slammed into Johnson's fingers once, but before Garth could reload, guards were upon him. He twisted and pulled.

"I'm gonna kill that nigger bastard," he shouted again and again as the guards wrenched him away from Johnson. The shouts turned to a painful shriek as one guard pulled Garth's left arm behind his back and bent the wrist so that the thumb almost touched the forearm. As he was being pulled backward along the cellblock, Garth heard the other inmates deriding the guards for their five-on-one tactics and taunting them to "let 'em fight it out. You scared he'll whip your man's ass?" Garth also noted that none of the shouters had made a move to help him. At the end of the cellblock his brother was no longer leaning against the wall, but he had taken no steps toward the fracas.

Garth managed a sarcastic grin despite the pain in his arm and somehow, he realized, his head didn't seem to ache as much.

*

One of the best things about solitary confinement, Garth decided, was that he did not have to mop the floor. And it was quiet enough for a man to sleep. There was little clanging of doors, or commodes flushing or guards' heeltaps *click-clack*ing along the corridor. There was privacy. Time to be alone. Time to think. He had never taken much time for serious thinking and often, as with Johnson, he reacted in his gut before the light came on in his head. More often than not, he was in the middle of a situation before he'd taken the time to plan his involvement.

He figured that the men on his cellblock already had divided his belongings, such as they were. There was not much to divide, he knew. Some cigarettes, clothes, shaving gear, magazines, a Bible, a picture of his sisters, Irene and Ruby, and some letters they had written. He knew he could not depend on Leonard to salvage anything. He could see his brother standing helplessly— and silently—as the others took what they wanted.

Garth's immediate reaction when somebody tried to filch his stuff was to grab a fistful of shirt, and chest hair if there was any, and slam the poacher against the bars. But he didn't need any more trouble after his bout with Johnson. He decided that he would be calm when he went back to the cellblock, find out what was gone that he cared about, find out who had taken what, and deal with them one at a time in a good way and in a good place. He would make a plan, for a change.

He didn't figure anybody would want the picture of Irene and Ruby, and that was the only thing he really cared about. His sisters had been more upset about his having to go to prison, he felt, than they had been about the other three brothers. They regularly wrote letters to him and asked him to give Leonard their good wishes. The two other brothers were in a different prison, so he did not know what kind of letters they got. They didn't get any from him. He wrote only to Irene and Ruby. Most of the time he told them about what was going on with Leonard, and sometimes he asked how the other two brothers were getting along.

Four brothers in prison. Sometimes he would grin outright when he thought about it. Other times he was saddened by the concern and disappointment that he knew his mother had felt while she was alive. He wondered if four brothers in prison at the same time for the same crime was any kind of record. He guessed not.

The prison status sheet did not explain what they'd done but simply listed burglary, larceny, breaking and entering, auto theft and resisting arrest. Lying on the bunk, his eyes closed and his hands clasped behind his head, Garth remembered again about the crime and grinned in the darkness. It surely didn't take much to put him under state care.

*

The four of them had been drinking homemade wine in their father's back yard one steamy August evening and they "got a little high"—a condition to which Leonard was particularly prone and a rationalization which the judge quickly discarded. Drunk and broke, they decided to go to the farm of a prosperous and well-connected Pennsylvania Dutchman outside of Lancaster and take some burlap bags from his barn. They planned to sell them for ten cents apiece. They thought it would be funny as hell to sell them to somebody who might resell them to the farmer. That rich prick could afford it.

They walked to the farm, entered the barn, which was un-locked, loaded about six hundred bags in the bed of the farmer's pickup truck, hot-wired it, and wove their way to another farm where, one of the brothers had heard, there was another pile of bags. They took about three hundred bags from that man's barn, then careened along a country road, back to the scrubby front yard of the Wade hovel. They parked the truck and went inside to stumble into bed.

When police saw the missing truck in the front yard the next morning, they refused to listen to explanations and acquiesced to the truck owner's demand that the four men be arrested. Garth refused to be handcuffed and a struggle ensued. Leonard broke loose and ran about ten groggy strides before he was tackled to the ground. The four men were held in the county jail for several months before trial because there was not enough money available to them or their father to arrange bail.

The judge, a longtime political crony of the first farmer, turned away every attempt at plea bargaining, saying he was unable to detect remorse in Garth's contention that the event was more a humorous escapade by four grape-headed drunks than a serious crime against society. After guilty verdicts were returned, the judge announced that sentences would be indeterminate—between ten and twenty years in a state penitentiary.

Garth thought it a high price to pay for burlap bags. As he lay now in solitary confinement he was not aware that the price was about to rise.

*

A key rattled in his cell door and he looked up to see the face of a guard leering at him.

"Let's go, Wade," the face said.

"Where to?" Garth asked as the door swung slowly open. He stood and scratched his head.

"Back to your block to get all your shit together," the guard said.

"Why?" Garth rubbed his eyes, wincing in the brighter light of the hallway.

"You're leaving."

Garth tried to smooth his hair with his hand, then jammed his shirttail into his pants as he walked through the doorway at the end of the corridor. Another guard was holding the heavy metal door and he grinned rather pleasantly, Garth thought.

"Thought you might be with us a little longer," the doorkeeper said. "Did you leave your key at the desk?"

Garth never had stayed at a hotel, but he recognized the facetious reference. He did not smile.

"Leaving?" he asked the guard who accompanied him. "Transferred?" The guard nodded absently, still looking ahead. "Where to?"

"Someplace where they can handle guys who like to fight guards," the guard said. He turned to Garth. "This is about the third or fourth guard you hit, ain't it?"

"Second," Garth replied. "The other time was another bird. Two in six years and both times they was fucking with me for no reason." They walked in silence. "So where's this place where they can handle me?"

"You'll find out soon enough," the guard said. "But I'll say this, it's a long ride and they tell me it ain't much fun when you get there."

"What's the big secret?"

"Ain't no secret. It just ain't my job to tell you. My job is to get you ready to go."

It did not take Garth long to gather his belongings. As he suspected, everything had been distributed except his Bible and the picture of his sisters. He started to leave the Bible, but didn't. Leonard appeared at the cell door.

"What's going on?" he asked.

"They're transferring me," Garth said.

"Where to?"

"I don't know. Said it was a long ride. Probably to Graterford. I shouldn't a hit that nigger guard, I guess. Probably cost me some time."

Leonard nodded. "I shoulda helped you," he mumbled.

"No, it was my fight. You'd a just got into trouble, too. But I'll tell you something," Garth said, lowering his voice and glancing over his shoulder conspiratorially, "solitary ain't bad for a while." He grinned, his big yellow-and-brown teeth barely discernible between his lips. "I gotta go. If you write Irene or them, say they moved me and I'll write myself soon as I know where I am."

Leonard handed him two packs of Pall Malls and, without as much as a handshake, Garth turned and walked away.

*

The car cruised slowly past a tiny building which could have been expected to house a security officer, though none was there, and continued along the drive beside the massive main hospital complex.

Looking up from the car window, Garth could see four levels of windows. Those at the bottom were not as tall as those in the middle two rows, and the windows at the fourth level were set only in the huge gables that protruded from the slate roof. They served mostly an ornamental purpose in that they looked out from the attic much as the bottom row did from the basement. There were other, smaller windows set here and there along the building. Every window he could see was striped with big, heavy-looking bars.

As the car swung around to the front of the hospital, Garth looked again at the bucolic scene, away from the ominous structure, and was reminded somewhat of the pastoral Amish landscape where he grew up, near Lancaster.

He thought briefly of his sisters and wondered if they would be able to find their way to see him here. He remembered the deputies in the front seat saying something about the hospital operating a farm and thought that perhaps he could be assigned to work outside if he established a record of good behavior. He could tell the warden or whoever ran this place that he had grown up on a farm. Maybe that would help. He quickly recalled how much he had despised grubbing in his father's fields, but he just as quickly decided that it was better than mopping floors every day.

The throbbing behind his right eye claimed his attention. He had been faintly aware of it when he awoke from a brief nap in Carbondale. Jesus, what a grimy, shithole of a town that looked like. He had heard inmates make jokes about towns and conjecture that if God were going to give the world an enema he would stick it in Cleveland or Pittsburgh or Camden or Trenton or Newark. Apparently none of those men had ever been to Carbondale.

"If this is a hospital, maybe they can find out what's causing these headaches I been having," he said as the car pulled around the administration building and stopped in front of heavy, dark-stained wooden double doors. Above the doorway, he saw the word RECEIVING carved in the stone. The driver stopped, turned off the engine, looked at his partner, and winked.

"They'll probably work on your head, all right," he said. "I hear they're pretty good at that up here." The deputies got out of the car and opened the right rear door. Garth swung his feet out the door and onto the pavement. Then he leaned forward to stand. He hunched his shoulders, twisted his head a time or two, and lifted each knee to get out the kinks from the long trip. He turned back into the car, reached his cuffed hands down to the floorboard, and picked up his Bible and the picture of his sisters.

Each deputy placed a hand above one of his elbows and together they guided him toward the double doors. Garth ran his eyes up the expanse of brick to the roof for one final look at the outside.

The door was opened by a heavyset man wearing a powder-blue short-sleeve shirt, a black bow tie, and dark trousers. Garth walked past him and stiffly climbed four or five marble steps before going through an arch that opened onto a hallway. Down the hall to the left he could see out the windows of the administration building entrance, the main entrance to the hospital. Through the windows he could see an almost empty parking lot.

The deputies turned him to the right and he stood before a set of thick steel bars that reached from floor to ceiling, wall to wall. Another man dressed in black and blue was standing at the bars beside a tall table on which lay a thick ledger book, where visitors signed in and out. On the other side of the bars stood a third beefy man, similarly dressed in what clearly was the hospital guard uniform. He twisted a key in the gate lock.

The two deputies registered, then guided Garth through the opened gate, followed by two of the Farview guards. Garth was briefly amused that he was handcuffed with four men in uniforms surrounding him. I bet they didn't have this many people around Lee Harvey Oswald, he thought. Then another man in black and blue came out of an office off the left side of the hall and stood in the doorway. He took a packet of papers from one of the deputies and opened it.

Garth looked straight ahead down the hallway and saw another barricade of bars stretched across it, with yet another guard standing on the other side. Behind him, Garth heard the tall gate clang shut.

"What did you bring us this time?" asked the guard who had come out of the office.

"Hot Shot here likes to mix it up with prison guards," one of the deputies said. "Knocked hell out of one at Western. The warden there says he has trouble getting along with people in authority."

"We get a lot of them kind here," said the guard, looking at the papers. "You fellas hungry? Why don't you go on to the dining room and get something to eat. We'll take care of this one. You know where it's at, don't you? Ernie here can show you."

"I think we can make it," the driver said. "We just go on down the hall and turn left at the kitchen, don't we? You sure you don't want us to stay here for a few minutes?"

"No, we can handle him," the guard said, looking at Garth, eyes the color of a new axe blade moving from the shackled man's face to his shoes and back. "Take them cuffs off and leave your pieces here in the office," he said to the deputies. "We'll lock them up and you can get them on your way out."

The deputies left Garth standing in the hallway and went into the office. Another guard was sitting at a desk. They took the pistols from their holsters and laid them on the desk. The guard selected a key from a crowded ring and inserted it into a drawer lock. He put the pistols in the drawer and relocked it.

The deputies walked back into the hallway. One of them unlocked Garth's handcuffs and removed them. He then looped them over his belt in the middle of the back. The deputies walked toward the second set of bars, were allowed through by the turnkey on the other side, and ambled toward the dining room.

The guard holding the packet of papers turned back into the office. "Bring him in and strip him," he said over his shoulder.

Garth had been massaging his wrists since the removal of the handcuffs. He looked at the guards, nervously glancing from one to the other in a measuring sort of way. They seemed to be poised for some kind of move from him. Their eyes, he noted, had been on him every time he had looked at them. One of them gave him a light shove in the middle of the back and said, "Get your ass in there and take them clothes off."

Garth had been through strip searches before and was not surprised at being subjected to one before he entered the hospital population. He removed his clothing and was again aware of a fear that nagged him every time he had to strip like this. He desperately did not want to get an erection in front of these men. Finally he was naked.

"Bend over and spread your cheeks," one of the guards said. This was a procedure that always amused him. He was determined that when he got out of prison he would not take any kind of job that required him to look at another man's asshole.

"Sit down and keep your mouth shut."

"So you like to hit guards, huh?" The axe blades flashed with the question from behind a desk where the guard stood. There was no doubt he was in charge, though he wore no bars or stripes.

(Matter of fact, none of the guards wore badges or name tags or any insignia that could identify one from another.) The others deferred to him. "Looks like this was the second guard you hit at Western. And . . ." he seemed to drag out the words, "you beat up another inmate and fought with the cops when they arrested you. You must think you're pretty tough, huh?"

Garth remained silent. He felt foolish and vulnerable sitting naked in the chair before the standing guards.

"You think you're a bad ass?" The guard's eyes narrowed perceptibly.

Still Garth said nothing. At the moment, he did not feel like a bad ass. He felt humiliated. He wanted to cross his legs or cover his genitals, but he felt that nothing looked so foolish as a naked man with his legs crossed, and he did not want to appear self-conscious. He gradually turned his head and saw the other guards watching him, seeming to enjoy his discomfort. One of them grinned menacingly.

"Think he'd like to try some of us, Lieutenant?" he asked, seemingly more for effect than in expectation of an answer.

"When I ask you a question, boy, you answer me," the lieutenant said. "And you say, 'Yes, sir,' and, 'No, sir.' "

"No, sir," Garth said. He could feel the air thicken with hostility.

"No, sir, what?" the lieutenant spat back.

"I don't think I'm a bad ass and I don't want to fight anybody." Garth was trying to be careful not to sound antagonistic. Not at five to one. Strange, he doubted that the guards were all that much older than he, but he felt immature, like a child getting a threatening dressing down.

"This is a hospital, boy." The Lieutenant sort of rocked back on his heels, then rocked forward, a little more assured of his position, a little more relaxed. "You look like a nice young buck. We got some rules here. You follow the rules, everything will be okay. You step out of line, you'll get your head busted. You keep your nose clean and your mouth shut, you'll get along okay. You want to start some shit, you'll get all you want. We don't take no backtalk. You want to get out of here alive, you just do as you're told."

He looked at Garth, the axe blades glinting in a long, challenging stare. Then he dropped his eyes to the desk top, looking at the Bible and the picture of Garth's sisters. He picked up the picture, removed the backing, and slid the photograph from the frame.

"Can't have this frame," he said to one of the other guards as though he were aware of something the other guards had not noticed. "Could make a weapon out of something like this." He jammed the photograph between the pages of the Bible and handed it out for one of the guards to take.

"Where do you want him?" asked the guard who took the book.

"On D-Ward," the lieutenant answered. "They got room, don't they? They got two or three up in R-Ward, sick. He can take one of the empty beds."

Garth did not follow the exchange. He was looking out a window, noticing that it not only was striped with thick steel bars, it was also covered with a heavy wire screen. Outside, the daylight had waned to a dull gray. He was tired from the trip, and the pain behind his eye was intensifying. He was hungry. He turned back to the now-silent lieutenant.

"Can I get something to eat and something for a headache? I got a bad headache."

The lieutenant raised his lake-ice eyes. "You missed supper. You can wait for breakfast."

"Can I at least have some aspirin? At Western they was giving me pills for this headache. You can check my records."

The lieutenant leaned forward and placed his fists, knuckles down, on the desk top. He was not particularly tall, maybe two or three inches shorter than Garth, and about thirty pounds shy of Garth's two hundred. But he had an intimidating, overbearing, almost bullying demeanor that rushed to the fore when he felt his authority challenged and when he knew he was backed up by bigger, stronger companions. He never became visibly angry. He became outwardly frigid and inwardly delighted at the chance to force his will on another.

He dropped his head toward the papers on his desk, leaving Garth to look at the top of his hair, a sleek, slightly wavy black pelt flecked with strands of stainless steel shavings. Garth could not see his slight smile.

"You ain't at Western, boy." The voice was flint-hard. "You at Farview from now on."

2

PAUL KIRCHOFF was trying to read his Bible, but he seemed unable to concentrate. He took off his glasses and held them away from his face to get a better look at the smudge on the left lens. He laid his worn book beside him on the oak bench, and the pages, soiled and wilted, lay open.

He picked up the tail of his stretched, dingy T-shirt and began to grind it into the lens. It was a futile activity and he knew it. The smear had been there for more than three years, yet reflexively he wiped at it with his shirttail at least two dozen times a day.

For a while, whenever a doctor visited D-Ward and Kirchoff was permitted to see him, he would point out the smudge and ask to have the glasses polished. In fact, he had started out asking to have the lens replaced. All his requests were routinely ignored, without a doctor ever looking at the lens. Most of the time the doctors did not even look at him. Mostly they kept their eyes focused on some kind of bureaucratic-looking form or other paper on the table in the little office off the ward dayroom. The office was supposed to be the nurse's station, but since there was no nurse, it was used by the charge guard, and the doctors would borrow it for the few minutes they visited almost every day.

Nobody, not even hospital personnel and supervisors, referred to the little room as the nurse's station, unless there were visitors about. It was the charge's office and the guard in charge of each of the three shifts occupied it. He ran the ward from there.

For the past two years, in an attempt to get around the doctors' indifference and get what he wanted, Kirchoff had been complaining that his eyes bothered him and asking for an examination. He assumed that whoever administered such examinations would at least look at the damned lens. He hoped that the examination would be administered by someone from outside the hospital, like it was seven years before, when he got his glasses.

On the rare occasions when he was allowed to see a doctor, his requests for an eye examination had been greeted with a "Yeah, yeah, we'll have the ophthalmologist look at them when he comes." It was just another way of routinely ignoring his requests, since an ophthalmologist had not been to the hospital since he received his glasses. Of course, one could be living at the hospital and he might not know about it, Kirchoff thought. But he doubted that the hospital would allow an ophthalmologist around unless forced to do so. What the patients couldn't see, they couldn't talk about.

Sometimes Kirchoff felt that his requests were niggling anyway. He knew of one patient who was slowly going blind with cataracts while the doctors made meaningless scratches on their papers. The only time Kirchoff had gotten any kind of reaction to his lens problem was when a doctor used the other patient as an example of how much worse things could be. That was not really true, he remembered. Dr. Zundel also had reacted to his request for an examination.

"You're just crazy as a shithouse rat," Dr. Zundel had said. But he said the same thing to every patient. That was his diagosis of every complaint from hangnail to hypertension to hallucination.

Kirchoff smiled bitterly at the memory of Dr. Zundel's consistent response. He had mentioned it once to the social worker, whom he had seen maybe a dozen times since he had been in

Farview. The man had half shrugged and half nodded and acknowledged that he had heard it before. Kirchoff had asked the
social worker how such an attitude affected the doctor's prescriptions of psychiatric therapy for the patients, and the man had
replied, "Not much. Dr. Zundel's not a psychiatrist, so he
wouldn't know much about therapy anyway . . . even if he cared
about it. He just prescribes whatever medication the guards tell
him."

Kirchoff later learned that none of the other doctors were psychiatrists either, except Dr. Dallmeyer, the hospital superintendent. But Dr. Dallmeyer was rarely seen on the wards. Kirchoff
had seen him a few times but had never spoken to him. Some of
the men who had been called before the staff for evaluation said
that he had been in the meeting but didn't say much. Kirchoff
did not know much about that. He had never been up before the
staff.

He looked at his glasses again and saw that the shirttail he had
used as a napkin at supper had made the lenses greasy. He looked
for a cleaner place on the shirt and belched. A harsh, acrid taste
filled the back of his mouth. It was the taste of tomato-based bile,
and he was reminded of the thin red sauce that had drenched the
gluey spaghetti at supper. He couldn't tell whether it was the
glasses or the heartburn that affected his concentration.

He looked around the ward dayroom, searching for some other
excuse, but everything he saw was pretty much as it had always
been, whether on this ward or any of the others where he had
spent roughly half his life.

He surveyed his world. Before him, walking in an oval around
the six thick, square pillars in the center of the cavernous forty-
by-one-hundred-foot room, were about half the hundred or so
patients assigned to D-Ward. Some merely shuffled along, heads
down, like derelicts searching for stogies. Others stared stoically
ahead, eyes burning with stern, almost angry intensity, teeth
clamped in determination as though they were hell-bent to complete one more trip around the pillars.

A few lurched spasmodically along, their arms and legs jerking,
almost clicking in motion as if they were attached to cogwheels.
Their faces were neither fiery nor downcast but were immobile as
masks except for eyes which flicked involuntarily upward. They
were rubbing their thumbs and fingers together as if rolling up

small wads of paper. They looked like victims of Parkinson's syndrome, but they were simply laboring under the effects of massive doses of Thorazine.

Other Thorazine patients were lying on the hardwood floor under some of the eight-foot benches which sat between the pillars and along the walls. Their backs were hyperextended like tightly strung bows.

The guards liked it better for the zombied cogwheelers to crawl under a bench or lie on a bench than to have them stiff-leggedly joggling around the ward, tongues protruding from drooling mouths. The ones on or under the benches were out from under foot and did not bump into other patients and cause disturbances. They did not talk, so they were not difficult to understand. They were out. Under control. Just the way the guards liked them. And nobody had to look at them.

As soon as a man started causing trouble, the guards started giving medication. The doctors would prescribe it, but the guards told them what to prescribe, how much to prescribe, and then the guards administered it. They always found out how much it required to drive a troublemaker to the floor. They kept adding to the dosage until they turned a man into a zombie.

Kirchoff knew that if a man did not want to be cogwheeled, he did not cause trouble, especially for a guard or a guard's pet rat. The rats ran errands or performed special favors for guards, favors that included anything from bringing a sandwich after working in the kitchen to snitching on other patients so that the guard could maintain control or look good in the eyes of his superiors. Occasionally it meant procuring a young patient for a guard's private pleasure.

In return for the favors, rats were given special treatment, which could include a semiprivate room off the corridor leading from the ward, or a good job either on the ward or off the ward in the laundry room or the kitchen or the farm, or the right to use the recreational or craft facilities instead of being confined to the ward dayroom all day.

Rats were hated by the other patients. And feared. But Kirchoff knew that all the music is not played by only one section of the orchestra. Having been a pet rat on more than one occasion during his two and a half decades inside the red-brick walls, he had come to know, and hate, the fear of retribution that pet rats lived with every minute. Not to mention the constant fear of screwing up and being cast back into a ward with no protection.

Kirchoff despised the rats and the role of being a rat, but he recognized it as the only way to improve one's lot at Farview, even if only for a little while, for as long as it took to make a mistake or become the victim of a snitcher who wanted to improve his own position.

It seemed to Kirchoff that he had been looking over his stooped, bony shoulders for almost three decades, constantly wary, self-protective, paranoid. But invariably he had failed to look often enough or diligently enough to keep from becoming implicated in some activity, never mind how minor, real or imaginary, and being bounced from a relatively good job or a relatively easy ward like W or X to one of the rougher ones like P or Q or N or this one. Most recently, another patient had knocked his supper tray from his hands, sending a bowl of soup and a cup of milk crashing to the floor and splashing onto a guard's shoes. The guard slapped Kirchoff and had him transferred from the relative peace of X-Ward to the chaos of D.

The accident also cost him his job in Main Dietary, the kitchen, where he had been in a position to eat good food like the guards ate, and enough of it, without having to bolt it down. Even without the better food, perhaps more important even, working in the kitchen was eight or nine hours off the ward, with the double benefit of being able to make some sandwiches to bring back onto the ward and give the guards and sell to the patients. It was his only source of income, his only means of bartering, the only way he could accumulate money on the hospital book for later use at the candy wagon or the Sears, Roebuck catalog. Not now. Now his job was on the bed-making crew and running the floor polisher on the ward. Neither paid money. For money, he had to shine guards' boots for a dime a pair, or fifteen cents sometimes. Since there were never more than six guards on a ward during any one shift, four during the night, and there were about one hundred patients, you damned near had to kiss a guard's ass just to be allowed to shine his shoes. And you couldn't shine shoes without shoe polish and you couldn't get shoe polish without money and you couldn't get money without having some kind of work that produced cash. Trying to figure a way out of that would drive a man crazy, Kirchoff was fond of saying.

Making beds in the dormitory room above him and pushing the polisher took up about two or three hours of his day. The rest of the time he sat on his bench next to the wall and read the Bible or watched television or walked in the circle. It was called a circle even if it was an oval.

His eyes moved slowly about the ward dayroom, scanning the oaken benches against the faded gray walls. He noticed that a few of the men on the benches had their hands in their pockets, vigorously agitating their privates. They looked like they had mice in their denims, fighting to escape through the fly, but the damp, dark stains betrayed the end results of their activity.

Along the wall to his right, Kirchoff saw a patient standing at one of the barred and screened windows, looking steadfastly into the leaden twilight. Another patient was seated on the floor beside the man, his hand wrapped around and stroking the standing man's stiff penis. He eyes seemed to be focused on some undisclosed target across the dayroom.

Kirchoff looked quickly to see if the guards were watching and saw that they were not. One of the guards was standing in a corner opposite the television set, talking to Dureen, a rat who operated his own canteen, practically a corner grocery. Dureen dealt mostly in cigarettes and young kids, but he also had candy and shoe polish and instant coffee and numerous other items for sale or trade. And cigars, of course. The Hawk liked his cigars and he liked them cheap. Good ones, but cheap. Free was best. Hawk was the guard in charge of D-Ward during the day shift, but in many ways he was the guard totally in charge of D-Ward because the charge guards on the other two shifts generally followed his lead, his philosophy. Hawk's policy usually was ward policy. Some things went on on the other shifts that he might not have approved in advance, but he always was told about them and he always backed up his co-workers. Even if they were wrong and he knew it. But he took no shit from them or from anyone else except his superiors. He talked and acted tough.

He was the one who allowed Dureen to operate and everybody knew it. Hawk never paid for a cigar from Dureen. He didn't pay for a piece of candy either. The guards didn't pay for what they ate or for what ate them, the saying went. They returned the favor by allowing Dureen to operate with impunity among the patients and privately with his own kid in one of the small rooms off the D-Ward corridor.

There were one or two others who operated freely on the ward, Kirchoff knew, including Coda, the greasy-looking, slick-haired faggot dressed in polished-cotton khaki slacks and a pinstripe shirt, who was talking with the shower-room rat across the room. Coda made ceramic doodads in the craft rooms in the basement and sold them for low prices to the guards for Christmas presents or simply for resale outside. He also painted portraits for guards who brought him a color snapshot of a wife or daughter. He made a lot of money and he could get anything he wanted, seemingly at any time he wanted it. He wore a nice watch and gave his kid a nice watch. He wore nice clothes, not the denim trousers and T-shirts with Farview State Hospital stamped on them. And his kid wore nice clothes.

Coda always kept his eyes out for a new kid. But by the time he was finished with one, he usually had provided him with a good job—a way to take care of himself. The shower-room boy was formerly a Coda kid. All he had to do was keep the shower room clean. It was one of two places where the patients could smoke on the ward—there and the bathroom—and he could decide when it was available for a smoke. He could close the shower room at any time, claiming that it was closed for cleaning. About all he had to clean up was cigarette butts. The patients were allowed to shower only once a week.

But the shower-room boy could rent the space for a few minutes of privacy to patients who wanted to be alone or alone with a friend and had nowhere else to go. Sometimes he was the one who wanted privacy.

The clothing-room boy, who ran the room next to the shower, where all patient belongings were kept on small boxlike shelves, and the boy who ran the storeroom upstairs, where all linens and blankets were kept, also maintained a more free and more private life than the average patient on the ward. They too were pet rats for somebody. The storeroom boy had the best job on the ward, however. He had a door to his room. And he could lock it.

Kirchoff looked around the dayroom and couldn't find the storeroom boy. That meant he was upstairs already, probably making hootch. But he did see Malone, a young black man with arms like steel cables and a head like a wrecking ball. Malone was sitting beside another black man Kirchoff knew only as Night Train.

Kirchoff had talked with Malone only a few times and had learned little about him other than that he was a teenager from Pittsburgh who had come to Farview from a juvenile detention center. Kirchoff knew Malone had a job in the kitchen, but it wasn't because he was a rat. He had a shit job. He cleaned the huge pots and vats, he didn't serve food or wait on tables in the guards' dining room. Kirchoff had worked in the kitchen and he knew how that system worked. The guards did not want blacks to touch food before it was served. Only after it became garbage.

Of course, even that job was better than being on the ward all day. And although there were no black employees at the hospital, there were plenty of black patients who would work in the kitchen washing pots and pans just for the chance of some decent food and a smoke afterward.

Kirchoff figured Malone's fists got him the job. They were clenched thunderstorms. The guards enjoyed unleashing them on other patients—usually another black with bottled lightning for a head and sledgehammers for arms, but a troublesome white would suffice if he needed a good lacing and the guards wanted a diversion and a chance to bet a little money.

Kirchoff had never talked to Night Train. He decided that he probably never would. Night Train didn't seem to like white people very much.

Kirchoff ran a hand through his thin, dingy gray hair and rubbed the back of his turkey neck. As he reached for his limp Bible, he heard the ward boy clap his hands twice, loudly. The ward boy, another one of the pets, was assigned the job of watching the door that led from D-Ward to Center. Center was the name given the area one entered past the second set of steel gates, where visitors and new patients went through security. Center was the original building of the hospital complex when it opened in 1912 and it housed the offices of the chaplain, the captain of the guards, a social worker and the sort of conference room where patients were taken for staff interviews, if they were fortunate enough to be selected for such a thing. Center was the hub of official activity.

Surprise visits from Center to D-Ward were not allowed. That was the ward boy's responsibility. His job was a step above that of

bed-maker, at least two steps above pushing the heavy floor polisher that seemed to whirr hour after hour. But God help the fool
who failed to alert the guards to approaching visitors. The guards,
adequately warned, could get out of their rocking chairs and hide
their nudie magazines.

The guards were not so worried about surprise visits by people
from outside the hospital, state officials or the like. The entire
hospital was alerted to those visitors. The ward boys were there
more to warn of incoming superiors or snitching rivals.

The guards were up now, magazines safely tucked beneath
rocking-chair cushions. Kirchoff and the other patients looked
toward the door. Some of those walking in the circle stopped and
others bumped them from behind, causing some minor bickering
and shoving that one of the guards stifled with a quick slap to the
face of the loudest complainer. The man standing at the window
and his seated companion seemed not to have heard the warning.

The door opened and two guards led a solidly built young man
through it. Although Kirchoff was sitting some sixty feet from the
door, he could see that the man was thick in the chest and shoulders, and had a neck as thick as a railroad tie. The arms looked as
if they belonged to a man accustomed to hefting sacks of grain or
cement. His forehead sloped toward a slightly protruding line of
bone above the eyes. He had high cheekbones and a prominent,
almost pugnacious, jawline. His hair was the color of a freshly
dug Idaho potato. To Kirchoff, Garth Wade looked about that
lumpy.

3

In another part of the hospital, Elroy Jones dreaded the approach of another winter in J-Ward. Sitting in the tiny concrete cell, in the corner farthest from the high, open window, he still could feel an occasional spray as the wind curled in on its chilly way south. He drew his naked thighs tighter against his naked chest and wanted to wrap his naked arms around his naked shins. The leather wrist cuffs, attached to the leather strap around his waist, prohibited such movement. His ankles were shackled, too.

He was in every physical respect a tiny man. Had he been brought up around horses, he might have tried to become a jockey. He had weighed only slightly more than 100 pounds when he had been committed to Farview eight years before. Now as he placed his head against his drawn-up knees he was a 90-pound embryo stuck to the corner of a concrete womb where he had been gestating for more than seven of his years in the hospital.

After seven years in the cell in the solitary confinement section of Farview, he was intimately aware of its every detail. He had spent endless hours slowly raking his eyes across each square inch of the gray, peeling wall. He knew where each new crack in the paint began—and when. He had watched them widen and lengthen. He had studied the details of the small, high window and the sky beyond until he knew every shade of blue and gray and purple and the clouds had gone beyond acquaintance practically to gabby neighborliness.

The light in the ceiling, several feet above his nappy head, shone constantly so that he knew night only by the shadings of color in the window. The door was of thick heavy wood, originally a sorrel color but darkened to light bay with the patina of age and the sweat of countless naked backs that had rubbed against it before Jones's matriculation. Centered slightly above his eye level was a three-by-five-inch rectangular opening through which different eyes stared at him at various times throughout the days and nights.

He had come to know the eyes, but he had never really figured out the minds behind them. He had decided that they were as dark as his skin, but he did not know why. He was sure that he was better off, for the most part, when the eyes stayed on the other side of the door.

He shivered and lifted his head from his knees. He scanned the floor for evidence that the spray from the light rain was beginning to cover it. At least it was not January or February, when the temperature frequently fell below zero. He had lost count of the times snow had blown through the window and melted on the floor during the day, then frozen into a light glaze for him to sleep on at night. During those nights his breath produced clouds of vapor that seemed to hang indefinitely and he thought that if he watched them long enough he would see granules of ice fall from them.

It was even worse when the guards decided to hose down the floor, to wash the accumulation of feces, dried sperm and urine into the small drain hole in the middle of the floor. There was a bathroom on the J-Ward cellblock, but much more often than not the guards would refuse to allow the patients to use it. Jones knew that many of the men on the row would relieve themselves wherever in their cells it was convenient, as the stench before a hosedown would attest. But he always tried to hit the drain hole.

Partly because it was a kind of game, a challenge, a diversion, but more because he hoped the guards would decide that his cell did not need hosing like the others. It never worked. The hosings were part of the institutionalism. It was like the army and labor unions and Saturday-night baths. When the guards hosed one cell, they hosed them all, whether they needed it or not.

Often in the winter they would wait until late in the day, sometimes into the night, before turning on the stream from the large, canvas-covered fire hose and soaking the cells and their occupants. Then they would open the windows to the frosty Pocono air and the floor would turn icy.

He looked at the hole. It was pretty clean around the edges. There were only a couple of places where his stool had brushed the side of the hole and had stuck. He almost never missed the hole when urinating. The worst problem about urinating was waking with a piss hard, aching to take a leak. The leather belt and cuffs would not allow his hands to reach down and bend his penis toward the hole unless he got on his knees or sat. Even then it hurt. Yet he would be unable to wait until he became flaccid and often didn't care. When he couldn't wait, he just closed his eyes, imagined that his cell was a South Philadelphia alley, and let fly. Sometimes he would hear a laugh at the door and turn to look through the small slit, where he saw eyes crinkling back at him in amusement.

When his bowel refuse stuck to the side of the hole, he would wait until it dried and knock it in with his toes. He never used his fingers because he had to eat with them when his food was brought, all mixed together in a metal bowl.

God, he did not think he could stand another winter of freezing solitude. But he knew he would not complain. Somehow he had survived seven years and he wanted that streak to continue. It had taken him the first full winter to learn to keep his mouth shut. He'd been repeatedly picked up by a guard and dropped onto the concrete floor every time he said something about the window or the water or the food or the cold. That's why he liked the eyes better on the other side of the door. It seemed that every time they came on this side, he ended up cringing into the cement.

He often heard shrieks from cells along the corridor and knew that somebody was getting an education in J-Ward behavior. Like him, they would learn not to complain. Like him, they would learn not to hit a guard. Or maybe they wouldn't learn and would end up in R-Ward and then on a slab.

He constantly wondered why he had been allowed to survive with occasional slappings and kickings and drops onto the concrete. He didn't know that the guard he had punched seven years earlier wanted it that way, had unofficially prescribed the long, sadistic punishment.

At least he wasn't dead, though sometimes he yearned to be. He clutched his thighs tighter against his chest and laid his chin across his drawn-up knees. God, what he would give for a blanket tonight.

But he had nothing to give.

*

Meanwhile, on R-Ward, Sullins was putting clean sheets on the bed where the geriatric had stopped breathing a few hours earlier. His hands were trembling and his eyes were darting furtively about the ward. It wasn't the fact of the old man's death, or that Sullins was unaccustomed to men dying, even though he was only twenty-six years old. It was the way the old man died that bothered him. That and the fact that he had seen it happen.

Sullins had been in the hospital since he was nineteen and had been working on R-Ward for three years. R-Ward was the medical ward of the hospital, and when men died at Farview that was where they expired. At least that's what the official hospital records showed. Every now and then a patient was carried or dragged into R-Ward from some other section of the hospital and Sullins was sure they were already dead. Certainly they looked like they were, and they might as well have been. Regardless, they did not leave the ward alive. Some who were still breathing when they were brought in breathed on for only a few days. For many it was the only way out of Farview. The ultimate discharge.

Sullins knew that the old man had not been expected to live much longer anyway, sick as he was with emphysema and just plain old age. He had lost all control of the basic bodily functions and was an object of disgust for those who had to clean up after him. But he was not really that much more trouble than some of the other geriatrics, and Sullins thought that if the old man had been in a regular hospital for the past few months something could have been done to help him. Even if he could not have been helped to the point of walking around or even sitting up, he certainly would not have died today.

Still, it was not that he had died, it was the way he died. That was what unnerved Sullins. Only two people knew how death had come. Three, if you wanted to count the victim. But he would never talk about it. So there was only Sullins and the man who did it. Sullins knew that he was not supposed to know, and he wished he didn't. He wished he had been looking in another direction when it happened.

He had been attending another patient not far from the old man's bed. He saw the figure in the long, white medical coat walk past, but he did not pay particular attention. A few moments later, he looked toward the old man's bed and saw the white-coated man standing beside it. Sullins stared in unbelieving fascination as he saw the man reach for the respirator at the old man's mouth and nose and pull it away. In the brief instants he looked, Sullins saw the old man's eyes widen and the face turn to a mask of fear. Then Sullins quickly turned and busied himself. He well understood the code at Farview, not only on the open wards but everywhere else as well. What was not seen could not be talked about—or asked about. Guards did not like knowing there were things that patients could hold over their heads. They never knew for sure if a patient was some other guard's pet and would pass damaging information to make life easier. Sullins assumed that the doctors were no different. He prayed that nobody had seen him watching the man in the long white coat.

He walked away from the patient he was attending and went to a section of the ward far from the dying man, but he could hear the struggling gasps as he walked away. When he looked back, the white coat was gone.

The only other outright killing he had seen, he had participated in. He was a slight, curly-haired teenager, just finished with high school, when he and a buddy met a man in a South Jersey tavern and ascertained two things over a few bottles of beer. One, the man was homosexual. Two, he had some money he was willing to spend.

Sullins and his friend agreed with the man that they should accompany him to his apartment. They agreed with each other that they should beat his ass, take his money, and run. Once there, however, the situation got out of hand and they were unprepared for both the man's ferocity and his strength. As the struggle became desperate and was swinging in favor of the intended victim, Sullins reached for a metal object and began to pummel the man about the head. Fight began to ebb from the man and finally he lay unconscious as Sullins and his friend fled.

They learned later that the man had died, somehow choked to death, and Sullins' fingerprints and the man's blood both were found on a large gilded crucifix.

He and his friend had been sentenced to die in the electric chair. But Sullins decided that if he were doomed to death, he would administer it himself. After an unsuccessful try, he was sent to Farview for observation. He supposed they were still observing him, but they didn't seem to be spending much time observing his mind.

Sullins always had thought of himself as more responsible than not, insecure rather than scared, more intelligent than the average patient at Farview, more observant than the average person, and blessed with almost total recall of things he saw or heard or experienced.

The memories of his first days at Farview stuck in his mind. He knew they would never leave. He was young and scared, then. He had been placed on D-ward initially, and when ordered he had tried to get under the cold shower. Really tried. But he couldn't stand it. When the guards began to kick him, he had screamed and flailed, and when they thought he had been subdued and let him up to resume his shower, he flailed some more. The guards had put him in leather restraints and strapped him to an oaken bench in the middle of the dayroom. He had stayed there through lunch, dinner they called it, and supper.

By bedtime he had settled down enough to have the cuffs removed. The next day he had gone to breakfast, then returned to the dayroom and sat alone on the bench. While he was sitting there, a man in civilian slacks and a button-down-collar shirt sat beside him. The man wore his hair combed straight back with liberal amounts of hair oil holding it in place. He looked like he could have been an emcee at a strip show or a gospel music singer or a Pennsylvania politician.

"You smoke?" the man asked.

Sullins nodded.

"Got cigarettes?"

"No," Sullins said softly.

The man extended a pack. Sullins looked at him and the man smiled.

"Go ahead and take one," the man said. "You'll have to smoke it in the toilet or the shower. Come on."

Sullins followed him into the shower room. They stood there and smoked their cigarettes.

"My name's Coda," the man said. "What's yours?"

"Sullins."

"You need anything, just ask. I can help you out."

"Yeah. Sure."

"I mean it."

"Okay."

Later in the day, two more times in fact, Coda gave him a cigarette. The next day, he gave him a pack.

They were smoking in the toilet when Sullins finally asked, "What do you want from me? Why are you trying to be nice?"

"I like you."

"Bullshit. What do you want?"

"Head," Coda said. "I give head. You go along, I'll give you a nice watch, clothes, coffee . . . whatever you want. You be my kid, I'll take care of you."

"What do I have to do?"

"Nothing."

"You setting me up?"

"Naw, baby . . . all you gotta do is be there. I'll take care of you."

"What if I don't?"

"Then you can go without a lot of things . . . and you can pay me back double for what you've already gotten."

Sullins was beginning to feel trapped. Rolling a queer was one thing. Participating with one was another. He thought of his mother and his sisters and his friends outside, and his face flamed with shame at what they would think if they knew.

"Where do you . . . we do it?"

"In bed."

"When?"

"At night. I'll get you moved to the bunk next to mine."

"Not where everybody can see?"

"Everybody'll know, baby."

Sullins fixed his eyes on the floor. He didn't know what else to say. Then he saw the Helbros watch Coda was extending into his line of sight. He took it.

That night, Bulldog, the evening shift charge guard, told him he was in a different bunk and showed him where it was. Coda was lying on the one beside it. When the lights went out, Sullins lay under his sheet, his body tensed as minutes dragged by. His eyes were squeezed shut. He felt a rush of cool air as his sheet was lifted near his thighs.

Tears glinted in the moonlight as they slid from the corners of his eyes and he turned his face into the dampened pillow.

It did not seem that much time had elapsed when his reverie was interrupted by Dr. Combest, who had been away from the ward for most of the day. The doctor had shouted at him from across the ward and had waved him toward the bed of the geriatric.

"This one's dead," the doctor had said when Sullins walked up. "Take him downstairs and put fresh linens on this bed. I'll get Dog Boy to help you."

Sullins had said nothing. He walked quickly to get a stretcher, and when he returned to the bed Dog Boy was standing there. It was easy to see where he got the nickname. He resembled a salivating albino St. Bernard. A canine mutant. He often whimpered when threatened by one of the guards or an inmate and seemed to slink away from difficulty, his ass dipped as though he were trying to tuck it between his legs. He was crude. A true cur.

"We won't have to clean up no more of this one's shit," Dog Boy said. "I hate it when they start shitting all over theirself and the bed and everything. That's the worst part of this job. It's worse when they thrash around and spread it all over the place. The guards should make them lay in it 'til they can't stand theirself no more."

Sullins said nothing as they dragged the body across the bed and, one at each end, swung it down onto the stretcher. They then carried it to the morgue in the basement and lifted it onto the single table. They stood for a moment, resting and catching their breath. Sullins looked around the room and settled his eyes on the jars that lined the shelves. He was fascinated by the organs drowning in them.

"They not going to do a autopsy on this one, are they?" Dog Boy asked, even though he knew Sullins had no way of knowing.

"Who knows?" Sullins said. "They may want to cut out his lungs and put it in one of these jars so they'll have one that shows what emphysema looks like."

"Well, they won't have to find out the cause of death," Dog Boy laughed. "He shit hisself to death."

Sullins looked at the rotund, fair-skinned man with jowls hanging loosely all the way from his eyes. He did not like Dog Boy and he certainly didn't trust him. Dog Boy had the run of R-Ward and he took advantage of it. He was mean, cruel, and sadistic. He enjoyed teasing sick patients and intimidating young ones. He was an active homosexual, and most of his freedom came from his association with Costello, a male nurse who was almost as large as he was.

Dog Boy had a room on R-Ward, unlike the slight, curly-haired Sullins, who presently lived on X-Ward and came to work on R-Ward each morning. Sullins often saw Dog Boy and Costello repair to Dog Boy's room for thirty minutes to an hour or more at a time behind a closed door. Sometimes they would take a third person with them.

The guards didn't seem to give a damn what Dog Boy did. Probably because he did some of their work and covered for them while they napped. If a patient was causing too much disturbance, the guards would assign Dog Boy to quiet him and Dog Boy eagerly complied. He would run errands for them and steal for them. More important, he seemed to have some kind of pull with their superiors. As a consequence, Dog Boy was surviving quite nicely inside Farview.

Sullins himself had relatively few complaints. He didn't like what was happening around him and he certainly did not like what happened to the old man, but as a rather recent graduate of the Coda school, he was in a good place. Like Dog Boy, he was able to get his hands on pills for sale or trade, and since Dog Boy did not like to shine boots, Sullins had that scam pretty much to himself on R-Ward. So he was never out of cigarettes and through the Coda connection he could get almost anything he needed to make life bearable inside this joint.

He and Dog Boy had returned upstairs after depositing the old man, and he was changing linens. As he picked up the soiled ones, he saw Dog Boy drape his beefy arm around the neck of a fourteen-year-old boy who had been placed on R-Ward ostensibly to protect him from the ravages of the open wards. The problem was that the boy, who had been institutionalized after swinging a little girl by the heels and smashing her head into a tree until she was dead as a sawdust-filled rag doll, enjoyed being ravaged as long as there was something material in it for him. He never hesitated to sell his participation, and once bought, he never hesitated to participate.

Dog Boy sort of carried the boy along and looked for Costello. When he saw the male nurse, he caught his eye and jerked his head toward his private room. Sullins saw Costello nod and walk toward the pair.

The three of them went into the room and closed the door.

4

GARTH WAS startled by what he saw as he stepped into D-Ward. He hadn't realized that he would be placed in one large room with all these other men. He had simply assumed that he would be assigned a cell to himself or with a mate. Actually he had not given the physical setup any real thought at all. Since learning where he was being sent, his thoughts had centered on what the system at Farview would be like, what would be expected of him, what he would have to look out for. Not the layout. He had not thought about that part of it, but if he had, he knew he would have had no way of anticipating this.

There seemed to be no pattern to much of anything going on in the huge room. In the far corner, about halfway up the high-ceilinged wall, a television screen displayed movement but he could hear no sound coming from it. Nor did he recognize the program. It wasn't a western. It seemed to him that there were a variety of muted sounds coming from radios and he thought he recognized snatches of Johnny Cash, then Aretha Franklin. He detected a plinking banjo mixed strangely with some kinds of horns. There seemed to be a steady milling of bodies, some bumping into others, some stopping to look at him or just to sense the atmosphere, like ants hesitating in their meanderings to register what their quivering antennae pick up.

Yet with all the aimless motion there were several bodies lying on benches and on the hardwood floor under them, instantly bringing to mind the stories he had heard at Western from men who had spent nights in fifty-cent flophouses. One man was standing at a window, looking out, while another sat at his feet, staring with glazed eyes in the opposite direction, his feet flipping back and forth like the windshield wipers of the police car that had brought Garth here.

Some of the men grinned at him, while others seemed to gaze through him with the same piercing, unblinking stare he remembered seeing on a crippled owl he had captured as a boy. There seemed to be an endless murmuring, and there were a few louder exclamations that made him jerk his head around in search of the sources.

"Hey, sweet meat!" someone shouted. "I'll kill that muthuh fuckuh!" came another. Garth looked immediately into a large ebony face split by a challenging, leering, almost senseless grin.

Some of the patients were beginning to edge closer and there was a rush of questions coming at him.

"Where you from?" asked a small rodent-faced man with a freshly sheared head of black stubble. "Gimme a cigarette," demanded another.

"You like me?"

"Fuck you!"

"What're you looking at?"

"Shake my hand!"

"I love you."

The questions and epithets came lobbing in like a barrage of mortar rounds, and Garth was momentarily bewildered. He took a slight step backward and tried to make sure nobody got behind him. He was feeling the first stirrings of fright. He had never seen anything like this. When he had first gone to prison he had been greeted more with hostile silence and measuring stares than with such verbal battering.

"Shut it off, you fucking maggots." It was a guard shouting. "Get back! Get the fuck away from here!" He grabbed the arm of one of the men nearest him and roughly shoved him away. The man stumbled backward. One of the blue shirts that had accompanied Garth onto the ward took him above the elbow and presented him, along with a large yellow card, to another guard.

"Here's Garth Wade," said the one with the card. "He knocked the shit out of a guard at Western." He handed over the card and left.

The guard who took the card was sturdy and short-legged. He had a tight seam of a mouth and eyes like wet coal. His dark hair was cut close above the ears and about the neck and he had no sideburns, yet on top it was rather long, parted on the right side, and combed at a sharp right angle from the straight, white line. His heavy face was pudgy and Garth thought he looked kind of like a bulldog.

He held the yellow card in thick, short fingers with dirty nails, and he looked at it for a long minute before moving his hard, bright eyes upward to meet Garth's.

"You mouthy?" he asked. The voice was almost nasal.

Garth shook his head quickly, negatively.

"They tell you out front how to answer, or you being a wise guy?"

"I forgot," Garth said quickly.

"Don't forget again." Then the bulldog face looked toward the shower room and the guard jerked his head backward, summoning the washroom boy, who came quickly.

"Get him a shower and some clothes." Several patients continued to linger around Garth. The guard's face hardened. "I said for you bastards to get away from here. Now move on!"

The shower-room boy moved toward the washroom and Garth followed. He looked back and saw that the guards who had escorted him to the ward had left, but that the eyes of the ones in the dayroom were glued to him. He counted six of them.

At the shower-room door he looked inside and saw that the walls were tiled and that there was a large, round stainless-steel community sink in the middle of the room, with a foot bar to control the water pressure.

"Get your clothes off," the shower-room boy said. Garth was

beginning to wonder if anybody here talked in anything but imperative sentences. Among the guards, words came out in belligerent, threatening barks and growls. There was no subtlety, no understatement, nothing veiled. Looking at the shower room, he remembered a sign in the boys' locker room at his rural high school: "The Best Defense is a Good Offense." Farview had put the slogan to practice, he decided.

As he began to remove his clothing he glanced back toward the open ward. Patients continued to linger nearby and were gradually coming closer again. Then a guard moved toward the shower-room door and another joined him. They formed a two-man shield between Garth and the other patients.

The shower-room boy turned on the water. Garth noticed an eager grin on his face. He looked young, not more than twenty-two or twenty-three, Garth decided. He had a flushed face and looked like he probably perspired heavily. But his wavy brown hair appeared to have been carefully combed and Garth figured him for a punkish drugstore jockey on the outside.

"Get a move on," the shorter of the two guards at the door said.

Garth was down to his underwear and he could feel a cold spray splashing from the floor onto his ankles. He was uneasy as he lowered his jockey shorts. This was one time he damned sure didn't want to get a hard-on.

An off-key symphony of whistles came from behind the guards, accompanied by a chorus of catcalls and derisive observations.

"Look at that white ass!"

"Fresh meat!"

"Whooo, ain't he pretty."

The taller guard turned toward the pressing crowd and shoved his arms straight out into the chest of the patient nearest him. Four or five men were sent sprawling backward and others scattered a few steps away from the door.

Anger was beginning to build in Garth. He was pissed off at what was happening to him. He didn't understand why he had to take a shower, for one thing. He did not like being subjected to any form of humiliation or being made to feel vulnerable. He felt both as he stood naked in the shower room with those leering, whistling bastards as spectators. As during the strip search, he felt the desire to cover himself from view but knew that to do so would only make him look more foolish. He couldn't understand why he was being made to feel like an ass.

*

Kirchoff had not left his bench on the side of the room opposite the washroom. He had seen this scene played so many times—had been in it himself once, of course, too—that he knew what was likely to happen next. The same thing did not happen every time, but almost. It always depended on how the new man reacted and whether he was white or black. When two or three new patients came in at the same time, it usually happened to only one of them. The others learned from that one and were spared a little pain, if not much else. But a man coming in alone almost always reacted from the gut, and he always paid for it. There was no way to warn him, and the man who tried was sure to pay too high a price for his interference.

It was usual procedure for an incoming patient to be given a shower when he came on the ward, although an occasional one missed the experience for some unexplained reason. Ostensibly the shower was for reasons of hygiene, but in reality it served as an introduction to the Farview existence. As far as the guards were concerned, it produced a multiple benefit. Mainly, it firmly established their dominance. It left no question of roles in the master-servant relationship that had obtained at the hospital for most of its half-century or more of existence. The patient learned early, if his mind functioned at all, that an order given was an order to be obeyed, immediately and without question; that punishment from guards would be quick and physical, and pain was the enduring payment for the slightest transgression.

The shower experience taught a patient that he would be punished for breaking rules that he might not even know were on the books, rules that in fact were written nowhere but were cataloged in the minds of the guards. It kept the patients unsteady, unsure of what they were allowed to do, how far they were allowed to go, and always looking to the guards for some sign of approval before, during, and after any act committed in the open. Patients were placed in the position of having to seek some sign of permission for every move, constantly looking over their shoulders, cementing a feeling of fear throughout the hospital.

The new man's shower also served to remind patients already on the ward not to step out of line, and reestablished the fact that the guards could and would act without fear of retribution from their superiors.

Finally, it assured the guards that the patients paid for whatever crimes they had committed against society, especially the ones committed against a policeman or jailer. Some patients had never stood trial for their crimes, having been judged incompetent to do so. They had been sent to Farview to receive treatment enough to make them competent. Others had been declared innocent of their crimes by reason of insanity and had been sent to Farview until such time as they could be safely returned to their community.

Neither circumstance made any difference to the Farview guards. They saw it as a part of their function to make sure that a man paid for his crime, regardless of the court's decision or whether a man had even gone to court. No, a man did not go back to his community without paying his debt. Temporary insanity was bullshit. Nobody would get away with that. Incompetent to stand trial? That was all right. A man did not have to go to trial to be sentenced. Farview was his sentence and he would damn sure serve it. After all, if a man didn't stand trial, he might never be sentenced. That would never do. Farview guards never left something like that to chance. Some judge somewhere had his chance and he had sent the man to Farview, so Farview would see to it that the man paid. By God, he'd pay.

*

Garth stuck his hand under the shower and quickly pulled it back.

"Goddamn, that's cold," he said, shifting his weight back and forth from one foot to the other.

"Get under there," said the taller of the guards at the door. "We ain't got all day."

Garth looked at the shower-room boy and the guards. The guards had their arms folded and the beginnings of scowls creased their faces. Beyond them he saw a group of watching patients begin to break up and walk away. No more taunts. But the shower-room boy was smirking.

"But it's cold," Garth protested.

"I said to get your ass under there," the tall guard said. He took a step toward Garth.

Garth slid quickly sideways under the heavy spray, then jumped just as quickly back out.

"Jesus Christ, it's freezing," he said. "Ain't there any hot water?" He saw that there were no controls on the tiled wall under the shower head. There seemed to be some kind of control near the door, where the shower-room boy was standing.

Now both guards were approaching Garth.

"Don't it suit you?" the shorter guard asked. "You think this is a fucking hotel?" Then he pushed Garth under the shower. Garth sliced through the water, hit the wall, and came quickly back like a boxer springing off the ropes. Too late he saw the tall guard's right arm rise in an uppercut toward his stomach, and with his feet slipping and his arms clinched against the cold water, he could not react in time to ward off the blow. The guard's fist imbedded itself in his belly and Garth doubled up. Then he went to one knee.

He never saw the foot coming at him, but he felt the instep dig between the point of his shoulder and his neck. He sprawled backward on his buttocks and slid into the wall again. He felt totally vulnerable. There was pain in his shoulder and his stomach, his entire body was exposed, and the cold water was cascading around him. The guards stood at the edge of the splashing, waiting to hit him again, but not really wanting to get wet.

Anger was rising in Garth and he was chilling under the shower. He was hurt, frustrated, and amazed at what was happening to him. He realized that he was trapped in the tiled room, outnumbered and apparently set up. He struggled away from the spray, trying to regain his bearings, put some distance between himself and the guards, and buy a little time to get a better sense of what was going on and how he could defend himself. He started to stand, slowly, gathering himself. But the guards were not ready to let him regroup. As they came at him again, he could see in the periphery that other guards were at the door. As he stood slouched and dripping, he saw one that had a bulldog face. It looked malevolent.

But the shorter guard was on him. He faked a kick at Garth's genitals and as the soaked inmate crossed his wrists in front to protect himself, the guard's open hand cracked into the side of his face, between the eye and ear. The pain was sharp, and Garth decided he had had enough of it. He swung his left arm, backhand, toward the short guard and had cocked his right to hit the taller one when he saw the other four guards advancing. He missed the tall guard with his swing and slipped again.

Both guards fell upon him and pinned him, face-down, to the shower-room floor. Now enraged, Garth wrenched one arm free and hammered his elbow into somebody's ribs. A knee came down on his ear and pressed the other side of his face into the concrete floor, and he felt a stabbing pain as the toe of a boot dug into his hip. Then the air went out of him as two knees landed heavily on his buttocks and pressed his testicles into the hard floor.

Garth struggled no longer. His head was throbbing but he could not determine whether the pain was worse on the outside or behind his eye. He heard somebody tell the shower-room boy to go get some clothes.

"He's a strong sonofabitch," a voice above him said. Then another broke through the labored panting. "Let this be a lesson to you, young buck. You do as you're told or it can get a lot worse. We don't mind dragging your ass out of here by the hands and feet if that's the way you want it. You understand?"

Garth said nothing.

"You understand?" the voice repeated.

Still Garth was silent.

A fist slammed into his kidney and shoelaces bit into his ribs.

"Answer me, motherfucker."

"Yeah, I understand," Garth said, trying to writhe and buck against the pain.

"Say, 'Yes, sir,' " another voice ordered.

"Yessir," Garth muttered.

"If we let you up, you gonna be a good boy and take a shower without any shit?"

Garth, eyes closed, nodded weakly. Another fist went into the small of his back like an air hammer attacking a sidewalk.

"You better work on your memory, cocksucker."

"Unnhh—yessir." Garth cringed.

The guards began to climb off him, one at a time until they were all standing over him.

"Get your ass up and take a shower . . . come on, get up before I bury this boot in your ass." Garth opened his eyes and followed the voice up to the bulldog face. It was hard, challenging, waiting as though it hoped he would not get up.

Garth tried to struggle to his feet. His entire body ached. He finally got to his hands and knees, but his head hung limp, looking at and almost touching the floor. His eyes had trouble focusing. He shook his head and blinked repeatedly. He placed one foot flat on the floor, then slowly got the other one under him. He stumbled into the wall and stood there, turning slowly to press his shoulder blades, then the back of his head against the tiles. His arms dangled at his sides. He tried to sort out what had happened to him and why. All this because he had asked about hot water? There had to be more to it than that. Would it have happened anyway? This must have been a setup. God, he couldn't let this happen again.

He straggled under the shower, which had been running throughout his ordeal, and he stood there with the water splattering onto his shoulders and racing in chilling rivulets down his beaten body. His eyes closed. He did not feel cold.

"That's enough," a voice said. Garth opened his eyes and stepped gingerly from under the water. The washroom boy shut it off. Some clothing came through the air at him. A pair of loose denim trousers and a white T-shirt. The same underwear he had removed earlier. He caught the shirt but the other articles fell to the wet floor. He did not stoop to pick them up.

When Garth looked at the door the guards were gone. The washroom boy was still there. Still grinning. He picked up the clothing and stepped closer to Garth, then he put his hand on the beaten man's back in a gesture that was supposed to have been taken as friendly.

Garth knocked the hand away. "Don't touch me, you little faggot," he said. "I don't have to take your shit."

"Yes, you do, asshole," the younger man said. "How do you think I got this job? You fuck with me and Bulldog will throw your ass in the peanut."

"Don't hit him," said a quiet voice in the doorway. "He's right."

Garth looked toward it. He saw a rather tall, slight man with hair the color of oatmeal. The man was wearing a dingy T-shirt and baggy bluish denim trousers like the ones Garth was holding. He was wearing glasses over eyes the color of stagnant water.

"If you hit him, they'll really beat the hell out of you," the man said. "And don't ask for a towel. They're just waiting for you to give them a reason to stomp your ass."

"What'd they just do?" Garth asked wearily.

"They do that to most everybody that comes here," the older man said. "Some get it a lot worse than that. They just touched you up a little. Just breaking you in. I gotta go. Put your clothes on and come on out and sit down."

Garth put on his clothes and the water on his body made the knit T-shirt stick to his skin in places and produce dark spots on the denims. The shower-room boy brought his shoes and socks.

"It pays to be nice to me," he said. "Sometime you might want to spend a little time in here alone. Or with somebody else. You can only smoke here or in the toilet and I run 'em both. If you need a place sometime, it'll cost you, but I can make sure nobody bothers you."

Garth finished tying his shoes and, without saying anything to the flush-faced younger man, he limped out into the dayroom. A few steps into the room he stopped, not knowing where to go or what to do. His first glance was toward the guards. He had learned one thing pretty quickly, and in that look he learned another. They were watching him, waiting for him to do anything that would require their intervention.

But when he looked at the other patients, he was surprised that none were looking at him, not even those who had besieged him on his arrival or hooted at him in the shower. It was as if he had been here all along.

Across the room, sitting on a long oaken bench, he saw the gray-haired man who had spoken to him at the shower-room door.

Garth walked slowly to the bench and sat down. Neither of them said anything for several minutes. He knew why he wasn't saying anything. The guards were still eyeing him and he was afraid that talking was forbidden.

Kirchoff was looking at his Bible. He was aware of the eyes on them, but he knew that in a few minutes the guards would turn their attention toward other patients, once they were satisfied that Garth would not cause further trouble.

Kirchoff removed his glasses and held them at arm's length toward a light in the ceiling high above. Then he brought them back to his lap and began rubbing the lenses with the tail of his dirty shirt.

"What are you here for?" he asked, not looking at Garth.

"I don't really know for sure," Garth replied. "I guess 'cause I got in a fight with a guard at Western. All they said was they was sending me someplace where they could handle me. I didn't know I was coming here 'til I was in the car. I heard this place was a sonofabitch, but what kind of hospital is it where they beat the shit out of you soon as you get here?"

Kirchoff put his glasses back on and looked out into the room. "First of all," he said, still not looking at the younger man beside him, "it isn't a hospital. They call it a hospital, but calling it one doesn't make it one. It's just another prison. They say it's for the criminally insane. I guess most everybody here has been charged with some kind of a crime, but not everybody here is crazy. That's for damn sure. I'm not, for one."

Then he chuckled bitterly. "I'm crazier than I was when I came here, but I don't think I'm crazy. Of course, the more you tell them you're not crazy, the more they're sure you are. I don't know how they'd know one way or the other. The guards are stupid as shit and the doctors are mostly just old G.P.'s."

"What's a G.P.?" Garth asked. He felt a little ignorant. The man seemed to have an air of calm resignation and sounded more educated than most of the people Garth had been around in his life.

"A general practitioner—a regular doctor. What I mean is they're not psychiatrists. They don't know anything about what's insane and what's sane. But they think we're all nuts and they don't really give a damn one way or the other. They just don't want to get hurt by somebody that really is crazy. Anyway, they just believe whatever the guards tell them, without checking about half the time. And they do whatever the guards tell them. The guards run the hospital."

Garth was listening to Kirchoff but looking around the day-room. The windows, blackened by night, were made darker still by the bright lights in the ceiling. Several men were watching television, several were reading large scraps of newspaper or single pages of magazines. Others were writing on sheets of lined paper and one man was drawing elaborate letters on a piece of cardboard while resting beside him on a bench was an ornately lettered sign which read: "Am I My Brother's Keeper?"

There continued to be a large, jerky, shuffling oval of men walking around the supports in the center of the room, several men prostrate under benches, and a double handful of men sitting or standing and wrestling with their private parts.

"Looks like a lot of them *are* crazy," Garth said. "What do you do here all day?"

"What you see."

"This?" Garth's eyebrows rose. "All day? You go to yard-out and job training and stuff like that, don't you? At Western they didn't like for you to sit on your butt all day. They bitched about your bad attitude if you didn't do something."

Kirchoff laughed. It was a low, almost grunting, sarcastic chuckle.

"They like it fine if you just sit. It would suit them if we all slept all day. All they want is to control everybody and sit in those rocking chairs. The less we do, the less they have to do. Sometimes we have yard-out in the summer. Not much. And there are some workshops, but they're mostly hobby shops and they only let patients go there if they can make some things for the guards to take outside and sell. No job training. They don't figure on many of us learning a trade. They don't figure on many of us needing one. They don't figure on many of us leaving."

"I'll be damned if that's so," Garth said. "I already served six years on a ten-to-twenty. If I hadn't a hit them guards, I could have been up for parole before too much longer. If I stay clean, I won't be here any longer than I was at Western."

Kirchoff's pond-water eyes peered at the younger man beside him and began to cloud.

"I was sentenced to thirty days," he said. He hesitated and looked away from Garth, his pupils flicking from side to side, seeking some undisclosed, elusive object near a ceiling corner. "Twenty-eight years ago."

5

KIRCHOFF REMEMBERED, could never forget, that sweltering summer day in the front yard of his mother's home in a rather shabby section of Northeast Philadelphia. He had just finished his second day in a new job as an accountant for the state.

It was 1938 and he felt he had finally found some semblance of security. The Depression still had people in cities like Philadelphia mired in failure, but he could sense that he and his wife and two small children were going to come through it after all. He had started working when he was seventeen and had attended the University of Pennsylvania at night to earn a degree in accounting. It was finally going to pay off.

He had worked at a number of companies, but one by one the Depression deprived the companies of anything to account for. The companies went under and the young accountant went job hunting, again and again. He did not think the state of Pennsylvania would go out of business.

Anyway, he had always believed that a man could get a job if he just looked long enough, did not give up. That's what irked him so about his younger brother. He had given up. Quit looking. All he did was whine and complain and take what little money their mother had and drink it up in beer. Kirchoff had no patience with that attitude and he frequently rode his little brother about it.

His mother, a German immigrant who spoke no English, was unhappy at the bickering between the two boys and, although she tended to agree with Paul's point of view, more often than not she defended her youngest, the one who still lived at home and had kept her company since the death of their father. Many of the arguments between the two brothers had become loud, even boisterous, with much name-calling and, invariably, threats which neither carried out.

This day, perhaps feeling a shade too self-righteous as the one who had made it looking on the one who had stopped trying, Kirchoff had walked onto the front porch at his mother's house, only to find his brother draining a bottle of beer.

Kirchoff made a snide comment, which was met with an equally snide retort. There was more rancor and Kirchoff walked off the porch, challenging his brother to come into the yard and settle the hash in a more physical manner. The brother obliged.

They stood in the front yard for several minutes shouting at each other, exchanging curses, and making threatening gestures. The mother added her shrill remonstrations. Apparently a neighbor feared violence or tired of the noise and summoned the police to quell the disturbance.

The appearance of the policemen angered Kirchoff. He protested that the dispute was a family matter that was of no concern to the police and could be settled without their intervention.

Not particularly enchanted by his attitude, the officers strongly suggested that Kirchoff come with them and that his leaving would certainly settle the disturbance. Twice he brushed off the hands of a policeman who tried to pull him away from his brother. The policemen, now angry, told him he would have to come with them, giving the tempers of both brothers a chance to cool and the gathering crowd a reason to disperse.

They took him to the nearby precinct house and placed him in a small cell. The young accountant was upset at the prospect of having to spend a night in jail, but was told that he could explain the disturbance to a magistrate the next morning.

His emotion changed from anger to fear. He did not want to be late to work his third day on the job with an explanation that he had been detained in jail.

He would never have the opportunity to offer the explanation.

The next day, he was taken before a magistrate who listened to the policemen describe the complaint. Then he turned to Kirchoff, who angrily chastised the officers for holding him for no reason and jeopardizing his job. He made a couple of denigrating remarks about the local system of justice.

The magistrate said three words: "Guilty. Thirty days."

As he was led back to his cell, he asked the escorting officer, "What am I guilty of?"

"Disorderly conduct," the officer said. "Disturbing the peace."

There had been no attorney present. There had been no jury. He was taken to the county prison to begin serving his time. He was angry and frustrated. The loss of the job that was to have given him a lifetime of security embittered him. Then he made a mistake.

When told by a jailer to enter his cell, he balked and was given a shove. He shoved back. The jailer reported the incident, and when Kirchoff's release day came he was told that his sentence had been extended because of the incident. He became furious and his relationship with those around him deteriorated rapidly. He protested to all who would listen that he had been "railroaded." He cursed the jailers and insisted that they were the reason he was being kept in jail and away from his family. He fought with a prisoner who laughed at him. He worried about his wife and children, and the frustration grew.

Summer faded into autumn and then late autumn. His expressed irritation grew. Then one day he was told that he would be taking a ride. Nobody told him where. The ride left him at Norristown State Hospital, a mental institution. Nobody told him why. His family was told that he was unable to control his anger and could not be released from custody until his mental state improved. His wife could not afford legal advice. His mother knew nothing about the American legal system. His brother thought it served him right.

At the hospital, Kirchoff maintained to any who would listen that he was being unfairly persecuted. The hospital decided that he was paranoid. One physician determined that "he continues to be friendly, talkative and smiling, but at times becomes insistent about the injustice of being committed here."

The longer he was held in the hospital, the more insistent he became. The hospital staff decided that he needed pre-insulin therapy. They induced thirty-one comas in him and by spring decided that they had achieved little success.

"He repeats continually that there is nothing wrong with him, that he is being tortured by the treatment and is being held here for no reason," the doctors said.

A year later, guilty of "progressive irritableness, insistence upon his rights, and illogical thinking," Kirchoff threatened a physician at Norristown.

A longer ride was prescribed for him. It ended at Farview.

*

"Why are you still here?" Garth asked, not realizing immediately how foolish the question was.

" 'Cause they won't let me go," Kirchoff said simply.

"I mean, why are they keeping you here?"

" 'Cause they can. 'Cause they want to. Hell, I don't know . . . maybe 'cause I don't have anybody on the outside trying to get me out. My mother's dead, but she wouldn't know what to do anyway . . . she didn't even speak English. . . . My wife's married somebody else, my children don't even remember who I was . . . they were too young when I came in. Maybe it's 'cause I don't give anybody any shit and I'm a good worker. I know it's not because they want to help me.

"I once asked a doctor here to let me speak to somebody that might be interested in my welfare and he told me I was crazier than a shithouse rat. Another doctor told me the longer I was here the worse I would get, but he didn't do anything to get me out. I don't know what you do to get out. I just try to make it as easy as I can while I'm here. I just try not to give anybody any trouble, especially the guards. If you show them you're mad or bitter, they'll just start riding you. They can make it rough as hell. You got to always watch out for yourself here. You can get the shit beat out of you just for saying the wrong thing or looking the wrong way. They've killed patients here."

"Nightshirts!"

Garth did not see who had barked the word, but it sounded more like a command than a declaration. He did see men begin removing their shirts.

"Take your clothes off," Kirchoff said. "They'll give you a nightshirt to sleep in."

"Nightshirt?"

"Yeah. It's like a woman's nightgown except that there aren't any titties inside them." He chuckled at his attempt at humor. "Everybody's got to wear them."

"A couple of guys over there are wearing pajamas," Garth said.

"Oh, the rats can sometimes wear pajamas," Kirchoff said. "It's a kind of privilege."

"Where do you sleep?" Garth asked, still separating himself from the mélange around him.

"Upstairs."

Garth began removing his clothes. Slowly. Self-consciously. "Where do I put these?" he asked, standing in his underwear and holding his T-shirt and denims. He was still wearing his shoes and socks.

"Just leave them on the bench," Kirchoff said. "There won't be anybody down here to steal them except the guards, and they'll take what they want anyway, if they want to. They took your money out front didn't they?"

"I didn't have any on me," Garth said.

"Well, you better figure a way to get some," the older man said. "You're going to run out of cigarettes soon. They'll give you some makings once a week, but you have to buy regular cigarettes."

"What about my billfold?"

"Leave it here, too. Tomorrow you can get a box in the clothing room if you got something you want to put in it, but the guards will get in there too if they want to. If they don't, the clothing-room boy probably will. It's damned hard to keep something to yourself in here."

For the first time since he came on the ward, Garth thought about his Bible with the picture of his sisters. He wondered who he was going to ask about its whereabouts. Rather than take a chance that that might be like asking for hot water or a towel, he decided he would wait until the next day and see if he saw it lying around the dayroom.

Within moments, the room was filled with naked men. Or at least mostly naked. Some were coming from the clothing room with dingy white cotton cloth which they began to shove their arms into and pull over their heads. Here and there men were reaching for others' genitals. Again, Garth felt foolish and vulnerable. He still had not pulled off his jockey shorts and he could not help feeling nervous and wary. He wondered what the guards would do if he pushed a fist into the face of anybody who tried to touch him that way. In prison he had learned immediately that a man was pretty safe from harassment if he simply demonstrated right off that he was not afraid to defend himself. Even if he lost to a group coming at him with rape on their minds, a man had to hit anybody he could and then later stick a shiv in one of the attackers. Cut up somebody. They might get him that first time, but if he showed he wasn't afraid to kill to protect himself, a man could get along all right in prison. Even a little man.

He didn't know about here, but he decided he would probably get a chance to find out.

Garth's conjecturing was interrupted by a rather nondescript man in a blue shirt and black slacks who handed him a large wad of white cotton fabric.

"Get out of them skivvies and into this shirt," the guard said.

Garth took the nightshirt, then looked past the guard's shoulder toward the center of the room, where a scrawny-necked man with almost no hair was going to his knees in front of a younger, pudgy-soft man with burred hair. Almost immediately a guard— the short, broad-faced one with the belly—stepped forward and kicked viciously at the kneeling man. The patient slid across the floor and quickly gathered himself into a fetal position, his arms practically engulfing his whimpering head.

"Get up, you slimy faggot sonofabitch," said the guard, standing over him. "You want to suck on something, I'll give you this boot."

Before the mewling man scrambled to his feet, the other guards, including the one standing before Garth, were on him. One slapped him in the back of the head, knocking him toward the others, who now ringed the patient. Again the patient wrapped his arms about his head, then stood shivering and moaning. One by one, the other guards shoved, punched, or kicked him until each had had a hand in the punishment, which had seemed sufficient with the initial kick delivered by the first guard. It was as if each guard were participating in a rite, following an unwritten code that required each to be as involved as the others in the activity before them. When the last one had hit the blubbering, skinny older man, they all walked away from him.

Garth noticed that virtually none of the other patients were watching the incident. They had not merely averted their gazes, they had almost all turned their backs.

Garth had scarcely noticed that Kirchoff had left when he returned wearing his nightshirt.

"What happened?" Kirchoff asked.

"Didn't you see?"

"No, and you didn't either, if you're smart."

Before Garth could respond, he heard another barking command.

"Line up!"

Then another.

"Turn them fucking radios off and get in line!"

Garth quickly pulled his nightshirt over his head and pulled off his underwear before the shirt fell below his waist. Within seconds there was virtual silence in the room. There was some almost-inaudible murmuring and mumbling and grumbling, some minor pushing, shoving and grabbing, but by comparison, the previous quiet seemed a din. The room was finally hushed. A guard walked the line and passed Garth uttering a count under his breath.

"Ninety-seven!" Garth heard him shout from the end of the line back toward the bulldog face at the head of it. The bulldog was looking at a piece of paper.

"And we got three on R-Ward," Garth heard him say. "All right, take 'em up."

The line began to move toward an open door at the end of the dayroom, on the side opposite a fireplace Garth was noticing for the first time. He wondered if it ever held a fire. As they were walking, Kirchoff turned his head and, taking a chance against getting caught breaking a rule, whispered, "If somebody gets in your bed and you don't want him there, kick him out. If you don't say anything, the guards will let it go. They don't give a shit what happens up here."

"Knock off the talking!"

Garth could not recognize the shouting voices yet, but he had a feeling it wouldn't take long. Faces and voices were the only forms of identification, apparently. He still hadn't seen a guard with a name tag and the guards didn't seem inclined to introduce themselves by name.

As Garth walked into the dormitory, he saw nothing but a roomful of beds, literally wall-to-wall, except for a center aisle, and a rocking chair at each end of the room. There seemed to be about a foot or so between the beds and there were two rows of them on each side of the room, heads toward the windows and feet toward the center. Each bed was covered with a sheet and a thin blanket.

The men in front of him were heading toward and between beds like rats threading a maze, but Garth was stopped just after he entered the room.

"Hey, you! New boy." It was the tall guard who had initiated Garth's Farview education in the shower downstairs. "You're in that one," he said, pointing toward any of a score or more of beds. "Near the wall. Next to that nigger."

Garth followed a line from the guard's thick, pointing finger until he saw the empty bed. Actually he had seen the black man lying on a bed next to an empty one. The man lay stretched on top of the blanket, his arms folded across his chest. He stared at Garth and his eyes did not flicker.

As he walked between beds to reach the vacant one, Garth noticed the well-muscled arms, and the penetrating eyes that never left him.

Garth lowered his body slowly to the bunk and lay back, feeling the ache settle in his muscles. He was looking at the ceiling when the lights went out. He continued to stare upward into the darkness and his mind began to race, backpedaling over the events of the day. It was a dizzying course.

He lay there for what seemed like hours, but he knew was not. He could hear deep snoring and the steady, rhythmic screaking of the guards' rocking chairs. He heard the rustling of sheets and the muted snatches of whispered conversation. He lowered his eyes from the ceiling and caught crouched silhouettes moving from one bed to another. He heard a scuffling body alligatoring under his bed en route to what he assumed was a liaison. He was becoming edgy again.

He turned to his side and pushed his head into the pillow. As he looked straight ahead, he felt a tremor jag down his spine.

He could see the whites of two eyes glaring back at him.

6

IT WAS still dark outside when the ebony eyelids sprang open like the lid of a jack-in-the-box. Night Train always came awake suddenly, completely. No eye-rubbing, yawning, stretching, scratching, reluctant arousal. And he always woke a few minutes before the lights came on and the guards started blustering and commandeering their way through wake-ups, line-ups, dressing, and pre-breakfast medications.

Those few minutes, sometimes five, sometimes fifteen, before the lights came on were invariably the best in the day for him. They were quiet, unthreatening minutes. All his. They were the only ones in the day that were only his. There were other stretches of time when he was not hassled, but at those times he was constantly watchful, wary.

In his private morning he could think about things in an orderly fashion, not having to block out the sounds of the ward or fend off some grab-assing fruitcake or control his flaring temper at some guard's name-calling. They were the only relaxing minutes of his day.

There had been 468 days for him at Farview. Now 469. He tried to think about how many minutes of peace, real calm and rest and relaxation, that meant he had had since he came. He quickly gave up counting. He had gone through the ninth grade—at least that's what his records indicated—but he had missed most days after the sixth grade and the relatively simple mental gymnastics of multiplication tables were beyond him.

As he looked at the ceiling high above him he could hear the sounds of restless sleep around him. The deep snores and the fitful whinings. Sometimes, though not this morning, he would hear the cries and screams of the victims of internal wars of paranoia and schizophrenia and he wondered what went on in the dreams and nightmares.

He thought he could smell bacon frying, and he took two audible sniffs of the dank air. His nose was tricking him again. It often took him back to his bedroom in West Philadelphia and let his momma run through the hallways of his mind. He could see her shuffling her heavy body around the kitchen, occasionally shouting warnings to his brothers and sisters about what would happen if they didn't pull their heads out from under their pillows and start getting dressed for school. Then he could see her walking to meet the bus that would take her out the Main Line to some big house where she would tend to some white children while her own were left to find their way through the days and ways of the slum.

Night Train rubbed his thick, flaring nose and turned his head toward the bed to his left. The new man was taking the deep, even breaths of sleep now, but he had spent a restless night, turning from side to side in discomfort and agitation. The man was thick and heavy and square but he had been no match for the guards. Nobody was, Night Train mused, and it wouldn't take them long to break down those muscles and turn him into a weak and flabby cur of a man. It seemed to Night Train that there was a contest on at Farview to see whether the mind or the body could be crumbled first. He knew he was a victim of the contest, even though he was trying to hold himself together while the hospital seemed to be tearing away parts of him little by little.

His mind was subsisting on hatred. Every time a guard called him a name, he fought against the temptation to split a skull. He knew he could not take on all the guards on the ward. He had tried that the first day in the shower, just as he imagined that the bulky man in the next bunk had tried and failed. No, Night Train was fighting to hold his rage until he could catch one of them alone. He knew he would someday. He was counting on it. It was a daily secret prayer he was certain would be answered. He hoped he could wait until the right time and place, but he had about decided that he was willing to be caught and killed if he could take one of the guards with him.

Night Train felt that his body was deteriorating faster than his mind and that concerned him even more. He got no exercise, no work really, except for pushing that heavy polisher. Nothing to tone his muscles. Every now and then he was allowed to take the floor with some little scum bag who was irritating him and whom the guards decided to punish or have some fun with. But he didn't consider those fights exercise. They didn't last long enough. He would hit them eight or ten times full in the face and a couple of times in the stomach and they would not get up. The main difference between him and Malone was that he hit them fewer times but with more force.

He had always been known as a man of formidable size and strength, with fast, hard hands he didn't mind using. He had often heard his friends on the street warn others, "Don't fuck with Night Train. Don't jump in Night Train's shit." He liked to hear them say it.

His name actually was Venance Lane, but his friends in the neighborhood had nicknamed him Night Train after the Detroit Lions football player. He kind of liked that too. In fact, he liked it very much. He thought it said a lot about him. It described his color, his power, his speed, and the time he operated best. He used to whistle at night and stop for nobody.

He got stopped, however, when he and a couple of friends robbed a corner grocer who said something about a "lousy nigger sonofabitch," leading Night Train to retool the grocer's face. One of Night Train's accomplices urged him to hurry with the beating and run, but he used the nickname in his exhortations. It was the only name the grocer remembered. The police quickly made an arrest, but Night Train refused to identify his associates and so went to trial alone on a charge of aggravated robbery.

At the trial Night Train said that he had not intended to hurt his victim, that he was unarmed and that he had attacked the man because the racial slurs enraged him and caused him to lose control of his mental faculties. He was pretty much repeating phrases drummed into him by his young, court-appointed attorney, who had assured him that some time in a mental hospital was preferable to time in prison.

The jury accepted his pleas of temporary insanity and agreed that he should be committed to a state hospital and remain there receiving therapy that would help him learn to control his volatile temper until the hospital authorities decided he was capable of returning to his community.

The jurors had no way of knowing that they were sentencing him to endless days of racial slurs, derisions, and a debilitation of the very mental faculties the hospital was supposed to strengthen.

He was about to enter his 469th day of being called "nigger," or "jigaboo," or "coon," or "jungle bunny," or worse. He didn't know how many more of them he could stand. After reacting to the name-calling the first four or five times and being kicked into submission and reticence, he had come to accept the futility of lashing out, "going on a toot," as the guards called it. All he could see it getting him was another six-on-one whipping and some time on the bench or in the peanut. But he could almost physically feel his resentment building and bubbling near the surface. He knew it would be only a matter of time—days, or even hours —before the resentment erupted into a thunderstorm of violence. Sometimes the feeling frightened him because he knew that he could not win against the guards. But even so, somehow he knew he would feel better for having unleashed the fury within him.

As he lay in bed he could feel himself tingle with the anticipation of feeling his fist crash into a face, smash through teeth, and drive toward tonsils. He could feel freedom in every aspect of the act, every inch the fist moved. He knew that he would never feel really good about himself until he let everything go one day and saw blood on the face of one of the blue-shirted devils who rode his ass, who made him bite his tongue, made him eat the slurs and the embarrassment of doing nothing about them, who taught him to hate with deep passion—especially anything in white skin.

The lights came on. With them came the intimidating voices.

"Get your asses up! We ain't got all day!"

Night Train rolled to his feet, accompanied by the symphony of groans and complaints from the more than one hundred men. The man in the next bunk was among them.

"Goddamn, I hurt," the white man said. "All over. My back, my ribs, my neck. Everywhere. My head too."

Night Train looked at the raw scrapes on the other man's knees and elbows, and the red welts on his face. The nightshirt covered whatever bruises were present.

"Tough shit," he said, and moved to the center aisle to stand waiting while the guards rousted those glued to their bunks.

When all the patients were standing in line there was a head count as there had been the night before. Nobody had left. They trooped downstairs to the dayroom and another head count. Nobody had escaped while descending the stairs. The patients went to their small piles of clothing, dressed, and lined up again for the walk to the dining room—K-3, it was called. Night Train knew he would have trouble calling the food breakfast.

A telephone call from the dining room to the charge guard in the office signaled permission for D-Ward to start walking toward breakfast. The walk, for Night Train, was so routine he could easily have accomplished it blindfolded.

Of course, somebody always screwed it up, and that had a way of screwing up other things in other ways. Not going along correctly and quietly to the dining room would invariably get a man kicked or slapped around. That would slow down the trip to chow. It also would set some of the really zombied freaks on edge and make them so nervous they would start acting out their fears and succumbing to their paranoia, and lash out at another patient or a guard; and that led to the guards jumping their ass. Such things did not happen only on the way to dinner; they could happen anywhere.

The trek from D-Ward to the dining room was mostly a walk down a long hallway with a bunch of right and left turns. The hall was lined with windows, all secured with heavy-looking bars painted gray, or silver that had turned gray, and thick wire screen.

To an outsider, the hospital seemed a maze of endless corridors like the one Night Train was walking along to K-3. The corridors formed four quadrangles within a quadrangle. The patient wards

—there were twelve of them, including the medical ward, the surgical ward, and J-Ward, for solitary confinement—formed the outer perimeter of the larger quadrangle.

There were other buildings outside the main quadrangle, three of which—AA, BB, and Z—housed patients not considered dangerous enough to require such stringent supervision as the others. There was a large, modern gymnasium and recreation building, the laundry, greenhouse, power house, farm office, and a building that at one time had segregated tubercular patients.

But on the way to chow, he could not see any of those buildings. He and the other men of D-Ward stopped and stood in a line outside K-3 while patients from another ward, having finished breakfast, were lining up in the same corridor for the return to their ward.

He saw a man in the other group turn to a patient behind him and say something. Almost immediately, and from outside Night Train's peripheral vision, came a hand that slammed into the side of the talking patient's head, knocking him into the wall, where he remained, cringing, his arms shooting upward to encircle and protect his head.

"No talking in line!" barked the owner of the hand, standing with clenched fists and looking up and down the line, challenging the others to make a comment or a move. None did.

Within a couple of minutes, D-Ward was filing past a cafeteria-type serving counter, each man holding a compartmented tray and a large metal soupspoon. They presented their trays to other patients who stood behind the steam table and served food. Each man received a spoonful of clammy, lumpy steamed rice, a piece or two of dry toast, and a cup of milk. The room was filled with men, one group leaving as another entered. From the time they entered until they left, they were urged to hurry.

Mealtime at Farview was an especially tense time for the guards. Mealtime and yard-out. At other times of the day, the patients were confined to a relatively controllable area—the ward dayroom or the dormitory, behind locked doors. But at mealtime and yard-out, more than one ward was present at a time in a less controlled atmosphere.

The guards were on edge, almost visibly scared, at such times and they wanted the activity ended and the patients back in the wards as quickly as possible. It was at mealtime and yard-out that patients from different wards could exchange information and contraband directly, if they were careful. The dining room was like feeding time at the zoo. The patients were always hungry and never pleased with the fare, which made them testy and grumbling. Yard-out was like a patient switchboard and exchange house. The guards hated both activities.

They could not refuse patients mealtime, but they could restrict the yard-outs. And they did. Night Train remembered that last year his ward was outside less than forty times. There was always too much rain or too much snow. Hardly any of the patients were allowed coats, and he was sure that that was intentional, so that cold weather could be used as an excuse not to have yard-out.

About the time Night Train sat down to eat his first serving, there was a call for seconds. He could not imagine who would want more than one serving, but he was pissed off anyway. Had the food been edible enough for him to want more, he would not have been able to finish what he had on his tray in time to get more. That's what always happened when he got caught near the end of the line. He didn't mind so much at breakfast, because it was seldom worth eating, seldom more than salve for hunger pangs. The other meals were little better, but they were more than steamed rice and he made it a point to be near the front of the line for them.

A powder-blue shirt came by, tapped him roughly on the back, and told him, "Eat up, nigger." He pretended that he was trying to eat faster, but the gluey mess was sticking in his mouth. He washed it down quickly with milk. Then he was ordered back to the corridor. On his way out he dropped his spoon into a box held by a guard. Then he and the others assembled in the hallway and waited while men and spoons were counted.

There had been no cigarette, coffee, or conversation. Breakfast had consumed seven minutes of his 469th day.

*

"Mr. Parton, can I talk to you?"

"Not now, Chamberlin," said the guard in charge of the dining room. "You through eating, go line up." He didn't like the slight, hatchet-faced patient, and he knew what the man wanted to talk about. The same thing he always wanted to talk about. Working in the dining room. Parton had been asked the same question four or five times in the past month or so, and his answer was always the same, and as far as he was concerned it would always be the same to Chamberlin.

Parton began moving toward the dining room entrance as a way of leading Chamberlin to the hallway and away from the crowded milling and standing and sitting of the dining room. He was moving him toward the hallway, where there were fewer patients than in the dining room and a better ratio of guards. The sandy-haired patient followed along as Parton had planned.

"I want to work in K-3," Chamberlin said as they reached the corridor. His lips trembled slightly and his red-rimmed eyes were fixed on the guard's face.

"I don't give a damn what you want." Parton was aggravated. He was now standing in the corridor, where everybody from D-Ward was assembled, except for Chamberlin, who was still in the doorway. All the D-Ward guards were there and a couple or three others. "How many times I gotta tell you no, you loony faggot? I don't want queers working for me."

Flames of hatred licked up Chamberlin's body and set off the black powder in his brain. Parton never saw the hand coming, but as it cracked against his face it sounded like a pistol shot going off next to his ear. He lurched backward for a split second, his left elbow rising to block the anticipated next blow.

The patient simply stood, lips still trembling, arms now dangling straight down at his side, until Parton lunged toward him. Time and people seemed frozen into immobility, eyes riveted to the scene. Garth's eyes and Night Train's were nailed there.

First Parton, then Chamberlin, broke the momentary still life as the guard lunged and the patient raised his arms to cover his head. Parton began swinging wildly, fists coming from far above and behind his head, but raining mostly on the patient's hands and arms. Then other guards moved toward the two.

Chamberlin tried to retreat from the storm and fell back into the dining room, pursued by the hands and voices of the guards.

"Grab that sonofabitch!" The shout broke the stunned silence and was followed by others rushing over each other.

"Get him!"

"Let me at him."

"You motherfucker!"

"What the hell you think you're doing?"

"Kick his fucking ass!"

The powder-blue shirts and dark slacks came together where Chamberlin had stood before he was knocked to the floor of the dining room. The guards surrounded the quivering form and began to kick and punch it savagely.

Chamberlin continued to try to protect his head from the repeated blows. His arms and hands almost had his head enveloped and he tried to pull his knees to his chin in a tight fetal position. The fists and feet of the guards standing over him shot into and out from the body, turning the scene kaleidoscopic.

The screams and moans from Chamberlin seemed to jerk attention back to reality and those standing by who dared to look saw one of the guards reach to the wall and pull away the long, heavy brass nozzle attached to the end of a flat, loosely coiled fire hose.

The guard pulled it toward the wriggling figure on the floor and began to swing it into the patient's head and upper body, once, twice, several times.

Suddenly a voice broke through the discordant choir of curses and crying.

"That's enough—get him on back to the ward. Any of you guys get hurt?"

Garth could not see who had interrupted the fracas. In fact, he had scarcely looked up from the floor to the faces of any of the guards involved. He had been transfixed by the kicking and stomping and the fire-hose nozzle directed at the patient. He had looked up the line of other patients once to see how they were reacting, to see if there would be some signal for him and them to leap into the fray in behalf of their set-upon comrade.

Nothing. The other patients had turned, or were turning, their heads away from the violence. It seemed that they were deliberately avoiding seeing what was happening to the man on the floor. Garth could not look away.

The incident seemed to end about as quickly as it began. Two guards were dragging Chamberlin by the feet along the corridor toward D-Ward. His blood-covered head and arms trailed along the floor like a scarlet bridal train. Garth's eyes followed the small procession and he remembered the times he and his brothers had helped their father pull a freshly shot hog by the back feet from the small barn to a nearby tree, except that almost no blood came from the small hole the bullet had left between the hog's eyes. Garth leaned toward the center of the hallway to maintain his view of Chamberlin and the guards.

"Keep looking, cocksucker, and you can take that same trip," said a voice behind him as he was roughly shoved back into the line.

7

WHILE THE men of D-Ward were lining up for a return to their dayroom, Malone and Spangler were at work in the kitchen. It was down the hall from K-3 dining room and practically in the center of the huge quadrangle. Its proper name was Main Dietary and strangely, perhaps in a nod to the paramilitary organization of the hospital, all the staff and many of the patients actually called it by its proper name.

Malone called it the kitchen. Had he served time in the military, he would have seen his job for what it was—K.P. He spent most of his time cleaning the giant pots, vats really, in which most of the food for the patients was prepared. He wondered if a very small man, a midget perhaps, couldn't crawl into one of the vats and hide. It wouldn't do any good at all to hide in one, of course. He was just speculating.

For sure, they were a job to clean. But he would rather be doing that than be confined to the ward all day. He knew the

81

guards didn't think of his job as one to be held out as a privilege, although it came after he had taken the floor against a beefy, baby-faced, bowling ball of a man and turned his face into strawberry jam. That was before his fists had established a reputation at Farview and the Hawk had won a lot of money on him.

All the jobs in the kitchen area were handed out as a reward for something, but, as on the ward, there was a hierarchy among patients in Main Dietary. As Malone looked around the vast room with its commercial-size bakery ovens and ranges and sinks, he saw that all the cleaning was being done by black men like him and Spangler. The serving jobs were held mostly by white patients. The best jobs, waiting tables in the guards' dining room, were all held by white men.

"The guards don't want niggers touching the food or the plates," said DeLuca, the man who ran the kitchen. That prejudice seemed to apply only before and during meals. The guards didn't seem to mind the blacks clearing away dishes and cleaning tables.

Malone didn't mind that job either. Just being in the guards' dining room had its advantages. The waiters had it best because they could become a sort of a friend to a guard and establish a contact that could lead to such favors as smuggling things in and out of the hospital or a shopping day outside with the guard as chaperone.

Not only that, but the guards' dining room was the best place to hear what was going on in other areas of the hospital and to find out which guards and doctors were particularly liked or disliked. For the most part, the guards and the doctors who ate there treated the waiters and busboys as though they were invisible. They talked about anything and anybody. They did more for the hospital grapevine than Yancey the candy-wagon man.

Malone didn't get to clean up in the guards' dining room often and he got to scrub the big pots and pans regularly. Nevertheless, he was glad for his kitchen job because it got him off the ward every day, damned near all day. Nobody seemed to mind if he worked ten or twelve or even fourteen hours a day. The truth of the matter was that he didn't care either. He didn't miss anything by not being on the ward except for potential trouble and total boredom. He gained quite a lot, the way he saw it.

In addition to being able to eavesdrop occasionally on guards and doctors, he also got to eat the same food as they. He had not eaten steamed rice for breakfast. He had eaten two bowls of cold cereal, two pieces of buttered toast and a couple of cups of coffee. He could have had eggs too, if he had wanted some. And he was allowed to smoke without having to go into the bathroom.

There was one other big advantage. In his spare time he could make up some sandwiches to take back to the ward at the end of the day and sell or trade for other things he wanted. He always gave one or two to the charge guard or one of the other guards and sometimes one or two of them would flip him a quarter. He was building up a little cash to buy cigarettes and candy with or to rent a nudie magazine for a half-hour or so. He had even accumulated a little money on the book. He was thinking about ordering something from the Sears, Roebuck catalog after he got a little more on the book. He didn't know how well that worked, though. He had heard about guys ordering things they never got.

Another advantage of working in the kitchen, of course, was that you knew not to eat the soup. It didn't matter what kind of soup was on the scheduled menu—pea soup, tomato soup, vegetable or chicken noodle. And it didn't matter what the recipe called for, or for that matter whether it was canned or homemade. They all had one common ingredient. Piss. Somebody always pissed in the soup. Malone guessed that sometimes more than one person did. Charlie most always did because he didn't want to take a chance on somebody else not doing it. Malone didn't know Charlie's last name, but he knew he pissed in the soup. He often saw him climb the short ladder used by those who had to stir the soup, or whatever, with the paddle.

Charlie would climb the ladder, hold the paddle with one hand and stir slowly, open his fly with the other hand and pull out his peter and piss in the soup. He never even looked around or appeared the least bit furtive.

There was almost no chance of getting caught at it. The patients who worked in the kitchen generally were not troublemakers, and the guards almost always stayed in DeLuca's office or in another little room with a table and drank coffee. And DeLuca was only in the kitchen a half a day at a time. He had a deal with the superintendent or somebody so that he could work only half a day and operate his own outside business the rest of the time.

Charlie would just wait until DeLuca went to the can or went off to his other job, then he'd climb the little ladder and let fly.

Nobody who worked in Main Dietary talked about the soup. They just didn't eat any of it and grinned when the food carts headed for the guards' dining room.

Malone smiled at the thought of it. Those bastards worried about black hands touching their plates and didn't know that a white man was pissing in their soup.

There was always talk of patients jacking off into the mashed potatoes, but he had never seen that. Nevertheless, he didn't take any chances. Just as he avoided soup at any meal, he passed up mashed potatoes.

He had one other job in Main Dietary and he could not sort out how to feel about it.

Every weekend, Friday afternoons and much of the day on Saturday, he had to fill boxes with foodstuffs for the wives of certain of the guards and doctors and other staff members to pick up. It was like being a grocery boy. He filled the boxes with canned goods and meat and other groceries, then carried them to the back gate where the delivery trucks entered, and loaded the boxes into the car trunks when the wives drove up.

He liked the job because it gave him a chance to get outside for fresh air and it kept him from having to wash as many pots on two days a week. But it made him mad as hell to think about all that food intended for patients going away in the trunks of automobiles. He had tried to talk to Spangler about it one day while they were unloading a grocery supply truck. But all Spangler wanted to talk about was escaping.

All he thought about was escaping. Always working on some kind of elaborate escape plan. Truth of the matter was that Farview wasn't hard to escape from—if you lived in Z Building, the bungalow. Malone had heard guards talking at supper one night and they said some twenty-odd had walked away from the place in something like eight or nine months. Of course all of them, or damned near all of them, had been caught and returned and had the shit beaten out of them. That had been pretty well advertised in the hospital.

No, escaping wasn't hard. Both Malone and Spangler knew that. Escaping from inside the main hospital building, through all the bars and locked doors, that was hard. But Spangler was dead set on doing it. That was all he wanted to talk to Malone about.

And Malone didn't want to talk about that. Malone was thinking. And what Malone thought about, he couldn't talk about to anybody. It had to do with loading the groceries for the guards' wives to take away. Lately that whole exercise was scaring the hell out of him. He really wanted to talk to somebody about it, but he didn't trust anybody that far. It even scared him to think about it alone, but he couldn't keep from doing that.

He wondered whether she would be there this afternoon. Or tomorrow.

Since he had been assigned the job of preparing and loading the food boxes, a couple of months before, she had been the only one of the wives who was even vaguely pleasant, much less friendly, to him. While the other women either opened their car trunks and got back inside the car or stayed in the car and gave him the keys to the trunk, she always got out and opened the trunk herself and stood there while he placed the box in the trunk.

Even from the first, she always smiled at him.

The last two or three visits had involved more than smiles. That's what bothered Malone. He was only a teenager from Pittsburgh but he figured he was street-smart. He could sense a few things. Trouble was one of them. In fact, he thought he had a damned good nose for trouble. He had been in quite a bit of it during his nineteen years and he had avoided more. He could sense that this woman was trouble he should avoid.

What scared and frustrated him was that she was the one forcing the action and he could not figure out why. For a time, he had questioned whether he was reading more into her smiles and moves than she intended, but he decided he was reading her right. He had been on the street enough to know the difference between red lights and green lights and he had spent considerable time observing the ways of the pretty foxes. This one was giving signals, and sitting where he was, in a heavily guarded mental hospital, he was confused about how to react to them.

He figured that she probably knew that, and it about halfway pissed him off and further confused him in trying to figure out why she was giving him the eye. She had to know what her signals were doing to a man locked inside a maximum security joint with other men. And she had to know that he could not follow up on any of the things she seemed to be initiating. Maybe that's why she was doing it, he thought. She wanted to be wanted and was flirting with him because she could see she was wanted yet remain safe from having to put her body where her smile was.

On the other hand, maybe she thought that he lived in the bungalow and could get away for a few hours from time to time without anybody at the hospital knowing for sure—or caring—where he was.

He let his mind race forward to a time when he would walk into the nearby woods and spread her before him. Or maybe he would do it in the back seat of her Oldsmobile. The front of his denims became constrictive at the thought.

He knew that white women sometimes had a thing for black men. He had decided that they were more curious than anything else, fascinated with the idea that they might be breaking taboo, that they might get up and see that some black had rubbed off on them.

And some, like the little social worker at the juvenile detention center where he had been before coming to Farview, seemed to be trying to wash away a couple of centuries of bigotry with a couple of hours of rutting frenzy. She had been so overt as to remind him repeatedly of what she had done, to prove she wasn't prejudiced. He often wondered if she told her friends about her proof. He had heard a lot of white men talk about their times with black women, but never to prove that they were not prejudiced. Her bullshit kind of got on his nerves but he just laughed at her and kept on laying pipe. Funny, she never threatened to cut him off.

He had to admit that the social worker had tried to give him more than tits, ass and freed-up soul. Had she not failed, likely he would not be at Farview worrying about how close to this newest sun he could fly without getting his butt burned. But she *had* failed. Her advice had been no match for the peer-group pressures he had succumbed to since he was a child.

Fights for acceptance led him to join a street gang, over the vigorous objections of his parents, who tried vainly to convince him that the dares and taunts of children did not matter. But they mattered to Billy Malone and he silenced them. His reputation as a street fighter grew and he became leader of his gang. The fights, while still growing out of little more than the taunts of children, graduated from fists to knives and guns.

Finally after a fracas with a rival gang one of the rivals lay bleeding in the street. Malone was charged and convicted of assault with a knife and stealing a car. He acknowledged having done both, but contended that if he had not used the knife better than the other boy, he might be in a box instead of a cell.

He was sent to the juvenile detention center and discovered that life inside was little different from life on the pavement. It was still a matter of doing unto others before they did unto you; and if they did it to you first, they had to learn that pay-back was a bitch.

His reputation as a fighter stayed with him and he was called upon to live up to it. His hands were fast as air hammers and just as unrelenting, and he never backed away from using them. To do so was to show weakness, an unaffordable option because the other men-children were ever watchful for a sign. He became the leader of a gang inside the center and discovered the only significant difference between gangs inside and those outside. Outside, when the cops came, it was not a mark of courage to challenge them, stand up to them, and get your cods cracked by a black-booted Pittsburgh Polack. There was a degree of glory, matter of fact, that went to the boys who could run away the fastest. Slipping the fuzz was cool.

Inside, however, there was no place to run and a gang leader was called upon to lead the gang not only against other gangs, but against a guard if the situation required. Intimidation was not condoned, even if to stand and fight meant an ass-whipping and severe discipline.

It was just such a physical confrontation with a guard, under the watchful eyes of peers, that gained Malone a ride to Farview. He had raped no one. He had killed no one. He had burned nothing. He was an uneducated black teenager from the litter-strewn streets who had resisted authority and hit a prison guard. The state had a warehouse for his kind. He had exhibited anti-social behavior and seemed to have difficulty relating to white people (nobody knew about the social worker). Farview was the place for him—and five or six hundred other black men—to learn to relate to whites. Of the more than five hundred people employed at the hospital, all were white except one, an assistant cook.

"Hey, you! Malone!" It was DeLuca's voice that interrupted the young man's trip backward. "You better start with them boxes. The list of what to put in 'em is back there on the table."

Malone walked toward the rear of Main Dietary and saw the list lying on the stainless-steel-topped table. He went to a stack of empty boxes that had contained canned goods trucked in that week. He placed them on the table. There was room for seven of them.

This time of year, on the verge of winter, he would fill the boxes with canned fruits and vegetables, milk, eggs, dry foods like rice and beans and cereal, meat and such nonfood items as bath soap and toilet paper.

In middle and late summer the boxes contained tomatoes, peaches, and other fresh produce grown on the farm.

Theoretically, the produce raised on the farm was to be consumed by the patients and was supposed to offset some of the cost of running the institution. At least that's what the Department of Public Welfare was telling the legislature. The farm would offset some of the cost, and as a bonus, farm work would have therapeutic value for mental patients.

Actually, the farm produced more milk and beef than anything else, the staff got more of the produce than the patients did, the patients hardly ever ate the fresh tomatoes, and scarcely more than a dozen of them (out of more than 1,300 in the hospital) were deriving the benefits of whatever therapy was available in farm work—a couple of them in gardening, three or four in the milk pasteurizing room, and eight at the barn. And there was considerable talk about the kind of therapy available at the barn.

Since the patients declined to eat the tomatoes, DeLuca, or somebody higher up, decided that the staff should take them home.

It was easy for Malone to understand why the patients turned down the tomatoes: They were presented in the dining room just as they came from the fields—covered with dirt or dust or mud, and insecticides or the insects that the insecticides didn't get. The patients could select a tomato as they went through the chow line, but there was no water to wash them with, and the patients were not allowed to take them back to the wards. Of course the patients could peel the skin off the tomatoes, if they could make the soupspoon work right.

Consequently, there was an ample supply of tomatoes for the staff. In fact, a couple of guards took several bushels each summer and sold them from an impromptu vegetable stand on Route 6, the Grand Army of the Republic Highway, which ran between Carbondale and Honesdale, the county seat. The guards would even get a trusted patient from the minimum security bungalow to run the stand for them. Pure profit, above the fifty cents a day or whatever they paid the patient.

There was plenty of milk and eggs for the guards and doctors, too, since the hospital had its own dairy and DeLuca refused to cook eggs for the patients except for hard-boiled ones very occasionally as a special treat. The guards insisted on having eggs served to them as a second meat dish at every meal, usually scrambled. But Deluca said it was too much trouble to cook eggs that way for the patients—or any way except in the shell in a big vat, about once every month or two.

That was one of the advantages of working in the kitchen or being a pet rat, Malone recognized. An occasional egg. He had even seen Dureen and Coda stand in the chow line sometimes and order an egg like they thought they were at the counter at a White Tower.

As he placed the groceries in the boxes before him, Malone thought about putting some kind of bonus item in the one for the smiling woman. There were a couple problems with the idea. He didn't know what he could put in that she would consider special, and if he could find something, she wouldn't know that she had anything in her box that the other women didn't. He laughed to himself at the unintended pun and wondered how she would react to a little word game when he saw her.

Maybe it would piss her off. Or maybe he would get caught. Well, if she got pissed off, he thought, he *was* caught. Maybe what he said would go right by her. Maybe she was just a hick broad that wouldn't catch on to anything he said that had two meanings. He didn't know much about her.

For one thing, he didn't know her name. Almost as much as anything else about her, he was getting curious to know her name. Who she was. Or more important, who her husband was.

When he thought about it, he didn't know why knowing her

name was so important. If he misread her apparent friendliness and said or did anything that pissed her off enough for her to tell her husband, it wouldn't make any difference who he was. Malone might as well give his soul to God 'cause there wouldn't be enough left of his black ass to say grace over.

But he would like to know who she belonged to so maybe he could at least see him coming.

Just thinking about the woman made him almost shiver with anticipation. Her last trip to the hospital, the one last weekend, was what was pushing him to the edge of disaster, causing him to consider doing or saying something . . . suggestive. On previous trips she had merely smiled. Stood there while he loaded the box into the totally empty trunk. And just smiled at him.

But last time she had put ideas into his head that she might as well have written into cement. They were fixed and they were frightening to contemplate seriously. It was nothing she said. It was what she did.

As usual, she had come to the rear of the car to open the trunk. This time, however, there were two other, rather large boxes in the trunk when Malone leaned under the lid to deposit the groceries. It appeared at first that the grocery box wouldn't fit between the other two, and he held it above them for a moment as he prepared to force them apart. His hands were on each side of the box as she moved in beside him, her thigh pressing against his when she reached across his right arm with her left and placed her hands on top of his as if she were helping him. Then she remained in that position while she appeared to be making certain the box was in the right place in the floor of the trunk.

She was wearing a thin flannel shirt and snug jeans in the crisp sunshine there had been last weekend, and the top two buttons of her shirt were free, providing, to one with the right angle, a glimpse of soft swell rising from a thin brassiere. She was not overlarge, and the plaid flannel disguised what charms were there. But as she reached her arms over his and leaned forward, she pushed her breasts into his arm. He did not take his hands away from the box as she continued to fuss with it and the ones beside it, her chest burning a trail across his bicep, her perfume smothering him in a veil of gardenia.

Then she looked up at him with a smile that could have been received as innocent or inviting. She stood erect and brushed her chestnut hair away from her face. Malone thought she could be any age from eighteen to thirty.

As she reached with him to pull down the trunk lid, she spoke. "Are you in the bungalow?"

"No . . . D-Ward," he replied, looking past her to where a guard was standing but not watching the exchange.

"The bungalow is better. More freedom. You should try to get there."

"I know."

"Well, see you next week."

Then she walked to the driver's side, climbed in behind the steering wheel, and drove away. She had not looked back. He still didn't know her name.

Malone had thought about her often in the ensuing week. She was a picture in his mind twice when he masturbated, and once she was the featured performer in a wet dream. Three or four times he thought he smelled her fragrance of gardenia.

"Shit," he muttered, looking down at his crotch as he felt it grow tight again. "You're gettin' like Lot's wife."

8

WHEN THEY walked through the door to D-Ward and into the dayroom, the first thing Garth and the other patients saw was the bedraggled, semiconscious Chamberlin prone alongside one of the oaken benches in the center of the room. The two guards who had dragged him from the dining room, just ahead of the other patients, were standing over him, breathing heavily from the exertion.

Once all the patients were inside the room and the door had been locked, all six guards gathered around the rumpled Chamberlin and continued what seemed to have been only a prelude in the dining room. This time, however, there was no fear in the eyes or actions of the guards. They were in no particular hurry to subdue the patient. This was punishment. Sadism. There were grins on the faces of the guards as their shoes and boots dug into the torso and legs of the patient who lay now like a sack of grain.

Chamberlin moved only when the force of the blows carried

him a few inches across the floor. And he made hardly any sound, save a few hoarse grunts and groans. No screaming or wailing as before. No protest or even pleading.

As if by common consent, the guards stopped the kicking. One, who had the look of a predatory bird, directed another to "go get the leathers." The second guard returned with a long leather belt, which he strapped around Chamberlin's waist and secured. Then he took the patient's limp arms and placed each one into a leather wrist cuff attached to the belt at the stomach. The complete ensemble usually was referred to as "restraints." Often the guards and patients simply called them "cuffs" or "leathers."

"Put him in the peanut," the man in charge said.

Two of the guards hooked their hands into Chamberlin's armpits and pulled him toward a heavy door at one end of the dayroom, almost in the corner. One of them unlocked the door and they pulled Chamberlin through that doorway to another door about four feet inside the tiny room. Another key unlocked that door, which, like the first one, had a small rectangular opening in the top center, with heavy-gauge wire crisscrossing it.

They dumped Chamberlin on the other side of the second door. He lay on a bare wooden floor which had absorbed the urine and vomit of countless men before him. Had he been able to move his arms, he could have spread them and touched both sides of the room. It was slightly longer than his almost-six-foot body, and high on the right side as one entered there was a small window.

The guards ripped the tattered remains of his bloody shirt from his body, jerking him off the floor and letting him land wherever he fell. Then they removed his trousers and left him lying red and pink and yellow-white like a side of pork. They locked the doors behind them as they returned to the dayroom.

Garth's eyes had been glued to the agonizing scene of sadism, again paying less attention to the perpetrators than to the victim of the brutal ganging-up. It was not until the two guards returned from the peanut that Garth took particular notice of the fact that these six guards were not the same ones who had led the patients to bed the night before. Not that he expected them to be the same, just that guards were guards, generally, and it took a little time in an institution for individual ones to matter to an inmate.

During the incident involving Chamberlin—Garth was yet to

know his name—the guards had seemed like a black-and-blue blur. Now he looked from one to the other, a quick, mental sizing-up. They seemed a little edgy, pacing like football players on the sidelines before a kickoff. Alert. Eyes darting from patient to patient. Anticipating. Frightened maybe.

When two or three of them met Garth's scrutiny with rather long, careful, measuring stares, he looked away and wished they would do likewise. He felt he had made a mistake in looking at them long enough to draw attention to himself. He was suddenly aware of a difference in himself, after less than a full day at the hospital. He didn't want to look any one of them in the eye. He was uncomfortable. In prison he would stare holes through a guard, almost daring the guard to make an issue of it. They were challenging, defiant stares. But here he shared the fright he sensed in the guards. He sure as hell didn't want to do anything to push them over the edge. They didn't seem to operate one-on-one. With him in the shower, and with Chamberlin at the dining room, they all piled in. A man had no chance against five or six or seven of them.

Garth wished he had not been caught looking so intently at the guards. He wanted to just blend in with the crowd, become invisible, avoid being the subject of anyone's attention. Too late.

One of the guards who had returned a stare approached. Still staring. He was sturdy and short-legged, but not fat. He did not have the paunch that seemed prevalent among the guards. He had blond hair, neatly trimmed instead of skinned up the sides and back as many of the other guards wore theirs. The face was crisp, lineless, tanned with the dull sheen of new leather. Almost pretty, but not quite. The eyes were green as seawater. The mouth held a steady sneer.

"You're new," he said, coming to a stop in front of where Garth sat. He stood with legs spread slightly apart, arms folded across his chest.

Garth didn't answer. He just looked up from where he had deposited his clothes before going to bed the night before.

"That nigger give you any trouble last night?"

Garth knew the guard could have been talking about any one of thirty-five or forty or more men on the ward, but he assumed the guard knew where he had slept and was referring to one person in particular. He looked around to see if he could spot the black man who had slept in the bunk beside his. Garth saw him standing only a few feet away, within easy earshot, looking from the guard to Garth.

"I don't know who you mean," Garth said. He was feeling squeezed and was searching for some safe middle ground. The conversation had trouble smeared all over it.

"The one in the bunk next to you," the guard said. His eyes were fixed on Garth, appearing to be unaware or unconcerned that the black man could hear what he said. "Night Train."

"No," Garth said. He quickly remembered. "I mean, no, sir. No trouble."

"You let me know if he does. I don't like coons. Do you?"

Now the exchange was beginning to trouble Garth. It was becoming a trap with teeth. He didn't trust the guard's appearance of offering help, and he sure as shit didn't trust that last question. He remembered what Kirchoff had said about the guards' attitude toward colored patients. So, now he was about to step in the trap. If he answered yes, that he did like "coons," he would more than likely find himself on this and every other guard's shit list. On the other hand, if he agreed with the guard and said that he too disliked "coons," did that mean he would have to keep an eye on Night Train and every other black in the joint all day long and then lie awake at night to keep from getting the hell beaten out of him in his sleep?

"I never thought too much about it," Garth finally said, hoping he was still on safe ground. "There ain't many of them around where I come from."

"What about that guard you got into it with at Western? He was a nigger, wasn't he?"

"Yes, sir."

"See what I mean? Niggers is no good. We got a saying in this hospital . . ." now he swung around to look at Night Train ". . . you can't shine shit. And that's what niggers is—shit. Don't matter whether they wear a uniform or not. Right?" He shifted his gaze back to Garth. "Right?"

Garth felt more cornered. He really didn't know how to answer. He didn't want to answer. He was sure the guard was pranking with him, but he was equally sure that a careless answer could cause him buckets of grief. He saw Night Train looking at him. Almost through him. Waiting for his answer. He could hear music coming from radios, a soft whirlpool of sounds and rhythms and lyrics. Beyond the guard he could see men already forming into the shuffling circle around the center benches.

"I don't know about all of 'em," he finally said, hoping he had found the thread between angering the guard or antagonizing the huge black man. But he refused to cave in completely. Some things on his mind he was going to say. "That one at Western sure was a asshole."

"Bed-makers! Upstairs!" The bellow from the door to the dormitory broke up the conversation. Garth felt as if he'd been released from the trap. At least for now. The voice belonged to a man of about his own height and weight, maybe an inch and ten pounds more. The man had a scowling, violent face with a nose like a hawk's beak, and was of no readily discernible age between thirty-five and fifty.

Garth saw Kirchoff and a few others gather near the guard, then go through the door ahead of him. Everybody else in the dayroom had continued to do pretty much what they had been doing. Most had not even been interrupted. But both the blond, stocky guard and Night Train had moved away from Garth, in opposite directions. He didn't know whether he had pleased either, neither, or both with what he had said about niggers.

He knew one thing for sure: He didn't like niggers any better than that guard did, but he liked them better than he liked guards.

Garth sat on the bench and watched them walk away. Then he gazed around the room at men stretching out under benches and on benches and others shuttling in and out of the toilet like bees entering and leaving a hive. Two thoughts occurred to him. Maybe they were not thoughts—more like urges or sensations or drives. He wanted a cigarette and he wanted food. He was hungry. He had missed supper the night before and had eaten damned near no breakfast as far as he was concerned. Being hungry always made him feel tense, ill-tempered. He remembered his mother saying there would not be any peace in the house until she had fed the tiger. Often there was not much to feed the tiger.

After he started smoking, it seemed to him that cigarettes sometimes curbed his appetite. Whether they did or not, he wanted his first of the day. He got up from the bench and walked across the dayroom toward the shower and the toilet, determined to smoke in whichever one was least crowded. Then he thought he might be able to smoke while taking care of another function, so he went to the toilet.

He took a step inside and was met by a stench so strong it almost made his eyes water. He noticed simultaneously that every commode was occupied and that men were standing against the walls filling the room with smoke. He wondered how they could stand there engulfed in the odor of human excrement and enjoy a cigarette.

He stepped out of the toilet and toward the shower room. As he started to enter it, a voice brought him up short.

"What do you think you're doing?" It was the flush-faced shower-room boy, leaning against the tiled wall just inside the door.

"I'm gonna smoke," said Garth.

"Not in here, you ain't."

"Why ain't I?"

" 'Cause I'm cleaning up in here. I've closed the room."

"Your ass. You're just standing around. You ain't doing nothing."

"I say I'm cleaning up . . . and there ain't nobody comes in here 'til I say so. Smoke in the toilet."

Garth did not want to do that. "How long before you're finished in here?"

"I don't know yet. Maybe an hour . . . could be two or three. I ain't decided yet. Meantime, you smoke in the shithouse 'til I say you smoke in here."

Garth felt his fingers ball into a fist. At that moment he felt that no price would be too high for him to be able to reach out and place his thick fingers around the small man's neck and run his head into the tile walls.

"Before I leave this hellhole I'm gonna squoosh you like a bug, cocksucker." Blood was coursing through the veins at Garth's neck and temples. His jaw was clenched and he was pushing the words through his teeth.

"Just touch me, you fucking ape, and the guards'll have leathers on you before you can spit. They'll fuck you up like they did Chamberlin there." He was pointing out the shower-room door, toward the benches in the center of the room. Then the red face split into a secure smile as one of the guards walked into view a few feet away. "Why don't you get out of here before I call him in here," the shower-room boy said.

Garth had seen the guard, too. He retreated toward the door with a parting admonition.

"Watch your back, motherfucker. Watch your back."

Still seething, he resolved to do without a cigarette rather than stand in the toilet and smell other people's fumes. He decided he would wait until the place cleared out a little, then go in and smoke a cigarette and take a crap at the same time. He could stand the smell of his own business.

He returned to his place on the bench he shared with Kirchoff and sat heavily, carrying an increasing load of anger, resentment, and frustration. And he was sore. The throbbing behind his eye was breaking into his consciousness again. As it had for two months, the pain had come and gone for the past two days. Not really gone, but dulled. Sometimes it was more intense than at other times, but he was sure that without medication it would build and become increasingly worse. The way it was beginning to do now.

He closed his eyes and leaned back into the bench. The pain in his head almost distracted him from the aches all over his body.

He didn't know how much time had passed—didn't really care —when he felt the bench jiggle under the weight of another occupant. He opened his eyes and saw that Kirchoff had returned.

"Does a doctor ever come around here?" he asked Kirchoff, but went on without waiting for an answer. "I gotta get something for this headache. What do you gotta do to see a doctor?"

"Ask Hawk," Kirchoff said.

"Who's Hawk?"

"Charge guard." Kirchoff sort of nodded toward the entrance end of the dayroom. "That one in the rocking chair . . . looks kinda like a hawk . . . Don't call him Hawk to his face—name's Kazbek. You better call him Mr. Kazbek." Kirchoff looked at the guard for a long minute before he continued. "He decides everything on D-Ward . . . during the day, that is. If he wants you to see the doctor, you see him. If he doesn't, you don't."

"Do I just walk up to him and ask him?"

"He isn't going to ask you, that's for sure."

"When do I ask him?" Garth did not notice that he was now including himself as a member of the madness. He was phrasing questions in the first person, not the second. It had taken less than a day.

"Before the doctor comes," Kirchoff said. "He only comes on the ward once a day, and Hawk isn't going to call him back unless there is a damned serious emergency." He looked toward the peanut, where Chamberlin continued to lie unconscious in leather restraints. "You notice they haven't called a doctor for that fool yet."

The guard was slowly rocking in his chair when Garth approached. He looked up but did not stop rocking as Garth asked the question.

"Why do you want to see him?" the guard asked, his cold, intractable eyes fixed on Garth.

"I got terrible headaches," Garth said. "Behind my eye. My right eye. This one here." He raised his right hand to it. "I've had 'em for a while now. Maybe two months."

"You just got here, didn't you, boy?"

"Last night . . . sir." Garth felt like a child before a school principal.

"You already starting to be a pest?"

"No, sir, I ain't being a pest. I don't mean to be."

"I think you are." The eyes narrowed. "And I think the doctor will be too busy with sick patients to waste time with a faker."

"I ain't faking. You can check my records from Western." Garth's brain was beginning to smolder. Here he was, a grown man, having to go through a bunch of shit, damned near beg, to see a doctor in a hospital, for Christ's sake. It seemed that everybody in the hospital tried his best to be a sonofabitch. Everybody except Kirchoff, and damned if he didn't seem colder today than he had last night.

"I tell you what I'll check." The Hawk stopped rocking and locked eyes with Garth. "I'll check your ass into that peanut, you fucking waterbrain. I don't take shit, I give it. I'll check your record when I'm damned good and ready and you don't tell me when that is." He paused to let the words have their intended effect. "Now, get your butt back over on one of them benches. If the doctor's got time to see you, I'll call you."

The Hawk flipped the back of his hand as if he were shooing a fly from a picnic lunch. "Get away from me."

Garth's hands knotted into hammerheads and again veins swelled in his neck and temples. He didn't know why he had to take this kind of abuse. He didn't think he could take much of it. But he saw two other blue shirts moving into the corners of his vision. He began to step slowly back, and back. He did not take his eyes from the predatory nose and scowling mouth. The Hawk was now rocking again.

Inside, Garth moaned at his own futility.

9

BEHIND HAWK'S eyes, hot, frayed wires of challenge and fear had touched during the brief confrontation with the new patient and, once again, had made him tingle with hatred for the animals he kept caged in this zoo. Part of him relished the thought of sinking the steel toe of his boot into the stomach—lower was better—of the hulking Neanderthal slowing backing away from him. Another part broke out in cold chills of apprehension at what he knew the patient would do to him if he got those blacksmith's arms around his throat.

He wanted to think he could handle himself one-on-one with all "them deranged bastards," but he knew—and loathed the fact that he never would make a move against one of them without ample help from other guards. And he was wary of ever turning his back on the men in white T-shirts and denim pants. He lived in fear of getting caught alone with more than one of them in a secluded part of the hospital. Or worse, outside the hospital.

Fear. He lived with fear, he was fond of saying with considerable bravado. His job was to control some of the most vicious criminals in the state of Pennsylvania. Killers. Axe murderers. Lunatics who would kill their mothers or rape little girls and boys. "Sure," he would tell anyone who gave enough of a damn to ask, "it's dangerous work if you don't know how to keep them under control."

He never really explained to an outsider exactly how he kept control, shrugging it off with "There are certain things you can do . . ." or "We got our ways." Sometimes, if his audience was more than passingly interested, he would launch into how "You have to train them just like you would an animal, a dog or a horse . . . some of them you have to teach not to pee on the floor. Grown men, these are . . ."

In truth, he trained them with the same fear he lived with. He used fear as a weapon. It never occurred to him that fear fostered hatred. In him as much as in the patients. Fear reduced a man's self-respect. Fear often led to humiliation, a feeling of inadequacy. A man who was afraid to stand up for himself was a man who was losing or had lost his self-esteem. That man began to hate himself and he hated the man who had stirred the fear and the sense of inadequacy that went with it. Fear bred hatred, then hatred fed on fear. For all of them.

Hawk did whatever he could to make a patient scared of him, intimidated, afraid to do anything or say anything he might not approve. That was better. That way, they seldom even came near him. Therapy was a bunch of crap and there wasn't any therapy that amounted to anything anyway. Fear kept them in line, he thought. Keep them looking over their shoulder for that boot in the ass and they don't think of much mischief. That was treatment. Shoe-leather treatment.

They used to give some shock treatments, he remembered, but they stopped that. Now about all they did was give some drugs. For his part, he just tried to make them all believe that he would just as soon stomp them to death as not.

Hawk worried that someday a patient would be released from the hospital and, carrying a heavy grudge, would seek him out and wait for him in the dark. Or get into his house and do something terrible to his wife or daughter. Or both.

The memory of Joe DeArmond was fresh in his and every other

guard's mind. A patient had not been out of the hospital a month when he came back with a pistol and shot Joe as he walked down the front steps of the hospital. Shot him in the stomach and paralyzed him from the waist down. Then the crazy bastard realized he had shot the wrong man, that he had meant to shoot one of the doctors. At least that's what he said.

You never knew what they might do. That's why Hawk never recommended any of the patients on his ward for even a diagnostic evaluation by the staff, much less a discharge. He could never count on the staff to turn down a patient for sure. The guy who shot DeArmond was an example. It was better to make the patient act out in some way, go on a toot and provide a good basis for recommending a longer period of treatment.

Treatment. A needle full of juice or some "M&M's," the slick-coated orange or pale-green or yellowish-brown, camel-colored pills of Thorazine or Mellaril. He liked to give the hard-to-handle patients a dose of prolixin on top of Thorazine and set them to slobbering and cogwheeling and looking like the fools they were. That kept them under pretty good control while he was around. He didn't have to worry about keeping an eye on them all the time. He saw to it that they took the medication whether they wanted it or not. Fuck 'em, he thought. He just didn't want to have to worry about them.

Hawk didn't think his job was such a bad one, as long as he didn't have to worry about getting sucker-punched the way Parton was by Chamberlin, or having a finger stuck in his eye or having a whole bunch of patients go berserk in a hard-to-control situation such as at mealtime or during yard-out or movies.

But having them all scared of each other and the guards as well went a long way toward keeping them from acting together. Of course, a lot of the real crazies would just as soon attack a guard as they would another patient. Either they didn't know the difference or they didn't care. They just wanted to hit something. Lash out. A lot of them were said to be brain-damaged, but Hawk didn't know how anybody at Farview would detect that, since there were no neurologists at the hospital, and the only psychiatrist was Dr. Dallmeyer and he didn't check any of the patients when they came in. Hawk figured they just put "organic brain syndrome" on the records when they didn't really know what was wrong with the patients.

Aside from having to deal with the nuts and the fear of the nuts, the job was a pretty good one, Hawk thought. Certainly the best one he ever had. The pay wasn't bad, and with people out sick or on vacation or what have you, there was plenty of overtime if he wanted it. There was civil service protection now and as long as there were enough patients in the hospital there would be a demand for guards.

It wasn't like in the coal mines. When the mines closed the jobs went. When he lost his job in the mines, there wasn't any such thing as welfare. And being in the union didn't make any difference if there wasn't a mine to work in. After the mines closed, he didn't know where to turn. There were just not any other jobs available in those scrubby, worthless mountains. Hell, one out of every five people who could work was out looking for a job.

Thank God for Walt Luker, he thought. Walt was the most influential politician in the county, maybe the most influential in Northeast Pennsylvania, as far as state government was concerned. He was influential enough that he never had to run for public office. He always got appointed to his government jobs and used his influence to help other men get elected so he could keep getting appointed.

One thing about Walt, Hawk thought. He didn't mind cramming his influence down another politician's throat. When the mines closed, Walt found state jobs for a lot of the miners. Republican patronage jobs. A lot of the guards were at Farview because Walt sent them there. Kazbek knew he was one of them, and like the others, he had become a Luker loyalist. He voted Republican, did his banking where Luker was a director, and patronized the other Republican businessmen and merchants who were in Luker's tight circle.

Through his control of the circle, Luker controlled the county, economically and politically. By building up the hospital's employment rolls through the dispensing of patronage, he came to control the county's second biggest employer. He was a director of the county's biggest bank, so he also controlled the lawyers who depended on the bank's business in real estate transactions and foreclosures.

Luker had a great deal to say about who in the area got state contracts, political favors, government jobs and any elected post from coroner to congressman.

Luker and Dr. Dallmeyer, the hospital superintendent, were quite friendly, probably because they had a common objective—to keep the hospital running with a maximum of state funding and a minimum of state interference. Hawk figured that was the primary reason that whenever a patient died, it was always due to natural causes or an accident, regardless of what the real causes might be.

Hawk remembered one death in particular that had been explained away so as to prompt as little outside investigation as possible.

One winter not long ago a seventy-seven-year-old patient named Mathison was in the infirmary, R-Ward, because his overall condition was generally deteriorating. It was about 5:30 in the morning and Mathison had been sleeping fitfully, sometimes awake, sometimes dozing. A patient named Brent awoke and had to go to the bathroom. On his way, he stopped by Mathison's bed to check on him. They had a brief conversation and Brent went on to the bathroom. A few minutes later, as Brent and a patient named Mincher were coming out of the bathroom, they saw another patient, Roger Krooger, on top of Mathison's bed, straddling the old man and choking him.

They ran to the bed, yelling for Krooger to get off Mathison, but he continued choking the old man. Finally Mincher pushed and punched Krooger enough to knock him off Mathison. By then, guards were on the scene and helped hold Krooger.

When the guards arrived Mathison was having trouble breathing and began gasping for air. They tried to keep him breathing by administering oxygen, but he stopped a few minutes later and was pronounced dead at 6:20.

An internal investigation was conducted by Lieutenant Pagnotti, and he determined that the two patients were telling the truth when they reported seeing Krooger choking Mathison. Dr. Dallmeyer then notified the county coroner's office about the death, but did not mention the report that Mathison had been choked.

The coroner performed an autopsy, still unaware of the incident of choking, and determined that death was due to natural causes. However, he did note that there was discoloration on the throat and that there were pettechiae and hemorrhage of the larynx.

Dr. Dallmeyer then used the coroner's finding of death by natural causes to discredit the eyewitness accounts of the two patients, Brent and Mincher, and wrote an elaborate report to state officials saying that "based on the autopsy findings and the unreliability of the patients' statements, death was attributed to natural causes."

That was the length to which they would go to explain away the testimony of patients about the killing of a patient by another patient. It gave Hawk and the other guards every reason to feel confident that the hospital authorities would go even further to protect them from statements or charges by patients, whether in eyewitness accounts or letters home.

Their ideas about the operation of the hospital were about the same as Hawk's on running his ward. He wanted maximum support from the front office and minimum interference. For the most part, that's what he felt he got. Especially with Lieutenant Pagnotti basically running the show. He pretty much let the charge guards run the wards, as long as there were not problems that could not be easily explained and forgotten, and as long as he got his share of the spoils. Of course, Pagnotti liked to make the decisions, but usually he followed the recommendations of the charge guards. Otherwise they would not be able to reward their pet rats or control the guards who worked under them.

Nevertheless, though Pagnotti professed to believe in strict adherence to the chain of command, Hawk knew that the lieutenant didn't vigorously discourage patients or lower-ranking guards from bypassing the charge guard and coming to him with a problem or some tidbit of information. Pagnotti had his share of pets on every ward, and it was rare indeed when something was going on in the hospital and he did not know about it. Usually in advance.

Patients often told him things in letters ostensibly intended for their families or friends or attorneys. The patients learned that every letter was censored in Center before it left the hospital. Pagnotti had a special person assigned to read each one, with instructions to report anything remotely intriguing. Hawk knew that several times patients—and some charge guards—had been surprised when Pagnotti walked onto a ward and knew precisely where there was a hidden weapon or a cache of money.

Those were the times when his eyes flashed like a blade fresh

from an emery wheel, then and when he had a patient begging
not to be sent to J-Ward.

But Hawk did not have Pagnotti making many surprise visits to
his ward. Patients on his ward had to submit their letters to him
unsealed. He, not Pagnotti, would find contraband and accumulated cash. Then he would turn it over to the lieutenant for dis-
posal or splitting up. And he, not some patient, would incur
Pagnotti's goodwill. Like it or not, Pagnotti ran the place.

Staying in Pagnotti's good graces was one way Hawk stayed
happy in his work. But there were other ways too. He rarely paid
for his cigars. Dureen provided those, and Hawk provided him
the right to operate his private shop in the corner of the dayroom.
Coda always supplied him with hot coffee. His uniforms were
laundered by a patient in the laundry and sometimes, only sometimes, he gave the man a quarter. Sometimes he gave him a dime
and sometimes he just gave him a hard look—which made the
quarter look much better.

It cost Hawk fifty cents to get his car washed and waxed, he ate
two meals free every day he worked, and his wife could pick up a
box of groceries each week.

Not all the guards got free groceries, although all of them got
tomatoes and peaches in season; but almost all of them got something extra. Some got a split of patients' Social Security or veterans' benefit checks; some got whatever they wanted from the care
packages sent to the patients by their families; some got whatever
they wanted—that fit—from patients' Sears, Roebuck orders;
some got cut in on pornography rentals or the sale of water laced
with a little whiskey.

Those deals were damned good, Hawk thought. Patients would
pay five dollars to rent a crotch-shot nude picture for half an
hour. They would pay twenty for a small Coke bottle filled half
with whiskey—the cheapest kind—and half with water.

Hawk and all the other guards always had shined boots and
shoes. It cost ten cents a pair and it was a good way for a new
patient to get started. The new guy would have to go into hock a
little bit at first in order to buy polish, but he didn't have to buy a
brush right off. He could buff with his T-shirt. Some patients
never stopped shining shoes. It was steady income and was not
very much trouble.

Anybody who wanted could lend money for one hundred

percent interest. There were a few patients who made loans to guards, but not at anything like one hundred percent. They were happy just to get repaid, and many times they didn't. But guards who lent money always got repaid, often in cigarettes at thirty cents a pack. Guards could bet with patients with small risk of losing—generally no risk—and they never had to pay for a snack or a pack of cigarettes or a cigar off the candy wagon.

Ceramics—everything from ashtrays to Christmas trees—from the occupational therapy shop made very nice, cheap presents, and Hawk had brought color photographs of his wife and daughter and a patient had made beautiful oil portraits the size of the one of President Kennedy out in Center. Hawk wondered briefly why patients painted so many pictures of Kennedy. Damned if everybody that went to the paint shop didn't do a picture of Kennedy. Him and Jesus. They were the favorites. And that nigger that led them marches down South. Martin Luther King. But only the niggers painted pictures of him. Him and Jesus and Kennedy. The white patients did Kennedy and Jesus and the niggers did Kennedy and Martin Luther King and Jesus.

They could sell a picture of Kennedy or Jesus, either one, to the people in the area, but Hawk didn't know anybody who would want to buy a picture of that nigger. Less than one percent of the population around there was black. They should limit the craft shops to men who would produce something that people outside would want, Hawk thought. Otherwise it just piled up in the basement.

On top of all those fringes, Hawk could come to work at six o'clock in the morning and leave at two o'clock in the afternoon to go work on his small farm.

So, all things considered, it was a good job. Stacking the dangers against the benefits, the benefits came out ahead. It was one thing to display scratches and other injuries incurred "subduing" a patient who had gone on a "bat," or a "toot"; but he and the other guards knew that the one real danger was that someday the hospital might not have enough patients to require all the guards presently employed.

There was also the danger that some patient would get discharged and tell somebody outside what was going on inside, but that was a remote risk. Who would believe a man who had been a patient in a hospital for the criminally insane? Hawk knew the answer to that question. Nobody.

Even when a patient's letter was successfully smuggled out without being censored, there was rarely a ripple. Letters to the governor got the kind of action the hospital appreciated. A recent one was routed through bureaucratic channels back to the superintendent, with a cover letter advising that perhaps the patient's letter could be useful in furthering his treatment. The letter was about all the gambling that went on inside the hospital, gambling between patients and guards. There was no question that the letter was used in the patient's treatment.

No, Hawk thought, the only other danger worth worrying about was that one of these fuckers would be released and come back to pay some debts, like the one that shot DeArmond. The answer to that was just to keep them inside. And while they were inside, keep them at the point of a boot.

The word "boot" brought to mind his good friend Boots Ringgold, who worked the 10 P.M. to 6 A.M. shift on D-Ward. He got his nickname from the steel plates in the toes of his boots and his inclination to "put the boots to 'em," as he was fond saying. Boots viewed the patients as prisoners, pure and simple. Prisoners sent to Farview to be punished. He'd even said as much the other night in a bar in Waymart while philosophizing over a few Stroh's.

"These type people—the prisoners—have got to be controlled somehow and some of 'em only understand a good lacing," Boots had said.

Everybody at the table had agreed. Hawk had nodded with the others, but with only half a mind. The other half was wondering why Boots was sitting there every night drinking beer instead of at home with that young, good-looking wife of his. Hawk thought she looked like she might have a roving eye, and if she were his wife, he damned sure would be doing his homework before somebody else did.

10

THE MORNING progressed about like most mornings on D-Ward, except that Chamberlin went into the peanut in worse shape than was usually the case when a man was confined to the tiny, dank room. But there was a patient in the peanut about as often as there was not, so other than the degree of punishment involved, the extent to which Chamberlin was battered, this day was not much different from other days.

Dr. Zundel had come, wearing galoshes as was his custom, rain or shine, summer and winter. He was picking his nose as usual, and he looked as though he had dodged the razor for the third or fourth straight day. As usual.

Also as usual, his once-white smock was soiled enough to have belonged to the service manager at a garage. And as was his practice, seemingly his studied practice, he attributed every patient's complaint to the same cause: "You're just crazy as a shithouse rat."

110

He went along with Hawk's determination of the dosages due the patients Hawk decided needed medication, wrote out the prescriptions Hawk requested, and left the ward without dispensing any medicine himself. He knew the guards would handle that.

One patient had resisted taking his medicine, resisted enough to require force. As was the custom in such cases, the patient was pinned to the floor by four guards and the dosage was administered by hypodermic—through his trouser leg.

Hawk had not allowed the new man to see Dr. Zundel about his headache. That was another favorite trick of his. Make a patient ask . . . beg . . . and still deny him what he wanted. Make the granting of each request seem like papal dispensation. The patient had to learn that he could not see a doctor whenever he wanted. He had to learn that he must depend on a guard's goodwill for everything, even for relief of pain. When the new patient was turned down, actually ignored, he would understand that a request to see the doctor was not routinely granted, even if this was supposed to be a hospital. Then the patient would try to please, even seek ways to please, Hawk and other guards in order to gain permission for something as usually fundamental as seeing a doctor—for whatever good that would do him even if he got permission. Two aspirin and back to his bench was about the best this new man could expect for his headache. Farview had no way to tell for sure that a man was brain-damaged, much less figure out what made a head ache.

There had been a couple of scuffles between patients walking around in the circle, mostly pushing and shoving that Hawk didn't let get out of hand. Four men were now sitting strapped to the center benches. They—and Chamberlin in the peanut— would remain in their present positions until Hawk personally said they could be released. That was true of any punishment. The guard who ordered punishment was the only one who could order an end to it. It was not a stated rule, it was understood. Both by the patients and by the hospital personnel, even supervisors. If a guard who ordered benching or time in the peanut was off for two days and forgot to end the punishment before he left work, the patient would continue in punishment until the guard returned.

Hawk chuckled to himself as he remembered an old guard, since retired, who benched a patient and then went on vacation for two weeks. The guard claimed that he just forgot to order the leathers removed, but when he came back to work, the patient was on the bench.

The relatively minor scuffles in the circle had been fairly forgettable incidents, and he made a mental note to tell Bulldog, the charge guard on the evening shift, that he could take the four off the bench whenever he wanted.

Chamberlin would need to be transferred to J-Ward when he woke up. That shithead needed to learn not to hit a guard. The transfer could wait until the afternoon. Maybe right after dinner.

The only other vaguely exciting thing about the morning had been the new man's trip to the crapper after the doctor had left the ward. Hawk had seen him go in. He always kept an eye on new patients, and especially ones as big as—what's his name? Wade. Garth Wade. And he could tell that Wade was pissed off about not being allowed to see the doctor. Anyway, Hawk had seen him go into the toilet. He figured he was going in to have a smoke. Or take a leak. Or else he was in for a little surprise, because he had not come to ask for toilet paper before he went in.

The toilet paper was on a roll hanging from the arm of Hawk's rocking chair. It was in about the same place on every ward, either on the charge's rocking chair or at the end of the center benches. Regardless, it was at a place where the guards could keep an eye on it and control its use. On some wards, a patient could come to the roll and take a sheet or two on his own. On D, at least when Hawk was around, only the pets could take their own paper. The others took whatever Hawk dispensed. Sometimes one square, sometimes none, never more than two.

Control of the paper reduced the opportunities for a bona fide nut to set fire to a roll or clog the toilets.

But the policy had another benefit. It forced a patient to come to the guards for yet another basic need, to come hat-in-hand asking for something to clean his butt with. It reminded Hawk a lot of a three-year-old yelling, "Mama, I'm through, come wipe me." It put the guards in the position of controlling whether a man has shit in his crack and skid marks on his underwear.

It was just another demeaning, dehumanizing weapon for the guards to use as they taught the patients how to live with society's rules and laws. Another weapon to teach them to respect authority. Like showers and shaves. Patients were allowed one shower a week and were shaved once every couple of weeks, depending on when the barber made his rounds. And everybody participated. Cooperation was a sign that the patient was making progress.

But there were conflicts for the more discerning patient to work out in his own mind. If he wanted to take a shower every day and practice the kind of personal hygiene that is generally accepted as good by society, he could not. But if he refused to take a shower when the guards decided it was time to take showers, he would be thrown under the shower kicking and screaming. The guards kicking and him screaming.

The same with shaving. If it was important to a patient's self-image that he shave every day, too bad for his self-image. Patients were shaved only when the barber came, regardless of how fast or how long whiskers grew, or how scruffy, itchy, or uncomfortable they became. Yet, facial hair—well-trimmed mustaches or beards—was not allowed.

They were issued no deodorant and all but the hustlers were limited to one change of clothes each week. Since there were no napkins in the dining room, and meat had to be picked up and eaten because the soupspoons would not cut it, hands and chins were wiped on T-shirts which soon began to smell of food and grease.

By the end of a week without a shower or shave or toothbrushing, or a change of clothes, even the patients who had not beaten off or peed in their pants looked and smelled like derelicts. Cur dogs.

The more sane among them knew it and hated it. The guards knew it and enjoyed it—almost depended on it. For them it was an important and obvious difference between the keepers and the kept. The guards seemed to need to have—and be able to see— such readily observable physical differences between them and the patients.

The contrasting quality of the food served to patients and guards was one easily recognized difference in how the two groups were treated. And anybody could see the difference between the powder-blue shirts and black bow ties and the grimy T-shirts and grizzled faces.

It was almost as if the guards—and the rest of the hospital staff too, for that matter—were afraid that if differences between them and the patients could not be seen, they might not be discerned. Or even be.

Garth had been sitting on a commode smoking a cigarette and was almost finished with his business when he looked up and saw the florid face of the shower-room boy he had already come to despise. Almost involuntarily, he closed his thighs. The younger man was grinning, almost laughing out loud at what he knew that Garth didn't.

Garth looked back down at the floor, took a final drag from his cigarette, and dropped it between his legs to a hissing drowning in the commode. Then he reached back to his right and looked behind to either side of where he was sitting and slumped slightly. He rested his elbows on his knees again and turned his head toward the man who had come into the toilet minutes before and had taken the seat to his left.

"Where's the paper?" he asked the man.

"Out there," the man said.

"Where?"

"It's on a roll on Hawk's chair. You didn't see it?"

"I didn't know this was what it was for. I thought there'd be some in here."

"Shoulda asked for it before you came in here," the shower-room boy said, grinning broadly, delighted at Garth's predicament.

"Fuck you!" Garth said, but it was hardly adequate and did not ease his embarrassment. Then he looked again to the man beside him. "What the hell do I do now?"

The man shrugged. "This prick can get you some, or sell you some, if he wants to," he said looking in the direction of the shower-room boy.

Garth did not want to ask the boy for a favor, but he didn't want to walk away without wiping his ass. What the hell, he decided. It didn't hurt to ask.

"Can you get me some?"

"I could," said the boy, still smiling, "but I won't."

"Why not? What the fuck's it to you to get me a piece of paper?"

"You got it. What the fuck's it to me if you don't have no paper? I'll sell you a piece of newspaper."

"Sell me a piece of newspaper? Why not toilet paper?"

"Newspaper . . . or you can use your hand. I don't care."

"Ain't got no money," Garth said.

"Cigarettes'll do. Cost you five."

"Five?" Garth reached down and pulled a rumpled pack from the pocket of the denims bunched at his feet. He couldn't see inside the opening well enough or tell by feeling how many cigarettes were in the pack. He tore the top of the pack completely open and counted seven cigarettes. He didn't see the shower-room boy counting them, too. He had another pack of the two Leonard had given him before he left Western. It was in his other pants pocket.

"Five's too many," he said.

"Then use your hand."

"You lousy faggot bastard!" His voice had risen and his eyes smoldered. He felt foolish sitting on a commode with his pants around his ankles, rather helplessly arguing with a red-faced teenager about how many cigarettes it was worth to wipe his ass with newspaper. His inclination was to pull up his pants, unwiped butt and all, and run his fist down the kid's throat. Better still, he would wipe his ass with his hand and rub the hand all over the shower-room boy's face. "I don't see how you've kept from getting your smart lip smeared around your ear," he said, too loud.

A guard appeared at the door. It was the blond one that had talked to Garth about niggers earlier that morning.

"What's going on?" he demanded.

"He don't have no paper," the shower-room boy said, nodding toward Garth. The man sitting beside Garth took a quiet swipe at his own bottom with the piece of tissue he had been holding wadded in his palm, pulled his pants up, flushed his commode, and scurried from the room without buttoning his denims.

"I was gonna sell him some newspaper, but he don't like the price," the shower-room boy went on.

"How much you asking?" the guard inquired.

"Seven," the young man said.

"He's a lying sonofabitch," Garth fairly shouted. "He said five."

"Seven," the crimson face said. "I said seven or he could use his hand."

"The motherfucker said five," Garth bitterly insisted.

"I don't give a shit what he said," the guard spat. "Give him seven or flush it and get the hell out of here."

Garth knew he had lost. But he refused to let the shower-room boy get anything out of his victory. He flushed the commode, then stood and pulled up his underwear and denims together. He looked with loathing at the kid and stomped between him and the guard into the dayroom. He looked back at them over his shoulder and both were smiling.

Hawk had seen him stalk out of the toilet and recognized the anger. He asked the blond guard about it and after hearing what had transpired he knew the new man would bear watching.

After dinner, as the midday meal was identified at Farview, Hawk decided it was time to relieve himself of Chamberlin. He was a pain in the ass and had been ever since he came over from Q-Ward. He probably had been a pain in the ass since he came into the hospital thirteen years ago. He had not been sent to Farview by a criminal court but had been committed by a civil court. He had spent some time on other wards and already had made a few side trips to solitary in J-Ward over the years, Hawk knew.

Dr. Combest called Chamberlin an "unreconstructed pervert," who was "without any control over his primitive urges." There was no question that he was homosexual, but it didn't take a psychiatrist to know that. It wasn't from any special medical training that Dr. Combest knew it. What he knew about psychiatry he had picked up from reading or seminars.

Chamberlin was always patting some other patient on the behind and starting a scuffle about it. And he was always having to be chased out of the toilet. Hawk had heard from another guard, a third- or fourth-hand evaluation supposedly, that Chamberlin could suck a dick until a man's head caved in.

He had been given several electric-shock treatments, but they had not seemed to change him substantially. He still had a combative nature and lacked self-control. Hawk didn't mind his patting other patients on the butt so much as he minded his hitting guards the way he had hit Parton at breakfast. Hawk had to send the man to J-Ward for that. If he let him get away with just the beatings and some time in the peanut, that would show other patients that they could hit a guard and get off with some boot shining. The next patient might do more than slap.

Hawk would have preferred to transfer Chamberlin to R-Ward instead. He would have liked to send him permanently. Let him check out of the hospital from R-Ward. Check out of the world from R-Ward.

He couldn't remember who had first described R-Ward as the place a patient was sent for the "ultimate discharge." One thing he knew for sure: Nobody died on his ward. They might stop breathing on D-Ward and their heart might stop beating in the peanut, but they died on R-Ward. Of natural causes. All the records would show how he died in the infirmary and nobody would know the difference. Probably nobody would care. Chamberlin's family had not visited him in more than a year, so they didn't seem to care. They were supposed to have plenty of money, they just didn't want to mess with their embarrassment of a son.

Hawk sent him on to J-Ward and passed the word to the guards there that Chamberlin was the one who had hit Parton. He felt certain that all the guards in the hospital knew about it by now, but he wanted to make sure. Maybe the men on J-Ward would find a reason to transfer Chamberlin to R-Ward.

It was almost time for Hawk and his crew of guards to end their shift. He sent one of his men on a final pass around the dayroom, a cursory inspection tour designed more to cover himself than to be assured of the well-being of the patients. He usually made the quick kind of last check himself before he left work, so that if something happened to any of the patients later, he could always answer the pitiful in-house inquisitors with a degree of truthfulness about how good a patient's condition had been when he last saw him, just before leaving for the day.

He had one of the other guards remove the leather cuffs from the four men who had scuffled with each other earlier in the day, deciding that he might as well not leave that for Bulldog to do. He got verbal assurance from each of them that they would be "good boys from now on." He didn't believe them, but he figured they didn't believe much he told them, either. For both sides it was pretty much a matter of promising rainbows and delivering rain.

Glancing along the benches against the wall, Hawk saw Garth Wade and Paul Kirchoff sitting turned in such a way that they were looking through a window to the gray, freezing freedom a few feet away.

Garth shivered and clasped his arms tighter against his chest, clamping his hands into his armpits as if it were becoming as cold inside as out. Although his eyes were facing outward, he was seeing something else. The picture of the raw and bloody Chamberlin would not go away. It frightened him, but it made him angry. He was about to complete his first full day here, and he already knew that he must control his temper. The beating he had received in the shower was like a woodshed spanking compared with the merciless pummeling Chamberlin had received for losing control of his anger for one brief moment. Garth wondered if he was still alive when he was taken away. Kirchoff had said that Chamberlin was probably going to J-Ward and that he would be lucky to come back alive.

Garth's eyes focused again on the softly falling snow outside the window, but he thought about the older man sitting beside him. Kirchoff had been here twenty-eight years, he said. How could a man take all this for twenty-eight years? This was worse than prison. Far worse. If you hit a guard in prison, like Chamberlin did, they sent you to the hole. Here, it looked like they would kill you.

He turned his eyes back to the room and they landed on Hawk and locked with his cold, impenetrable ones. They held for several seconds, neither man having intended it, but each unwilling to avert his eyes in what had become the start of a private war.

Hawk lost the first secret skirmish. He looked out the window near his rocking chair again. A strong wind was blowing the snow in swirls. The mercury already had dropped below freezing several times at night in the Moosic Mountains, but according to the weather forecasts he had heard on a patient's radio, the temperature would dip well into the teens this night, and it was not yet December.

Winter came early to Farview. And stayed late.

PART II

The one means that wins the easiest victory over reason: terror and force.

—Adolf Hitler

11

JONES LAY pressed against his cell wall, trying to wedge his frail, nude body into the concrete corner to avoid the frigid wind and the thin swirls of snow forced ahead of it through the open window above him. He was huddled in the right corner of the tiny cell, at the opposite end from the door. He debated moving.

In this his seventh winter inside the cell, he still was not sure which was the warmest corner. He did know that a corner was warmer than along any of the walls, and he was absolutely certain that a corner was warmer than any place in the middle of the tiny cubicle, where wind could surround him. The truth of the matter was that he had tried every inch of the perimeter of the cell and knew for a fact that the warmest place was against the wooden door. At least it was warmest to whichever side of his body was pressed against it. But it presented two problems. One: The other side of his body had to face directly toward the window and the wind. Two: Lying against the door took him out of the view of guards looking in through the small rectangular hole in the door and gave them an excuse to open the heavy door abruptly, shoving his manacled body roughly ahead of its sweep before he could scurry out of the way. That would be followed by a kick and orders to sit where somebody could keep an eye on him.

He didn't know where they thought he would go, and he knew they could not be worried about his suicide. There was no way he could take his own life, even if he had wanted to, which he didn't. He had often thought about going to bed warm and never waking up. But he only thought about that in the winter and he didn't think that meant he wanted to kill himself.

He pulled his arms tighter around his gray-brown legs and tucked his head between his knees so that his ears were covered. Even so, he could hear the sounds coming from the cell next door. The muted wailing like a distant train whistle.

It had been going on for almost two months, by Jones' count, sometimes worse than it was this particular late January afternoon. Or was it February already?

All he knew was that they had brought the man into J-Ward sometime around Thanksgiving and that he was in bad shape then. They had carried him in, hands and feet. Jones had seen that much through the small slot window in his door. He had seen the man as they carried him past. There was blood all over his clothes and his eyes were closed.

He knew that the guards had stripped the man, because he saw one of them walk back down the corridor with the red-stained shirt and slacks.

Jones remembered that it was the day after Thanksgiving that he learned the man's name. He heard the charge guard say something to another guard about a package arriving for "that Chamberlin cocksucker."

"What's in it?" the second guard had asked.

"Just some toothpaste and shaving cream and shit like that," the charge said. "You want it?"

"Sure," the second guard said, "if it's the kind I use."

"C'm'on," the charge said. "You kidding me? You use the kind that's free."

Jones heard them laugh and later saw the second guard flipping the can of shaving cream end over end and catching it, again and again, as he paced the middle of the corridor.

He had heard Chamberlin's name repeated often in the ensuing two months and he had heard the rise and fall of moans and screams. He saw Chamberlin dragged to a shower and back. He saw guards walking away from Chamberlin's cell just after the screams had been loudest.

This late afternoon they were not loud. Then they seemed to be not at all. There was a quiet that seemed almost startling. Even the guards noticed it. One walked to the door of Chamberlin's cell and looked in. Then he motioned to another at the end of the battleship-gray hallway. The other joined the first at the door and looked in through the small rectangle.

Jones unwound from his frost-stiffened hunker in the corner and crept toward his own door.

He stood at this doorway and looked sideways through the tiny opening, toward Chamberlin's cubicle. He saw the two guards and heard their whispering, but he could not make out exactly what they were saying. One of the guards walked away from Chamberlin's door and past Jones, headed toward the charge's office. Within what seemed to be only a few seconds, the guard returned, accompanied by two others, one of them the charge. A guard rattled a large key in Chamberlin's door lock and opened the door, then all four men disappeared from Jones' view. He could not see what they saw when they entered the cell, but he heard one of them mention R-Ward in a normal tone.

A couple of minutes later the four of them came back into the corridor. The patient, a guard at each arm, one at each leg, sagged between them. He looked raw and bruised and welty.

As the guards lugged their pitiful burden toward the door to the main corridor—where an immediate left turn put one almost at the door to R-Ward—one of them looked toward Jones's door and locked eyes with the diminutive patient.

"Pull your fucking head back and look out your window," he growled. But he did not follow up the implied threat and shared the load on to the main door.

The guards reached the main door about the same time Yancey was coming down the main corridor from the commissary. He pushed his candy wagon before him and had to come to a stop as the door to J-Ward opened and the guards and their fragile freight entered the hallway.

He looked to see who was hanging between the black trouser

legs, but the man's head was falling loosely backward from the shoulders like that of a chicken with a broken neck, and Yancey could not see the patient's upside-down face.

As the four guards shuffled toward R-Ward with Chamberlin, Yancey turned to the guard who was holding open the door to J-Ward so that the candy wagon could be pushed through.

"What happened to him?" Yancey asked, careful to keep a disinterested tone. "He fall down?"

"I don't know," said the guard, just as carefully staking out his safe ground. He trusted Yancey as much as he trusted any of the patients. More, probably. But he wanted to strike the right note to indicate noncomplicity in Chamberlin's recent past or dismal future. "You know who it is, don't you?"

"I didn't really look too closely," Yancey said, underlining his casual pose.

"That's that queer sonofabitch that jumped on Parton in K-3 back around Thanksgiving," the guard said, following Yancey and the candy wagon into the J-Ward corridor. The door closed and locked behind them. "You heard about it."

Yancey remembered. Chamberlin. And he remembered that Chamberlin had not jumped on Parton according to all accounts he had received. He had slapped the guard and then was mauled. Yancey also remembered seeing him cuffed and strapped from time to time to the benches on D-Ward and knew that he had been transferred from the peanut there to J-Ward sometime before Christmas. Yancey remembered. He kept up with everybody who had an account in the book. But he didn't convey such recognition to the guard.

"Yeah, I guess I heard something about it," he said, presenting a subtle claim to no more than secondhand knowledge. "Don't look like he'll be jumping on anybody else anytime soon. Is he sick or what?" Yancey's string-along technique was more than adequate.

"I guess so," the guard lied. "He's been saying he didn't feel too good for several days. Maybe more than that."

Yancey knew the man had not done any business with the candy wagon since his transfer to J-Ward. Nobody on J was allowed much more than cigarettes from the wagon, unless a guard wanted something. But Yancey usually saw a portion of a face through the tiny rectangle in the door. He had not seen Chamberlin since before Christmas.

"I wonder what made him sick," Yancey said. It sounded like a question.

"Probably a bad heart," the guard said, looking at the well-kept candy-wagon operator through eyes halved by drooping lids. There was suspicion in them, as if he were looking for some sign that Yancey knew better than he was being told. He didn't get such a sign.

"Probably," Yancey said.

"Gimme a pack of Camels and put them on his account," the guard said.

"First, I better be sure it's who I think it is," Yancey said, seeing an opening and deciding to force the guard to offer information.

"You know who it was," the guard said with a tinge of anger. "The one who was in the cell next to that little nigger. Chamberlin."

"Well, that's who I thought it was," Yancey said, trying to appear offhand with his comment. He turned a page of the ledger in his hands. "Is he being transferred to the infirmary or just being taken in for a couple of days?" He held a pencil poised over a page as if ready to make a notation. He looked at the guard as if waiting for an answer.

"Transferred," the guard said.

"Then I better not charge anything to him," Yancey said, "until I go onto R-Ward and find out what kind of shape he's in. If he gets well, he may want to see the book. You know Chamberlin. He gets mad as hell if he thinks he's been cheated."

"Give me a pack of Camels, Yancey, and mark 'em up on him," the guard said in a suddenly cold voice. "He ain't going to get well."

12

ON D-WARD, Hawk had just lit one of the cigars Dureen had given him that morning, and was casually puffing on it. He was satisfied by a robust lunch of ham steak, macaroni, and a soup that seemed a little bitter, and he was leaning back heavily into his rocking chair. Through the window he watched the white flakes of a beginning snow fall slowly and softly past the dark landscape in the background and turn all outdoors into dotted swiss.

He was wondering how many inches of the stuff would pile up by the next afternoon and how adversely it would affect the turn-out at the bingo night his church's men's club was sponsoring in Honesdale, when his mind was jerked back inside the dayroom by two loud claps from the ward boy and the subsequent entry of Yancey and the candy wagon. After hearing some of the grousing by the patients who had not enjoyed their fried bologna at lunch, Hawk figured Yancey would do a brisk business again today.

126

If there were such a thing as a trusty at the hospital—nobody here was totally trusted—Yancey would have to be considered one. He lived in the bungalow with the twenty to twenty-five other patients who shared the more relaxed facility with a couple of doctors and a handful of guards. It had been built originally, more than fifty years earlier, as a dormitory for the doctors and guards when the area was even more remote, roads were worse, and automobiles a rarity. It contained private and semiprivate rooms and only one guard was assigned there each shift.

Operating the candy wagon was only one of the functions Yancey performed at the hospital. He also had the hospital paper route for both the morning and evening Scranton newspapers, and he worked in the canteen from which the candy wagon was stocked. Those were his official duties.

Unofficially, he was a private messenger between wards for the patients and a private snitch for some guards. How else would he have the best job in the hospital? He talked when it helped him, kept his mouth shut if it didn't. He was a conduit for some contraband, smuggled mail and money out, whiskey and pornography in. All done through his friendship with certain guards and always at a profit. In the previous year he had accumulated more than three thousand dollars, which he sent home to be banked.

What he was constantly looking for was the chance for a really big score with the superintendent or Lieutenant Pagnotti. Something that would put him in solid enough with one or both of them that he could perhaps get off the hospital grounds for several hours at a time. Then he could move things in and out of the hospital himself, without having to pay guards. Then he could make a lot of money, maybe get laid a time or two, and perhaps work his way into a discharge.

Of course, he knew he would have to be careful about becoming too good a worker. If you were too good a worker, the hospital never would let you go. He knew some older patients who had been in the hospital for years and years, and he had heard guards talk about how they couldn't let so-and-so go because he was too good at his job. Coda, for instance. He was too good at making ceramic things. They would never let him out. Same thing with another guy in the ceramic shop. He was almost as good as Coda. Coda was trying to teach him some things so he could be really good, too. So then maybe they would let Coda leave. Probably not.

Anyway, it was operating the candy wagon, a rolling snack cart actually, that gave Yancey his special status, his unique position among the other patients. The wagon was allowed into every section of the hospital, and since the guards were not going to be bothered with pushing it and keeping up with the transactions, where the wagon went, Yancey went. Thus he became the main vein in the hospital grapevine. He delivered messages accurately and confidentially, unless it was of major benefit to him to do otherwise. He had a way of knowing whom he could trust and a way of nurturing the trust others had in him.

More importantly, he kept "the book." That was the ledger in which he recorded how much money every patient in the hospital had in his personal account, with which to purchase anything from soap to Salems to Sears, Roebuck shoes. When patients gave him money for the book, they knew it would be entered correctly. When guards wanted to steal from a patient's account, they knew he would pick a patient who was such a vegetable he would never know the difference.

Best of all, he did not cheat on the books himself. He never took anything that was not his. At Farview, Yancey was special.

He had been in the hospital for seven years, and he knew that when he got there and for the next couple of years afterward he had been sick. Mentally ill. Whacko. Fortunately he was not aggressive or abrasive, or "assaultive," as the hospital staff liked to call anyone who became angry enough to hit someone, regardless of the reason. Also, as sometimes happened, he had been given some medication that worked for him, that helped bring about a remission of his paranoia, which had lasted more or less for the past five years.

Yancey was in Farview because he and some friends had robbed a bank. Actually, he did not rob the bank, did not go into the bank. He was supposed to drive the getaway car. But he didn't. He stood beside the car while his friends ran from the bank. There had been a gun battle, and a policeman had been killed. Still, Yancey stood beside the car. An hour later, when police had everything under control, Yancey was still standing beside the car. It was as though he wanted to be caught. The police finally obliged him and charged him with bank robbery, too,

In truth, he didn't know where he was. Acquaintances testified later that they had seen him in a store the morning of the robbery and had spoken to him, but that he didn't know who they were.

His lawyer pleaded successfully that Yancey had to be crazy to stand beside the getaway car of a bank robbery waiting to get arrested, and that he was incompetent to stand trial. Yancey was sent to Farview for observation and treatment until he was found competent to face trial.

For the first two years he cared about nothing. He was not bothered by no-shave, no-shower, no-napkin, no-toilet paper. But then he began to improve and decided he was spending about as much time observing the hospital as the hospital spent observing him. More time actually, since he was observing all day. He began to have a growing awareness of what was happening around him.

He had been kicked around and smacked about and he remembered feeling like a bumbling, disoriented child desperately groping for something that might please his elders. As he became more aware of those around him, he saw that some of the patients were regularly, constantly, brutally abused, while others seemed to be left virtually alone, almost ignored. He saw that some men had everything, even their most insignificant possessions, stolen from them while others were stealing at will and getting away with it. While some had no cigarettes or candy, others had plenty of both to sell, trade, or give away. Yancey decided that although life inside the hospital was meaner, more frightening, more brutal, and more dangerous, otherwise it was just like life outside.

Freedom, he determined, had a great deal to do with how much you had in your pocket. Slowly and carefully, he began to fill his.

However, as his renewed awareness spurred a renewed sense of what was right and what was wrong, he saw a lot that went on in the hospital that he didn't like. He had no trouble rationalizing his own actions as items in his personal survival kit. He helped guards steal from the zombies because he felt he had to do it to keep his job, his freedom on a leash. He had even been able to conclude that candy-wagon theft, stealing from the book, was minor, nickel-and-dime—well, thirty cents, counting cigarettes —and he classified his participation in it as "going along to get along." Looking out for Numero Uno. Doing what he had to do to get out of the hospital eventually, and to make life bearable— and as enriching as possible—while he was inside.

He knew that several thousands of dollars a year was stolen from patients through the candy wagon alone, and he figured that several thousands more was stolen from bed-ridden geriatrics and zombies who were supposed to be getting Social Security and veterans' benefit checks. Shakedowns and surprise raids always netted a few hundred bucks for the guards, and the betting and loansharking were out of control.

Yancey knew how it worked. He helped run a lot of the scams. He picked up numbers bets as he went around from ward to ward, picked up bets on horses that were supposed to be running at Belmont or Aqueduct or Pocono Downs over in Wilkes Barre. He always took the money to the horse room, where he could almost always find somebody, a guard or doctor or social worker, on the telephone with a bookie. Much of the time they just used patient money to bet. Reduced the risk. Occasionally a patient would get a little money back and be told he had won. That would keep him and his friends interested in playing along. Truthfully, such wins happened so rarely that occasionally was the wrong word.

There were always poker and dice games going on, mostly in the clothing and supply rooms on the wards, but it was not hard to find a game in the john or the shower room, either. And whenever there was yard-out there were big games. Patients were allowed to bring blankets outside and they would gather around the edges of them with excited eyes and cash-filled fists. Some of the guards would play, too.

That sort of pissed Yancey off. While the guards were playing or watching the games, the queers would take over the portable toilets and stay in them for the duration of yard-out, forcing everybody else to wait until the whole crowd went back inside before they could take a leak. Naturally, a lot of the men sneaked around to piss against the building or down their legs. If they were caught with their peters out, pissing against the walls or in the grass, they would get hell slapped out of them, while nothing ever seemed to happen to the queers who caused the problem in the first place.

About as much as anything else, the guards like to bet on fights between patients on the wards. These occurred wherever the charge guards decided to let two patients take the floor against each other, but for the most part they were limited to D, N, Q, and P wards. Sometimes the fights were rather spontaneous, just two men who got mad at each other and wanted to fight, with the guards holding them off for only the few minutes it took for benches to be rearranged into a kind of ring and wagers to be made. At other times the fights were planned enough in advance that guards in other sections of the hospital could get a bet down.

Usually the planned fights would be staged between two pretty good fighters, sometimes friends but not always. More often than not, they involved two black patients.

The fight would go on until one of the men could not get up, could not move at all. There were no referees, no gloves, no counts, no rules. The men would fight until one was a sleeping mass of protoplasm. Then the man who lost stood an excellent chance of being kicked and beaten and tossed into the peanut by the guards who lost money on him.

They were brutal events to watch, but fascinating.

Billy Malone was one of the best fighters. Fact was, Yancey couldn't remember Malone ever losing. He fought as though his very life depended on the outcome. Yancey figured maybe it did. Sometimes the guards would punish a particularly troublesome patient by making him take the floor against Malone, or Night Train Lane, or Alexander Reed over on Q-Ward, or Willie Cate on N. They were all strong, with hard heads and fists. Malone's hands were quick as hiccups, and Yancey once saw him hit a patient so hard beside the eye that the eyeball came out of the socket.

He always bet on Billy Malone.

Yancey finished his business on D-Ward. He had given Hawk three cigars from the account of a patient who was sick on R-Ward, and had taken care of the other guards by making similar charges against the accounts of patients he saw cogwheeling in the dayroom or asleep under a bench. He sold Dureen several dollars' worth of goods with which to restock his corner grocery and delivered a watch to Coda.

He had whispered three or four messages from patients on

other wards and had taken a letter and a five-dollar bill from a patient when none of the guards was looking.

He had one more stop, one more ward to visit, before gathering his newspapers for the afternoon delivery. The state paid for a dozen papers each morning and each afternoon for patients to read in what passed for a hospital library and in other selected areas, but the doctors and staff took all of them for their own use and left the patients to buy their own copies or do without. It always made Yancey laugh. Patients were not allowed to have cash, but the rule could be broken if their having cash saved a dozen staff members twenty cents a day.

As he wheeled the candy wagon toward the door to leave, Yancey saw the same kind of active commerce he saw on every other ward. Patients who had bought cigarettes on their book accounts were now giving them to guards for a quarter or thirty cents a pack.

They were trying to put some freedom in their pockets.

13

FRIDAY CAME as Fridays all that winter had come for Malone—full of anticipation. He waited all week for two, three, five minutes beside the woman who smiled at him. That was the way he identified her, now. The woman who smiled. She was the only one of the guards' wives who smiled at him. He didn't really give a damn whether the others did or not. Most of them were jowly, greasy-looking Italians and Polacks, often with hair in curlers and a cigarette hanging from a scowling mouth. He was just as glad that they stayed inside the car and gave him the key to the trunk. The trunk was better to look at.

But the woman who smiled kept him moving through the days like a carrot at the end of a week-long stick. She had been receptive to the word games. She had initiated them, in fact.

"I wish you'd put something special in my box for Christmas," she had said the weekend before the holiday.

"Yeah?" he replied. "Like what?"

"Can't you guess?" she teased.

Then he knew the gate was down. He felt like he was stepping off into a lake when he spoke.

"Think I'd fit?"

"It might be fun finding out," she said with that same winsome smile, part innocence and part invitation. Then she slipped a five-dollar bill into his palm—"Merry Christmas"—and walked quickly around to the driver's side, got in her car, and drove away.

That had been almost two months ago and only in his mind was he any closer to having her under him. The word games had continued each week that she came to pick up groceries. Two or three times she had not come. She said she had been ill. Flu or cold or something. But when she came, she always managed to press against him. The trunk of her car always had other boxes or items inside that needed to be pushed aside to make room for the groceries. But the thick winter clothing she wore flattened her contours and made the touching more mental, more emotional than physical.

Malone, of course, was not given even a jacket to wear outside. In addition to the naked cruelty of such deprivation, it was an insurance policy against his trying to sprint through the arched gateway and across the snow-covered fields. So he was clothed in denims and a flannel shirt his mother had brought when she and his father visited before Christmas.

He had asked the woman her name, but she had said he did not need to know it until he got transferred to the bungalow. Naturally, he had volunteered his when she asked. At first he thought he had been foolish, but later decided she could find out anyway if she wanted, and it was better for him to tell her than to have her asking around among people who would wonder why she wanted to know.

He was placing groceries in the trunk of another car when she arrived. Involuntarily, he raised his hand in greeting as he turned to trot back to the kitchen to fetch her box of groceries.

When he returned with them, she was still sitting in the car. He stood by the trunk as she got out quickly and came around to unlock it. She was not wearing the thick layers of coating, but had on only a pair of slacks and a sweater. He observed the obvious.

"You're just wearing a sweater."

"All the better to feel you with, my dear." She grinned.

"True. But it could be better."

"It would be if you were in the bungalow," she said, reaching across his arm in their well-practiced maneuver.

"Yeah, well, I don't make those decisions"—working his elbow into her breast. She clamped his arm to hold it against her.

"It must be hard," she said, with the proper pause to complete the double entendre, "in there." Then she moved away and reached up to pull down the trunk lid.

"It is," he said. "Sometimes."

She winked. He winked at her. She got into the car and he turned to run back to the kitchen.

Neither of them saw the guard who had been standing inside, behind the woman. He had been unable to hear anything, but he saw Malone wink at Boots Ringgold's wife. It never occurred to him to wonder why she didn't seem to take offense.

*

Inside D-Ward a social worker was finishing a conversation with Bulldog in the charge's office. They were looking through the large glass window into the dayroom.

"Look, Luhzinski," the social worker said, "the man's been here more than twenty-five years. For Chrissake!"

"So what?" Bulldog said, his right jowl snuggling into a fleshy palm. His elbow was resting on the arm of the chair and his body seemed to slouch in resentment. "I don't give a shit if he's been here fifty years."

"He don't cause you no trouble. Why not let him see the fucking doctor? He's supposed to see one every six months or every year or something like that."

"When's the last time he saw one?"

"He never has."

"Why you getting on my ass? This ain't the only ward Kirchoff's been on. What about them other wards? Why didn't they let him see the doctors? See? It ain't only me."

"Yeah, but you and Hawk give me more shit about it than the others. And, hell, I just noticed a little while ago that he ain't seen an outside doctor since he's been here."

"Then, you're the one with a problem, not me. You're just trying to cover your own ass."

"Look, Luhzinski, it's the law. We got to let him see an outside, independent doctor. Once a year . . . or maybe it's twice a year, I don't know. But it's damned sure more often than once every twenty-five years."

"Don't hand me that crap, Shipler. The law says I can't kick 'em in the ass, too. Fuck the law. They broke the law. That's how come they're in this place."

"What the hell is it to you if some out-of-town sonofabitch asks him a few questions?"

"Mainly 'cause he'll probably bug the shit out of me trying to find out what the doctor said about him. Whether he can get out. Whether he can go to staff." Bulldog was waving his meaty hands in the air before him as though he were trying to get more volume from an orchestra.

"If this fucker gets a lawyer, he can sue our ass off for not following the law, Luhzinski. And he'd probably win."

"Shit. He ain't going to get no lawyer. Every time he writes to one they stop it out front and put another letter on top of his telling whoever reads it what a crazy fucker he's dealing with. He ain't going to get no lawyer. None of the rest of them is neither, if they didn't already have one when they got here."

"Well, maybe not. But I'd feel a lot better about it if we just made a pass at doing things the way we're supposed to."

"Supposed to, my ass. We're supposed to keep these bastards away from the rest of the world, that's what we're supposed to do. And we do that damned good."

"But Kirchoff's harmless. He's absolutely harmless. He wouldn't hurt anybody." The social worker paused. He thought he had an opening. "Why don't you just let him go answer a few questions from the doctor. If nothing else, it'll help his morale."

"Aww, fuck his morale. How many you got to have?"

"I got to have enough to make it worth the doctor's time to come here. He gets paid according to the number of patients he sees."

"Don't tell me how to make a clock, Shipler. Every time I ask you what time it is, you want to tell me how to make a fucking clock. How many you got to have from D-Ward?"

"Five."

"Bullshit."

"All right, four."

"Bullshit."

"No, I really do. I need at least four."

"Four?" Bulldog now was leaning forward, both elbows on chair arms, his hands loosely clasped in front of him.

"And one of them needs to be Kirchoff."

"Yeah, okay." Bulldog continued to study the dayroom. "Kirchoff, Dilworth, Gladstone, and Burack. How's that?"

"Sounds like a law firm," Shipler said.

"Shit," Bulldog said. "Bet Kirchoff's the only one of 'em who can read and write. Them others can't hardly find their assholes without help." He chuckled loudly. "I guess they get plenty of help."

He stood and rapped his knuckles on the window, getting the attention of one of the guards in the dayroom and motioning him around to the office. He gave the guard the names of the four patients and told him to bring them to the office, one at a time.

"I think Gladstone's out, ain't he?" the guard said, looking through the window toward the open room. "No, there he is. Hell, I thought he was under a bench a few minutes ago."

He left the office and went back into the dayroom to retrieve the patients. Kirchoff was the third one summoned.

Bulldog asked him two or three perfunctory questions, then said to Kirchoff as he had said to the previous two, "If you keep your nose clean, you can see a doctor about what kind of progress you're making here. How would you like that? He'll be here in a couple or three months. April or May. Give you lots of time to get ready. We're pretty nice people, huh? Okay, go on back."

Then, as he had with the first two, he called after Kirchoff.

"Hey! Don't fuck up or you can forget it. Understand?"

Kirchoff nodded that he understood. He wasn't sure he did understand completely. He understood the part about not fucking up. He didn't understand why, after twenty-eight years, why all of a sudden he was being allowed to talk to somebody about— what had Bulldog said?—his progress. Did this mean he was going to staff? Or just to talk to one of the doctors? Would they give him some kind of test?

By God, this might be it. This might mean he was on his way out of this hole. Somehow he had known that if he stayed out of trouble and did his work like he was supposed to do it, it would pay off. But twenty-eight years was one hell of a long time to make it work. Still, there were others who had been here longer than that. Sometimes it just takes a while for things to work out.

Did Bulldog say it'd be a doctor? Did he say that for sure? Planning that far ahead, it must be something more than routine. When did he say? April or May. By God, this was the first step. That would be time enough to think up some questions and come up with some good answers. Sure hope this isn't one of those deals where they bring in a doctor to see fifty or sixty guys in a day. He had heard about those sessions. Four or five minutes and you were out. Nothing ever came of those. But Bulldog said this would be talking about progress. It would take more than four or five minutes to cover twenty-eight years. By God, this is the chance.

Garth had been pushing and pulling the polisher around the floor. He had seen the guard take the four men into the charge's office one at a time. He had seen Kirchoff go in and had seen a different Kirchoff come out. The other three men did not seem much different after coming back into the dayroom, but Kirchoff looked different. There was a hint of a smile playing at the corners of his thin lips and he ran his liver-spotted hand repeatedly through his cirrus wisps of hair.

Then the older man crossed his arms across his chest and stretched his skinny legs out into the floor from the bench he was sitting on. He gazed at the ceiling, then to the floor. He unclasped his arms and put a slender finger to pursed lips. His eyes would squint in thought, then widen in speculation. His entire body, which had seemed tired when it went into the office, was animated now.

A few minutes later Garth was allowed to leave the polisher. Another patient took the handles and fought to keep the heavy piece of equipment under control. Garth walked to where Kirchoff was sitting at his familiar place on the bench.

The two of them had not had much to say to each other since Garth's first couple of days on the ward. They didn't have anything particular in common other than their presence in the same place. Kirchoff read his Bible every day, seemingly all day. Garth had not opened his since his second day on the ward, when he found it on the floor under a heavy oak chair near the clothing room. He had placed it in his small shelf cubicle in the clothing room. The picture of his sisters was still pressed somewhere between the pages.

Neither man was much into the hustles on the ward because Kirchoff did not smoke and had few other needs that hustling could fill and Garth was content with rolling his own cigarettes from the bag of Bugler tobacco he was provided every week at state expense. And unlike most smokers, he could easily make it through a day smoking only three or four cigarettes, although he sometimes smoked the equivalent of more than a pack of ready rolls, as the manufactured ones were sometimes called.

Neither of them was particularly gregarious, and beyond the usual introductory amenities of how they got there and what kind of joint it was, they didn't have a great deal to talk about.

But Garth was curious about what had happened to Kirchoff when he went into the charge's office.

"You get a parole?" he asked after he sat down on the bench beside the older man. He was grinning and trying to give the question a friendly lilt and at the same time convey to Kirchoff that it was meant facetiously.

"No," Kirchoff said, recognizing the intent of the question. "But I'm going to get to see a doctor for a special session about my time here."

"No shit. When?"

"Sometime in the next couple of months." That seemed like a long time away, but he would not let a glimmer of skepticism creep into his demeanor. "April or May," he said as positively as he was able.

Garth had two questions: Why was it so far off? and What was special about the session?

"What's special about it? I mean how is it different from seeing the doctor here on the ward?"

Kirchoff knew that he had used the word "special" to lend added significance to the impending session. It was special to him, but that did not mean the session per se would be anything special at all. He was somewhat put out that Garth had lit upon it.

"Maybe it's not all that special," he said. "Bulldog said we would discuss my progress. That's what he said."

"How often they do this?" Garth said, allowing the sense of

anticipation to float from the older man and take root in himself like spores from a wood fern.

"I don't know," Kirchoff said. "It's the first time for me." That's why it was special. One time in twenty-eight years makes anything special.

He told himself to be careful about reading more into the meeting than was actually there, but still his thoughts ran to fantasy. And almost without knowing it was happening to him, he began to see things that he expected to happen when he left the hospital. He visualized his son and daughter greeting him outside the hospital. Both of them were constructions of his imagination because he could not remember what they looked like. He had not seen either of them since they were children. Their mother had divorced him shortly after he was transferred to Farview and, according to the last letter he had received, she thought it best that the children were spared the frustration of not being able to see their father. She forbade them to write letters to him and she assured him that his letters would not find their eyes. She moved away from Philadelphia and took the children with her. He did not know where his children were, the children he visualized approaching him with arms wide.

He visualized various poses he would assume, expressions that would be on his face. He wanted to have the right expression when his children saw him. He debated about them in a mind that was beginning to move toward discharge and freedom as a fait accompli. How should his children see him? How did he want them to see him? Standing tall and straight. A slight smile? A look of stern wisdom? A wide, mouth-open, teeth-parted, deliriously happy more-laugh-than-smile? It had to be just the right look. Something to show that he was a man who had survived. A man who had overcome adversity. Not the look of a refugee from a loony bin. It had to be the right look that his children would see when they laid eyes on him for the first time in twenty-eight years.

Every time he thought about how long he had been in the hospital, it brought him jerking back to reality. And brought up more questions. Questions for which he had no answers. Like most of his questions. Why was he seeing a doctor after twenty-eight years of virtual neglect? He had not made any more progress

during the past year than he had made during the past decade—
or during the first decade, for that matter.

He never had been given a psychological or psychiatric examination, he never had received any kind of therapy. He had met
with a social worker a couple of times, but all he was ever asked
was how he was getting along and what he thought about the
hospital and why he thought he was here. And he always said he
thought he was getting the shitty end of the stick and that he felt
he had been railroaded and that the hospital was doing him no
good and his life was being wasted for no reason. The comments
had not helped him much, apparently. He was still in the hospital. But it had been several years since he had seen the social
worker, until today in Bulldog's office.

It certainly would be nice to walk out of the hospital a free man
and run into Bulldog and tell him to take that polisher and shove
it up his ass. Or tell that nutty Dr. Zundel that *he* was crazy as a
shithouse rat. Or maybe just ignore them. Run into them somewhere and have them say, "Hey, aren't you Paul Kirchoff from
up at Farview?" and say back, "Fuck you, you despicable scum."
It would be better if there were a lot of people around to hear it.

"There were four of youse guys that went into the charge's
office," Garth intruded on Kirchoff's fantasies. "Is that different?
Different from other times? All four of youse going to see a doctor? I mean, does this look like they might be sending more guys?"

"I don't know about the others," Kirchoff said, sensing that
Garth's hopes were beginning to take on a vague swelling. "You
don't always know when somebody sees a doctor off the ward.
You generally know about somebody going to staff, because they
can't keep quiet about that. They always think that means they're
getting out. Then when they don't, you hear them bitching about
how somebody on the staff fucked them over."

"Are you going to staff?"

"No. They didn't say anything about staff. I think they just said
'a doctor.' "

"They say what kind of doctor?"

"I'm sure it's a psychiatrist."

"Is this gonna help you get out?"

"I hope to hell it is," Kirchoff said honestly.

"I hope it don't take twenty-eight years for 'em to get around to me," Garth said. "I been waiting three months to get something for my headaches. And you know what else? Ever since that first night, when I got here and they kicked the shit out of me in that shower, I get a sorta shooting pain in my hip and thigh. Damned if it don't sometimes feel just like a needle was sticking in me. You know what I mean?"

Kirchoff had drifted away from Garth's end of the conversation. He was thinking about what he'd wear out of the hospital. He would wear a tie. He would start working toward getting a tie. And a white shirt.

✻

It was late one night the middle of the next week when Spangler was awakened by the *click, click, click* of boot-heel taps on the floor of the D-Ward dormitory. It could have been sometime past midnight. But his eyes came open and he raised his head off the pillow to look in the direction of the sound. He knew who owned the boots. Shortly after he arrived at the hospital he had complained about a guard deliberately clomping through the night, keeping him awake. His complaint had been contained in a letter he wrote to the superintendent. A response was contained in the palm of the guard's hand, slamming against his cheek. He never complained again, but unlike with the other patients, he was invariably awakened by the heel taps. Usually Boots would make only a couple of *click-clack*ing passes down the center aisle, then go to his rocking chair and doze off. That's when Spangler slept.

Spangler was lying on his stomach and had only to lift his head a couple of inches to see Boots coming down the aisle. Then he lowered his ear back to the pillow and closed his eyes, knowing sleep was a few minutes from return.

The steps stopped near the foot of his bunk. He opened his eyelids a slit, then shifted his head almost imperceptibly in order to bring the guard into view. He was standing at the end of the bunk beside Spangler's. Malone's bunk.

Spangler closed his eyes, but he heard the shuffling sidesteps of the guard moving between bunks. Malone was asleep, lying on his back, breathing deeply and steadily.

Then Boots stopped shuffling. He had stepped alongside Malone's bed to a point even with the patient's head. He stood silently staring at the face below him. Slowly, he brought his right hand to his waist, grasped the tongue of the zipper between thumb and index finger, and lowered it. There was hardly a sound as his fly came open. He reached inside his trousers and freed his penis. It was beginning to swell as he reached out his hands toward Malone's head.

One hand grabbed Malone's right ear. The other slapped him three or four times very quickly, then roughly went to the back of the patient's skull and yanked it toward the guard's groin.

"Open your mouth, nigger," the guard raged. "Suck the cock that's been fucking her."

Malone was struggling in bewilderment. The blows had blasted his sleep and the hand twisting his ear was bringing excruciating pain. His mouth was about to scream when the guard filled it. Malone gagged in hatred and humiliation. He tried to push away but couldn't. The vise grip at the base of his skull held his face firmly to the guard's crotch. The guard's other hand continued to twist the ear.

The guard began to slam his pelvis into Malone's face, using each thrust to punctuate invective.

"You look at my wife again and I'll cut your balls off . . . you gorilla bastard . . . you want white meat . . . have it, you . . . nigger . . . black . . . ape . . . cocksucking . . . coon . . . sonofabitchin' . . ."

Malone tried to protest what he could sense was almost upon him. He tried to shake his head but the grip tightened firmer still.

"Unh, unh," he moaned. "Unh, unhhhnnn." To no avail.

"Swallow, nigger bastard," Boots said as perspiration trickled down his sallow face. "Swallow if it chokes you to death."

Malone had stopped struggling. His torso was held off the bed solely by the hands that continued to clasp his head. Tears slid from the corners of his eyes and into his ears. When the guard had spilled himself, he pushed the teenager's head away, down onto the pillow, as though he were pushing a hard basketball bounce pass.

"Don't you never look at another white woman, nigger," he spat. "You ain't gonna ever get a chance to, if I got anything to say about it."

Boots was raising his zipper when Malone bolted from the opposite side of the bunk and hurried gropingly toward the bathroom. The guard watched him go, then shuffled between beds toward the center aisle.

"Go ahead and puke, you wool-headed bastard." he screamed behind Malone. "Throw your fucking guts up and choke on 'em!"

Spangler watched the guard standing in the middle of the room and he saw several other heads rise from the surrounding bunks, awakened by the commotion. Then he saw the guard walk toward a rocking chair, the *click-clack*ing of heel taps mixing with sounds of retching and heaving in the bathroom, and the voices of other guards assuring the rousing patients that they should go back to sleep. He had been stunned by the scene that was played before him. Fascinated, yet frozen. But now his mind was working, jumbled and confused, but active, thoughts and feelings squirming over each other like worms in a bait can. Yet one idea was constant and dominant. He knew he must get away.

Inside the bathroom, revulsion welled inside Malone, but hatred engulfed him. He pressed his forehead against the cold toilet seat. His knees were digging into the floor before this vile altar, but he was oblivious to their ache. He made two vows: He would hate all white men from this minute forward, and he would not rest until the world knew about the horrors of Farview.

14

WINTER SEEMED to live in the mountains of Northeast Pennsylvania and a wicked, biting wind was a permanent houseguest. In mid-May patches of snow remained in shady spots on the slopes of the Moosics and in secluded corners of the Farview yard.

These vestiges of the usually frigid winter, and the damp areas in the sunshine where snow had melted, were reasons enough for the guards to continue to resist yard-out. The longer they could keep everybody inside—and remain inside themselves—the better they liked it. For that reason, many of the patients who thought about it, and most did, seemed to think that the best time to run away was during bad weather, snowstorms or heavy rains that made the search as difficult as the escape. During those times, guards didn't even want to search the interior grounds, much less look into outbuildings and beyond.

But Spangler's disposition was much like the guards'. He did not want to be outside in the cold and he did not want to walk miles like a drenched rat. Even now, though he knew the time had come to make his break, he was not happy at the prospect of cold, hungry nights in rugged terrain about which he knew virtually nothing. He knew that Carbondale was not too awfully far in one direction and Honesdale somewhat farther in the other, but he didn't know how long it would take him to get to either place by going through the woods. All he knew for sure was that he wanted to get away from Farview, get to civilization, get to a bus and get to Philadelphia, where he thought he could get lost long enough for the authorities to forget about him.

He had about eleven dollars in his pocket and he was pretty sure that would not be enough to get to Philly. He thought he could make it with twenty dollars more, but that presented another problem. He didn't have a friend close enough to lend him that much money. Malone would have done it, but Malone was now out of money, since he had lost his job in the kitchen and had no way to get sandwiches for sale to guards and patients on the ward.

Spangler knew that his best chance lay with Yancey. The candy-wagon man had plenty of money and was willing to lend it, but he sometimes wanted to know why it was needed. Yancey often found that once he knew why money was needed, he could fulfill the need rather than supply the money and improve his position with less risk and more profit. Spangler was not eager to confide in Yancey. For one thing, the candy-wagon man could not be expected to want to lend money to a man who never intended to see him again. For another, it was not good to let too many people in on something as important as running from the hospital.

He knew from his days in prison, however, that very few escape attempts were known only to those involved. Somebody else always knows about what is going to happen. Spangler knew that he himself had talked so often about wanting to escape that nobody who knew him would be surprised that he had tried. He could not remember to whom he had mentioned his plan. There had been several and all of them had laughed or merely walked away. What the hell harm would it do to tell Yancey about it? And promise to mail him back the money when he got to Philadelphia. Yancey had helped a lot of other patients. What was twenty dollars more or less to him? But Spangler knew that twenty dollars was important to every person inside Farview and he decided that argument would not impress Yancey. But everybody said he could be trusted. At least he would not squeal. If he refused to lend the money, Spangler thought he knew where he could steal some.

He did not see Yancey until the next afternoon when the latter came into the kitchen for a cup of coffee, as he was allowed to do because of favors he had extended to DeLuca. Spangler waited until Yancey was standing apart from others in the kitchen before he approached.

"Would you do me a favor?" he asked.

"Depends," Yancey said, looking evenly into the black man's eyes but somewhat repelled by his grubby, unshaven, soiled appearance.

"I need some help, Yancey," Spangler said, beginning to feel inferior to the man who ran the candy wagon and who stood before him with clean slacks and shirt, clean face, and carefully coiffed hair. "You the only one can help me, man."

"Whatcha need?"

"Twenty dollars."

"What for?"

Spangler looked warily from side to side, the very essence of suspicion.

"I'm leavin' this muthuh fuckuh."

Now Yancey looked about furtively, apparently more afraid of hearing what Spangler was saying than Spangler was afraid of being heard saying it.

"When?" Yancey asked.

"Soon as I can. Tonight, if you give me the money. I send it back to you soon as I get to Philly and get back on the block. I promise, man."

Yancey knew better. "That's bullshit," he said. "You know they open all the mail that comes in. I'll never see that twenty. You gotta think of something else."

Spangler's mind was whirring. "I send you something you can sell for more'n twenty."

"Like what?"

"I don't know, man. I think of something. Just help me out."

"How are you going to get out?"

"I got a plan."

"If you get caught, they'll kill you."

"They ain't gonna catch me."

"You bet," Yancey said sarcastically.

"I am bettin', Jack. You gonna help me?"

"You get caught, you better have an answer for where you got it."

"I been selling sandwiches. I ain't talked to you about nothing."

"Okay, come get something from the wagon and the twenty will be there. You pay back forty."

"Sure," Spangler said, hardly listening to the last stipulation. He would agree to anything, he knew, and he would pay back nothing to Whitey.

Yancey figured pretty much the same thing. But he knew that the wrong reaction to the black man's request could cause him more trouble than twenty dollars could cover. Spangler could pass the word that Yancey had refused to help him escape when he could have helped without any problems to himself. Part of the code of conduct for inmates anywhere required a man to help another to get out unless it was impossible to give that help. It didn't do a man any good to keep another from leaving, Yancey knew. And it didn't do a man any good to have the word get around that he had fucked a buddy when he didn't have to.

He slipped the money to the slender, pidgeon-toed black patient and wished him a muttered good luck. Then he completed his rounds with the candy wagon about the time he usually started his paper route.

As he delivered the afternoon newspapers, he was on the look-out for Pagnotti, the flint-eyed lieutenant. He always tried to make it appear that he was going out of his way to give the lieutenant a free newspaper. He was about the only guard worth brown-nosing constantly.

Pagnotti's assistant said he thought his boss had gone to the room provided for the patients who liked to wear women's clothing. He said Pagnotti thought it was funny to watch them. Shipler, the social worker, said he thought Pagnotti was visiting X-Ward.

Yancey came to X-Ward first and when he approached the charge guard's office, he noticed that the door was slightly ajar. Yancey wore sneakers and his appearance at the door was unannounced. He was about to say something lighthearted, but the sounds caught in his throat as he looked into the room.

A rather large black man stood with his back to Yancey and the door. His legs were slightly spread. He had one hand on the desk to help maintain his balance and his head was bent forward a few degrees. His eyes were looking toward his feet.

Yancey's went there, too. But on the way down the man's body, his eyes stopped at the man's buttocks, which two thick-fingered hands were clutching. The hands were white and on one was some kind of large ring. The hands were protruding from shirt-sleeves of sky blue. The hands seemed to be tugging the buttocks rhythmically forward.

Yancey's eyes went on to the floor and he could see between the patient's legs that black slacks encased the knees that were planted at the patient's feet.

It was a guard, Yancey could tell, but he could not see the man's face nor even his upper body. He didn't recognize the ring either, but he was sure that Pagnotti did not wear one like it. In fact, he could not remember seeing Pagnotti wearing any kind of ring.

Yancey made no sound as he backed quickly from the doorway. He walked down the short hallway and handed a newspaper to the guard who had been standing inside one of the patients' double rooms, bragging about how he had kicked the shit out of a man who did not come out of a bathroom as quickly as the guard would have liked. The guard took the newspaper and unlocked the corridor door, allowing Yancey to depart the ward. He hardly skipped a beat in his bluster.

Yancey went to try to find Pagnotti at the room where some of the patients were allowed to express their transvestic leanings. He decided against saying anything about Spangler's plan. The scene in the charge's office had been enough to make him believe that Spangler was doing the only thing any patient should think about doing. Getting away was about the only thing that made any sense. The only thing that held out hope. Hustling for money was nothing more than a way to make life easier inside and have something when you got outside. Maybe even help get you outside. But everything was, or at least should be, pointed toward getting out. Spangler was simply trying another way. He would probably fail anyway, Yancey thought; there was no use deliberately trying to screw him up.

Yancey knew he could never try to run away because he was afraid of getting caught and of what would happen if that occurred. He could have walked away just about any time he felt like it, but he knew they would come looking for him. He had a feeling that they would find him no matter where he went. He felt certain he would be allowed to leave the hospital some day fairly soon, and he was truly afraid of doing anything that could mess that up. He acted gutsy and glib, but that was bluff. Inside, he was constantly worried. Worried about his wife and kid. Worried about his mother and dad. Worried more than anything else about the future. Not the long-away future. The tomorrow future. The five-minutes-from-now future. He was constantly thinking about the kinds of things that could get him into trouble. He sometimes did them anyway, if the price was right or if the risk seemed low. Like right now, he was worried about the twenty dollars he had given Spangler. But that was low-risk. Even if Spangler squealed about where he got the money, which was pretty unlikely, it would be his word against Yancey's. No question who the guards would believe in that case. No, there was little risk, but he worried about it anyway. When he thought about it, it seemed to him that he was scared almost all the time. Maybe all the time. Yet he was in the hospital ostensibly because he was a paranoid-schizophrenic type. It seemed to him he was more paranoid inside than outside. He didn't think that should have been the situation.

As he turned a corner in the hallway, he saw Pagnotti a few feet ahead. His eyes went immediately to the lieutenant's hand. There was no ring. The fingers were smaller than those of the man Yancey had found on his knees. And the nails were cleaner.

Pagnotti saw him approach.

"You got a paper for me?" he asked.

"I got this one but I was going it to take to Recreation," Yancey said, knowing better.

"Fuck you, Yancey," Pagnotti laughed. "And fuck Recreation. Gimme that paper."

Yancey handed it over and walked to the canteen with a silent wish for Spangler's good fortune.

15

Out in Center, not too far from where Yancey encountered Pagnotti, Kirchoff was waiting to see the doctor. He was edgy, sitting on a hard oaken chair similar to the ones in the ward dayrooms. In his lap, one hand was clasping the back of the other. His right leg was draped across the knee of his left and was pumping slightly, without any apparent effort on his part.

His dingy hair was unevenly parted but oiled into place, the result of some obvious concern but little practice. His trousers were rumpled and bagged out at the knees, but his shoes were shined. His thin socks were loose and slipping toward his ankles, leaving an expanse of skin showing between their tops and the trouser hem.

He was wearing a white shirt. It was somewhat yellowed and without stays for the collar, which curled up a bit on either side of the inch-wide green and maroon-striped tie he had tied in a tiny half-Windsor knot that was not quite centered at his collar button.

Attempted respectability was written all over him. In his mind this was his one chance and he was going to try his very best to make the right impression, do his utmost to win the approval of a person he never had seen, a person he thought held the key to his freedom. His future. He knew from his days as an accountant, his days as what he saw as an executive, that success, like beauty, was often in the eyes of the beholder, and that first impressions were often lasting ones.

Had there been anyone nearby capable of such emotions, the view of Kirchoff sitting there waiting for his chance to show somebody that he should not be in the hospital would have evoked pity. Even sadness. He wanted so desperately to look like a normal, everyday, mature, self-respecting man. But everything about him just missed, missed enough to cast about him the aura of fool.

The turned-up collar points and the narrow tie that was almost a decade out of style, worn over baggy denims. The socks tumbling about the ankles, the hair closely sheared high up the neck to a point above the ears, and parted with more detours than a road under construction, then slicked down on top. He had been shaved earlier in the day, but had been the subject of a half-assed job.

Sadder still, he didn't know the image he was giving. He had done the best he could do with what he had to work with. And he thought he had done well. He thought he looked good.

"Kirchoff!"

He was aroused from a reverie that reviewed a quarter-century in captivity. He looked up to meet the eyes of the guard who had spoken and was speaking again:

"Let's go. Your turn."

Kirchoff stood and entered the room. It was located on the opposite side of Center from D-Ward. He did not know it, but it was where patients were brought for staff evaluations, known only as "staff" by the patients and employees. "Meeting staff," it was called by one and all.

That was the one meeting that mattered. It was the one where the decision was made to release, transfer, or retain a man.

Heavily barred windows like the ones on the wards lined one wall. A large conference-type table was in the middle of the room and wooden chairs were placed here and there. A bespectacled man who appeared to be in his midforties was sitting at the table. A thick, bushy ring of curly hair created a dark halo around a rather sizable bald spot on top of his head. An unruly mustache was smeared across his upper lip and much of it seemed to curl over his lip and into his mouth. He often bit off pieces of the mustache and picked the tiny hair ends off his tongue with his finger and thumb. His suit was about as rumpled as Kirchoff's denims and the knot of his wide tie had been pulled well loose from his neck. To his left he had a stack of papers that looked to be mimeographed forms. To his right were two stacks of files in manila folders. One pile was considerably larger than the other. When he picked up Kirchoff's folder, there was only one folder remaining in the stack.

He had not looked up when Kirchoff entered the room, or rather been ushered in by the guard. The guard had guided Kirchoff to a seat opposite the doctor. Kirchoff remained standing. It was part of his plan, his idea of good manners. His idea of making a good first impression. Remain standing until the doctor indicated that he was ready to have him sit down. The only thing that kept Kirchoff from extending his hand for shaking was the doctor's continued fascination with something printed he was holding in his hands. He hadn't looked up.

Then he did, with apparent irritation.

"Sit down," he more barked than said. "What are you waiting for? We don't have all day here, you know."

"I'm sorry," Kirchoff said, sitting quickly and sagging a bit as though some of the wind had left his sail. He had hoped for a sort of have-a-seat-and-make-yourself-comfortable round of pleasantries, but that obviously was not to be the case. He was already more frightened than he'd thought he would be.

"You Paul Kirchoff?" the doctor asked, looking up from the folder.

"Yes." Kirchoff tried to smile.

"Looks like you've been here several years. How have you been treated? Okay?" The questions were brusque, not conversational.

Kirchoff looked quickly from the doctor to the guard sitting a few feet away, then back to the doctor. Trap question, he thought. The guard is waiting for a criticism that he can report to Pagnotti or Dr. Dallmeyer or somebody.

The doctor was waiting, looking at the paper before him on the table, his pencil poised above it. He looked up when Kirchoff's answer was delayed in coming. "They treat you okay or not?" he asked again, his impatience showing.

"I suppose so," Kirchoff said.

"Do you know why you're here?"

"Not really. I got into a big argument with my brother and there was a lot of noise. Threats and shouting and like that. I was the one they took to jail. But I was the one with a job."

"Yeah, and you hit a guard and you threatened a doctor, didn't you?"

"Yes, but not really. I mean, nothing really serious. I shoved a guard because I was hot and he had shoved me first. I didn't really threaten that doctor. I mean, I did say some things, but I didn't really mean those things. I mean, he kept saying that I was crazy and that I didn't understand reality and stuff like that. He never listened to what I said. I just said some things to make him pay attention, to make him listen to me. That's all that was."

The doctor was not looking up. He was jotting words on the page in front of him and the messages in Kirchoff's eyes were lost on him.

"You've been here a long time," he said without responding to what Kirchoff had said. "What have you accomplished?"

"Accomplished?"

"Yes. What have you done since you've been here?"

"You mean where have I worked? Things like that?"

"Yes, that'll do."

"Well, I've worked in the kitchen and the dining rooms. I worked in the upholstery shop for a while. I've polished floors and made beds."

"Is that all?"

"I don't know that I've accomplished much. I don't know what there is to accomplish here. I've read a few books. The Bible, mostly. I've played some chess."

"Do you think you're getting any better?"

"Well, I doubt it. I don't get to play very much. There's not anybody much to play with."

"No, no, no, you misunderstand. Your outlook. Your condition. Do you think that's improving? Do you think you are making progress?"

"I'm sorry," Kirchoff said, not knowing why he should apologize for following the conversation. "Uhh, I don't know how much progress there was for me to make. There was nothing wrong with me in the first place and I don't think there is anything wrong with me now. I think I could go out and make a living, if I were given a chance.

"One doctor told me I was crazier than a shithouse rat, but another told me there was nothing wrong with me. He said that the longer I stayed here, the worse I would get. I don't know if that's true. He's dead now."

"I see you were married. Twenty-eight years is a long time without a sexual relationship. What do you do about that?"

"What?" Kirchoff had heard the question, but he had not expected to be asked it. He looked again toward the guard, who was sitting with his arms folded, obviously bored with the procedure.

"You heard me," the doctor said.

"Why do you ask something like that? Why is that important?"

"I'll ask the questions. You answer them."

"But I don't see . . ."

"You don't want to cooperate?" The doctor began to reach for a folder.

"Sure, but . . ."

"Then answer the questions. I'm not going to beg you."

Kirchoff did not want to antagonize the doctor. He felt the stakes were too great to get into an argument over the propriety of a question.

"It isn't too bad," he said. "I get along okay, I guess. I try not to think about it too much. Some of the men, that's all they think about. I try to keep my mind . . ."

"Okay, that'll be all," the doctor interrupted. "You can go now." He looked toward the guard and said, "You can take him back now."

"That's all?" Kirchoff said. "That can't be all. How long have I been in here? I bet it hasn't been five minutes."

"You got as much time as anybody else," the doctor said. He nodded to the guard, who took Kirchoff's arm and tugged him firmly toward the door. Kirchoff did not resist.

Once outside, Kirchoff continued with the guard.

"How can he learn anything about me or anybody else in five minutes?"

"He ain't there to learn nothing," the guard said. "He's there to satisfy the law. The law says everybody here is supposed to be examined by an outside doctor every so often. He's examining. I bet he's done more than thirty of 'em today. Twenty-five, anyway. He gets paid for each one he does, so you know he ain't gonna spend much time on any one."

They were at the door to D-Ward. It was unlocked from the inside and Kirchoff was escorted through it. Then he was taken to the dayroom. The other patients were lining up for the walk to supper.

Kirchoff stood near the doorway for a moment, then stepped to the side along the wall as the procession started out the door.

"How'd it go, Kirchoff?" It was the blond guard.

"What'dya mean, 'How'd it go?' " Kirchoff raged suddenly and loudly. "It was a fucking joke and you know it."

He did not see the rolled-up magazine that landed above his ear and propelled his head into the wall. For a moment the lights seemed to have gone out and when he could focus again, he was sitting on the floor. White flecks of light floated in his vision like so many single-celled animals that came to life, flashed in tiny explosions, then disappeared. He could hear the sounds of sirens, so faint that they must be miles away. Or maybe it was a radio signal.

"You know better than to talk like that, Kirchoff." It was Bulldog standing over him. "Ain't you learned nothing in all these years? Show a little respect." ·

16

SPANGLER DID not try to escape that night. He had thought that he could be forgotten in the confusion of supper and make a run for it from the kitchen across the big yard to the arch gate at the rear corner of the complex, the only place in the main quadrangle that was not connected building-to-building.

It was the same path Malone had taken with the boxes of groceries for the guards' wives, and he often told Spangler about the apparent lack of attention the guards paid to what went on at the gate. Even though Malone was no longer doing the grocery-packing job, nor even working in the kitchen, Spangler assumed that the guards were as lackadaisical as Malone had maintained.

But every time Spangler looked from the rear of the kitchen to the arch gate, he saw a guard standing either in the archway or near it. He discarded what already was a skimpy plan.

A couple of weeks later, however, he and a half-dozen other kitchen workers were taken to the gymnasium recreation area for an afternoon of unplanned activity. They learned later that they were on exhibit for a small group of people from Scranton who were touring the hospital.

It had been easy for the guards to round up some of the kitchen workers and march them straight from the kitchen, down the main corridor, between W-Ward and X-Ward, and on to the gym.

The patients in AA-Ward, were also brought over to the gym, which was virtually next door to them. Some of the patients played pool with a guard or with a man assigned the job of recreation therapist. A couple of men were given roller skates and skated on the asphalt path outside the basement of the gym. A handful of men went into the small room that served the hospital as a library.

An impromptu basketball game was started on the gym floor upstairs. It glistened with wax and lack of use. There were bleachers that could be unfolded and extended to accommodate spectators. One section was partially extended for some reason.

To the untrained eye, there appeared to be considerable activity, and the patients, unaccustomed as they were to such privilege, carried smiles that served the purpose of the men conducting the tourists and made the tourists feel better, too.

The disorganized basketball game was a flurry of missed shots and ball chasing while the tour group stood at the corner of the court nearest the door and the steps to the pool tables and other activities below. The guards smiled benevolently and addressed one or two of the patients by their first names.

"How's it going, Jimmy?" one of them asked, but received no response, leading anyone who was paying attention to wonder whether there was a patient named Jimmy on the floor. "You doing okay, John?"

As the group turned to be herded through the door leading to the floor below, all eyes, including those of the patients, fascinated by the crowd of strangers, were directed away from the basketball court and toward the door.

Spangler's mind ignited like the engine of a getaway car and his reflexes went into gear as rapidly. In a few very quick steps, he was behind the partially unfolded bleachers and moving deeper under the folded ones, into the darkness of hiding.

Within minutes a voice was calling the players off the basketball floor and the large gymnasium was a cavern of silence. It was then, and only then, that Spangler began to consider his next movements. He decided to wait until nightfall and then explore the recreation building for a way out and away from the hospital.

He was not thinking properly. He would be missed in the kitchen long before dark, more than likely, even though DeLuca had left early, as he did every day. In any other place than the kitchen, it would not take long at all for a patient to be missed and a search begun. There was less scrutiny in the dietary jobs. Nevertheless, Spangler should have expected to be missed when it came time to wash pots and dishes.

He was.

And it did not require much time for the guards to trace his whereabouts during the day up to the recreation period put in for the benefit of the tour group. A couple of people remembered seeing him in the gymnasium. Nobody remembered having seen him since then. A check of D-Ward disclosed that he had not been taken back there.

Five blue shirts went to the recreation building. It was still light enough to see without the aid of lights, but they turned them on in the basement, anyway. There was no sign of Spangler in the library or around the pool tables, or under them. He was not in any of the two or three tiny rooms off the library, where a rare few of the privileged were allowed to play an occasional guitar. He was not lying down beside the three rarely used bowling lanes and he was not in the supply room. He was not in the yard outside.

When they went upstairs to the basketball court they did not turn on the lights, but Spangler knew they were present because he could hear the tapping of heels on the highly varnished hardwood.

His entrails climbed into his throat when he heard the sound of footsteps, and he seemed not to breathe as he waited to hear the direction they would take.

For the guards' part, it did not take long to look around the bare court and see that the huge room was empty, unless there was something or someone behind the bleachers.

"I'll go get a flashlight," Spangler heard one of the guards say. He impulsively looked about him for a better hiding place, but in the blackness of his position deep along the bleachers and against the wall, he could see little even though his eyes had grown accustomed to the darkness.

"Get me one while you're at it," another guard called.

"Why don't we just pull the bleachers out and look between the boards?" one of the other guards asked.

"That'll take too long," came the response. "We get a flashlight and we can just go under one end of the seats and walk a little ways in and shine a light under the whole thing. Then we don't have to put them back up again."

When the guard returned with the flashlights, two of the party went to check under the bleachers on the other side of the floor and the other three remained on the side nearest the door.

Spangler did not know what to do. He was afraid to move, for fear of making a sound. He was afraid not to move for fear of being found. He thought he would have a better chance of escaping notice if he were lying on the floor in the far corner at the lowest point of the bleachers. Lying down was better, even against the wall, where the bleachers reached high over his head. He took his white T-shirt off and wadded it under his stomach. He hoped that his black head and black body would blend into the darkness and evade detection in the flashlight's beam.

He lay tightly against the floor and pressed into the wall. He closed his eyes and he could hear his heart making the sound of African tom-toms. He thought it sounded like more than one heart beating inside his chest. It seemed that he was hardly breathing. Fear washed over him and he shivered. He felt cold without a shirt, yet he was perspiring. He heard shoe leather scraping and tapping along the floor and the sounds seemed louder in the confines of the bleachers' cave.

"Put that light back over there against the wall," he heard a guard say, and he turned to granite. "No, lower. Near the floor. Yeah, that's it. What's that?"

Spangler could not feel the beam of light bathe his body, but he knew it must be on him.

"That's him, ain't it?" he heard a guard say, then follow up with: "Hey, boy! Get your ass up from there."

Then there was the shout. "Hey boys, we got him over here!" And the approaching footsteps.

Spangler trembled.

"I said for you to get your ass up," growled the guard. "Move it!"

Spangler opened his eyes and looked up into two bright beams. He could not see the forms or the faces behind them. His pupils constricted and were like two nailheads in the center of white saucers. He was immobilized with fear.

He did not see the foot coming, but it struck him in the side, barely below the ribs. Almost all his breath left, air rushing from him as through the neck of a filled balloon.

He rolled to his back, and began to buck and squirm, struggling for oxygen. He was able to utter only grunts, but he extended his arms before him, palms out in a silent plea that the kicking be stopped. He shook his head from side to side. To no avail.

With the lights shining in his eyes, he never saw the blows coming at him. He never knew from which direction or person the next would come. He could hear the voices, but was concentrating more on covering his body than on identifying the attackers.

"Thought you'd run away, huh?"

"I told you to get up, you wool-headed bastard!"

"Move over a minute and let me shine my shoes on that shithead!"

"We'll fix your ass for running."

All Spangler could do was roll from side to side and squirm and wriggle and try to dodge the feet flying at him from all sides now. He had no way of knowing how many he evaded. Not all, for sure.

His breath returned and he put his hands together in front of his face. He pulled his knees into a fetal position just before a foot lodged in the small of his back, knocking him forward and sending his hands from his face to his kidneys. It was then that another foot dug into his abdomen and he felt his sphincter loosen. His bowels released their contents and he seemed to have no control of them.

"Please don't hit me again," he begged. "I didn't mean to run," he lied. "I'm sorry. I'm sorry. I'm sorry."

From somewhere above him a fist made a sledgehammer landing on his mouth and he felt an enameled stone on his tongue.

Then his tongue found a gap in his teeth. He spit out the tooth and tried to get to his feet to escape the agony. He got to his knees, his arms flailing before him in search of something to grab. He was pushed from behind and his nose and cheekbone tried to dig a trench in the hardwood.

Still he tried to get away, not knowing that he was surrounded. Again and again he was kicked, until finally he felt a heavy foot come down firmly into the middle of his back, seemingly trying to pin him to the floor. He rolled over under the foot and heard the guard lose his balance and fall.

Spangler came to his feet, only to have his feet cut from under him by a soccer-type kick to his ankles. He lay motionless and heard one of the men above him say, "We're gonna make you think twice about running away, you stupid, stinking, thick-lipped sonofabitch."

Then the helpless patient felt someone grab his legs above the knee and almost simultaneously felt the shooting, searing pain that came when one of the other guards stomped on a shin and fractured a bone. While Spangler was writhing from that blow, the guard stomped down on the other shin and Spangler screamed as a bone in that leg also cracked.

"You ain't gonna run for a long time, asshole," a voice in the darkness spat. "You try this again, we might fix it where you don't walk again."

Spangler lay moaning, hoping that the kicking had ended. He didn't know if he could take more. The fight was gone from him. The stench of his soiled clothing was threatening to suffocate him.

"Let's get out of here," one of the guards said. "Better take him to R-Ward."

"Yeah," said another. "Let them clean the sonofabitch up." He and one of the others grabbed Spangler's arms and started pulling him along the floor.

"God, he smells awful," said another. "Heard of kicking the shit out a man, but I didn't believe it could really be done."

"I hope I didn't get any of it on my shoes," said one of his comrades.

17

Tension began to gnaw at some of the men on D-Ward that evening after they returned to the dayroom from supper. They all had heard that Spangler was missing. One of the guards had blurted it out after the report of his absence came from the kitchen. But he had just barely beaten the grapevine. The kitchen workers were telling anybody who would listen as they came through the chow line.

Some of the patients on D-Ward wanted his escape to fail, probably because it was he and not they who had the chance. Or so they thought. The black patients, especially Night Train, seemed to be begging inwardly for his success. They whispered animatedly and their brows were furrowed and they paced nervously, like expectant fathers awaiting word.

For others, the nightly ritual seemed unchanged. Some were reading torn-out sections of magazines, a small crowd was smoking in the bathroom, and a larger one was shuffling around in the circle. The television was tuned to network news.

On the screen came film footage of Muhammad Ali, accompanied by a voice-over explanation of the latest skirmish between the heavyweight boxing champion and the United States government. The black faces near the television set were staring at it intently. They hardly saw the hand reach up to switch the channel, it happened so quickly. Almost simultaneously came the gravel voice of a guard: "I don't want to hear any more about that chicken-shit nigger traitor."

There was a chorus of protest from the patients who had been concentrating on the newscast.

"Hey! Whattaya doing?"

"Turn it back!"

Night Train reached up and turned the selector back to the Muhammad Ali coverage.

"Don't touch the TV, boy!" It came from one of the guards at the end of the dayroom opposite the television.

"I want to watch this," Night Train said. His anger was rising. He was becoming increasingly interested in the Muhammad Ali case, which he knew about only through television, and he was becoming more fascinated with the Islamic philosophy, or what little he knew about it—that, too, stemming from what he was able to glean from television, but mostly from his admiration of Ali.

"I don't give a damn what you want, nigger!" There was venom in the voice. It belonged to Bulldog, who had walked from his rocking chair near the door to a point not far from Night Train. "You sit your coon ass down and shut up."

"But I . . ."

"I said shut up. Right now."

Still, Night Train stood. Veins in his temples were popping and ligaments along his ebony neck were straight and hard and prominent. His fists were clenching and unclenching and clenching again. When he spoke, his words came out slowly, with one-at-a-time emphasis, firm and filled with a mix of pride and hatred.

"I am extremely tired of being treated with racist attitudes by people here," he said, looking directly into the eyes of the charge guard. "I am not an animal, a nigger, a jigaboo, or a coon. I am a man!"

The other guards began to close in, looking as though they were waiting for Bulldog to give them some kind of sign to subdue the patient. But with a slight wave of a hand he held them off. Still, he refused even to let it appear that he was conceding a point to the black man.

"Big fucking deal," he said, turning to walk back toward his rocking chair. Then he turned again and looked at Night Train.

"We'll see how much man you are," he said. "I suppose it's about time you and Malone took the floor. Me and Boots have been waiting for a chance to get you two jungle bunnies together." He took a step or two toward Night Train. "My money'll be on Malone . . . not some traitor-loving motherfucker with a big mouth. We'll do it one night next week. We'll see if you got more in common with that chicken-shit Clay than a loud mouth and a BB brain."

Night Train was left smoldering, but silent and motionless. He wanted to shout a challenge to the potbellied guard to take the floor himself, but he knew he had said too much already. He had said too much, but he was glad he had. There was a feeling of release. Of freedom. He had said what was on his mind and had stood up the way he thought a man should. He looked around to see how the others had reacted to his confrontation with Bulldog. He hoped, even expected, to see some looks of respect, admiration. Perhaps awe. He thought he would see some quiet, private smiles of congratulation.

He saw what he had always seen in that room. He saw men with their heads down, their eyes averted, some still scanning the far corners of the ceiling, in search of angel wings. Or peace.

The only men looking at him at all were Malone and Wade. Wade was wearing the private smile. Malone seemed to be measuring. It was not until then that the gravity of his actions registered. He knew what it meant to take the floor with another patient. He had done so several times. But he had always won the fights. Now he became poignantly conscious of what had happened to the men he had whipped and the men Malone had whipped.

Some of them had been literally kicked from where they had fallen, practically comatose, to the peanut. Some had been stripped and drenched with water in the peanut and then exposed to the frigid Pocono winter that blew through the opened window in the tiny cubicle.

The guards did not like to lose money. And the man who lost their money was a man who lost more than once, and in more than one way.

Night Train did not want to lose to Malone, even though Malone was his friend. He did not want the added punishment at the hands, or feet, of Bulldog and his friends. And he did not want to lie naked and raw in the peanut, even if it wasn't winter.

He knew that Malone would not want to lose either. He knew what had happened to the younger man that night when Boots raped his face. He had watched the eyes burn with hate.

Malone rarely spoke to others, patients or guards. In fact, he never spoke to a guard unless an answer was demanded of him. He seldom looked other men in the eye. There was a quiet rage inside him. And an avowal to do whatever was necessary to get out of the hospital and tell the world what was going on inside. He had decided that he would do whatever anybody asked of him. He would run any errand, take on any unpleasant task.

His parents were working with their minister and his political connections in Pittsburgh to obtain a competency hearing for him to show that he was able to serve his time in prison. The minister did have influence.

Malone knew that now was not the time to be derailed from his plans. He knew as well as Night Train that losing fighters often were finished for good at Farview. Sometimes they died.

They both sensed that the loser of their fight would not survive to fight again. Nor go through the gates alive.

*

When Sullins saw the condition of Spangler's body as it was brought to R-Ward he was immediately reminded of the way Chamberlin had looked that day a few months earlier when he was dragged in from J-Ward. Spangler's face and arms and legs were swollen, and even though his skin was dark, it was as discolored as Chamberlin's had been. His chest and back were scraped raw. He was dazed and what little speech he could muster was mostly incoherent grunts and groans.

Spangler's mouth was cut and bloody and a tooth was missing.

Sullins did not remember that Chamberlin had lost teeth, but he remembered his having been much more nearly dead when he got to the infirmary than Spangler was. Chamberlin had been too far gone to say anything, maybe even feel anything.

In many ways, perhaps in every significant way, Sullins thought that the story of what had happened to Chamberlin, both before his death and in the months following, was the story of how Farview really operated.

The orderly knew that hospital records indicated that Chamberlin had been transferred to the infirmary unit "for rest," but that he had been there only briefly before he died.

As he looked at Spangler, Sullins' mind sped back to the morning Chamberlin had expired, and he recalled the subsequent events almost as vividly as if they were presently occurring around him.

*

Chamberlin had stopped breathing at 7:55 A.M. and about an hour later, at 9:12, Dr. Dallmeyer sent a telegram to the patient's family, telling them that their son had "died suddenly." By 2:10 that afternoon, Chamberlin's mother had informed the hospital that she would permit a legal autopsy of her son's body and she provided instructions for transferring it home.

That same day, Dr. Dallmeyer hastily scheduled an autopsy. He and Dr. Zundel and two other doctors on the staff, as well as assorted guards, hospital employees, and a patient or two, gathered in the basement of R-Ward.

Even though the death was considered sudden, the county coroner was not notified and no representatives of his office were present. It was a private autopsy rather than a legal one.

As far as Sullins knew, the examination of the body was rather detailed, and one of the doctors was taking notes. In fact, he found it strange when Pagnotti came by afterward asking questions about the autopsy.

Sullins learned later that no postmortem report of Chamberlin's death had been prepared and that notes of the autopsy could not be located. Nevertheless, Dr. Combest, who was not present at the autopsy, completed the death certificate and attributed death to pulmonary embolism.

Dr. Zundel's notation on the Department of Welfare's death notice form had said that death resulted from an acute coronary thrombosis, coronary occlusion.

Later that night men came from a funeral home in Scranton to pick up the body and prepare it for shipment across the state to Beaver Falls. Dr. Combest was there when they arrived.

"What'd he die from?" one of the undertakers asked.

"I think he got the hell beaten out of him," Dr. Combest said, knowing that embalmers were likely to recognize the evidence of one-sided combat.

Sure enough, during the embalming it was noticed that Chamberlin's right wrist was broken, as were two ribs. The embalmer also could hardly fail to notice that the body contained no internal organs.

The brain had been placed in a display bottle and left on one of the shelves in the Farview morgue. According to Dr. Dallmeyer, the other organs had been examined and disclosed no remarkable findings. Except for the heart.

The embalmer replaced them all with wadded newspaper and sent Chamberlin to his mother.

About a month after the body was sent west, Dr. Dallmeyer wrote a letter to Chamberlin's sister in which he described her brother's death as "abrupt," having occurred "so unexpectedly that we were all upset."

Still, the fact that she had inquired into her brother's demise prompted the hospital administrators to arm themselves with an internal investigation report in case somebody at the state level heard about the "sudden" death of a man named Chamberlin.

Pagnotti was assigned to conduct the investigation. Although he was unable to locate either a postmorten report or notes of the autopsy, and could not find any two people in agreement on who had been present when the autopsy took place, he interviewed some people and determined that Chamberlin had been transferred to R-Ward in the first place in order to be treated for a head injury he incurred while trying to escape from J-Ward.

That was the story concocted by guards on J-Ward and enhanced by the eye-witness testimony of a patient, Elroy Jones.

Jones was a man who happened to have been in the right place, Godforsaken as it was, at the right time. He was not slow to seize the moment.

Pagnotti always liked to have the statement of a patient included in any investigation he conducted. He thought it added considerable credibility to what otherwise was a compilation of comments from men, guards, who had a direct stake in the result of the investigation. A patient who was not directly involved in an incident could not be shown to be prejudiced one way or another.

So when Jones was approached by the men in blue shirts, he was alert to his opportunity. He became especially alert when they removed the leather restraints.

"You remember a man named Chamberlin?" Pagnotti asked him.

"Sho," said Jones. "I feel sho I do."

"What do you know about him?"

"I know he was in here."

"You know where?"

"I think so. Why you ask me all this stuff?"

"We thought maybe you could give us a little help."

"Maybe I could and maybe I cain't."

"You want to help us or not? You gonna cooperate?"

"Why should I? You gone kill me if I don't? I'm gone die in here anyhow."

"Maybe not."

Jones could feel the good news building.

"You gone get me outta here?"

"I might be able to arrange something. Could get you off of J."

"You ain't gone put me on no P or Q or D, is you?"

"That depends on what you know about what went on in here with Chamberlin."

"I can know a lot." The deal was within reach.

"I can put you on G or maybe BB."

"I want W or X or the bungalow."

"Not the bungalow."

"X, then. And a good job."

"Okay."

The bargain was made.

"What you want me to say?" Jones asked. He did not give a damn what really happened to Chamberlin. He had an idea that the man was dead when he left the ward, but he didn't know for sure. And he didn't care. He would go along with anything Pagnotti wanted, if it got him off J-Ward.

"He was in the cell next to you, right?" Pagnotti was careful. He might lead Jones to go along with anything, but Jones would be the one to make the statement, Jones would have to answer the questions orally in front of a witness, and he would have to sign it. Pagnotti called two of the regular J-Ward guards into the cell to hear Jones. When they were in the cell, he repeated the question and Jones repeated his answer:

"Right."

"Sometimes you saw him outside his cell, right?"

"Right."

"You never saw him get beaten or kicked by anybody, guard or anybody else, right?"

"That's right."

"You never saw him get mistreated, right?"

"Right."

"But you remember the time he tried to escape, right?"

"Right." Jones was trying to hold on to the line.

"You saw him break away from the guards, these two here, and run toward the door, right?"

"Right." Now Jones was following the course again.

"And you saw him trip and fall headfirst into the door, right?"

"Yeah, that's right." Jones was almost ready to laugh. These guys could cover up anything by claiming it was the result of an escape attempt or subduing. But this was one time he didn't care, and it was so easy to go along with the program.

"All right. Write your name right there." The lieutenant indicated a blank line at the bottom of a sheet of paper filled with typewritten lines.

"What's it say?"

"It says what you said, stupid shit. Sign it before I grind your head into that concrete wall."

Jones laughed a low, gravelly laugh and wrote his name.

Pagnotti looked at the paper, then looked to one of the other guards.

"Get him something to wear and take him to D-ward," he said. "Tell Hawk to make sure the little fucker gets to the horse room in the morning sometime."

"You said X-Ward," Jones shouted. "You fucked me."

"Yeah, I fucked you," Pagnotti said. "You can go to D or you can stay here and get what Chamberlin got. I don't care which."

"But you made a deal."

"Well, I broke it."

"Then I take back everything I said." Jones was almost pouting. He looked humorous, pitifully humorous. Pagnotti laughed out loud.

"Fuck you. It's on paper and I got two witnesses, plus me. You think people will believe us or a crazy little shit who's changing his mind? Go to D and shut up. I'm giving you a break."

Jones knew it was true. It was all true. He had been double-crossed, nobody would believe a crazy man and he was getting a break. He nodded his head and followed the guards into the hall-way. He put on a pair of denims that were too big and a T-shirt and a pair of shoes and socks. It was the first time he had worn clothes in more than seven years.

He wished he could have taken a bath.

*

Sullins had heard about Jones and the Pagnotti report from Yancey, who had daily dealings with the tiny black man now that the latter was working in the horse room, cutting out pictures from nudist camp magazines so the guards could rent them to patients.

And as Sullins looked at Spangler he knew the hurting man would be fortunate indeed to survive the repercussions of an actual escape attempt, instead of a fabricated one. But maybe not, he thought. Maybe the fabrications were worse than the realities. Maybe they were the same. Maybe the guards and doctors had no more idea than the patients about where reality began or ended.

Sometimes he thought everybody at the hospital was crazy. Sometimes he thought nobody was. Just different. Different personalities, different physiques, different minds. All scared. Maybe the only thing insane was the way the place was run, everybody scared of everybody else. Or maybe that there was such a place at all. Maybe the system was crazy and not the people. But the people were the system.

That was the problem with Farview. Both the system and the people in the system were rotten. And hidden. And forgotten about.

That was how a man who tried to run away got his legs stomped on and broken.

18

As THE week progressed leading up to the fight between Night Train and Malone, excitement mounted, nowhere more so, perhaps, than on D-Ward. The two men lived on the ward and often were forced by the guards to look into each other's eyes.

There were frequent arranged fights between patients, sanctioned combat that provided the hospital's only live entertainment as well as an opportunity to wager on the outcome. And sometimes two patients who wanted to fight each other, either to settle a score or because of temporary anger, were allowed to take the floor and impromptu betting occurred.

But this fight was different. This was more than live entertainment, and it was more than another chance to wager. In this fight, two guards had a personal stake in the outcome. Boots Ringgold hated Malone and Malone hated him. Bulldog may not have hated Night Train any more than he hated any other black man, but he hated what Night Train had done to him in the television incident. Night Train hated Bulldog.

Each of the guards wanted to be rid of his particular antagonist, but neither of them had either sufficient cause or the stomach to personally do the job. Each was investing heavily in the fight. Each was making significant promises to the man he was backing. And both had gone higher in the hospital administration for assurances to back up their promises.

The fight would be worthwhile for the winner, if he were not maimed beyond the value of freedom.

Bulldog had guaranteed Malone that if he won he could go to staff, equipped with a recommendation that he be allowed to stand trial or return to prison or whatever was necessary before he could be released into society.

Boots had arranged virtually the same future for Night Train, and had promised him half of the money he won on the fight.

Both men had been promised the peanut and J-Ward if they lost, a promise neither had needed to hear.

Betting throughout the hospital was active, and more or less evenly split. And for about a week both men had more friends than they had known existed. And more enemies.

For Farview, it was the ultimate sport. It was rural and earthy and dirty. It was classic and pagan, and Roman as their church. It was animalistic, it was gladiatorial. It was blood and money. It was to the death.

It was a human cockfight.

Betting on the fight had been steadily building all week, and it had not started out slowly. Both men owned solid reputations and fast, hard hands. Both men had won a lot of fights and had sent men to R-Ward. Malone had a feeling that he had killed a couple of patients in previous fights. He had never seen them again afterward. And the time he knocked a man's eye out of its socket was imbedded in his and other peoples' memory.

Yancey was betting on Malone. All he could bet. His new friend, Jones, already was hustling pornographic pictures for himself by stealing a couple of the ones he cut out and peddling them, renting them actually, on the ward. With several hundred men who were in the market for fantasies to masturbate over, the guards did not begrudge Jones his handful of merchandise. He had made a few dollars and was betting it all on Night Train. He wanted to double his money. He was in a hurry to make up for seven years in isolation.

In the guards' dining room, conversations centered on whether Bulldog's nigger could whip Boots's nigger. Bulldog had fanned the interest by taking all bets against Malone.

"My coon can beat his coon," Bulldog told anyone in range. "My nigger's got a harder head, harder fists, and he don't have chicken-shits for heroes. My nigger's got guts."

Then he would laugh and shake his head at the amount of money he had wagered on the fight and say, "And if he don't win, I'm gonna kick his ass all the way through that peanut."

All Boots said, over and over, was, "A nigger that'll suck a dick can't be much fighter."

Both Malone and Night Train heard the guards and the patients discuss the fight on the ward. Malone's hatred for Boots deepened, if that were possible. He didn't want to be anybody's nigger.

Night Train heard the talk and decided that this would be his last fight, win or lose. He was feeling like a Tom, doing whatever the guards said, always saying "Yessir" and "Nosir" and "Mister." Shining shoes and standing in line. He felt like a child instead of a man. That's what had been so good about standing up to Bulldog about the television set.

He had a feeling that it wouldn't make any difference whether he won or lost the fight, as far as Boots's living up to his promises. He figured Boots would renege and he would be beaten up about as bad as Malone, all for nothing. The only people who would gain anything from the fight would be the ones who had bet on him. It wouldn't do him any good.

Except if he lost, he probably would not live long. Boots would be mad as hell and probably wouldn't let a doctor get to him for a while just so he would have to lie in the peanut and suffer and bleed.

No, he thought, he had to win this one. He knew Malone would not hold back. Malone wanted his freedom too badly. He had heard Malone say he wanted to get outside and have a shot at Boots when it would be just the two of them. Malone believed Bulldog's promise. He would do anything to win, Night Train knew. And that might mean beating him to death, just to be sure there was no question about the winner.

Night Train had decided that if he won this fight he would stand up to them and not fight any more. He had decided to live like a man if he lived. If they killed him for not doing what he was told, he would die like a man. But he would be nobody's nigger after this.

The fight was planned for second shift on Friday, sometime after seven or seven-thirty. Boots would come in early. All the hospital supervision would be gone home. They knew about the fight, of course. Some of them had bet on the outcome. In fact some of them seemed to spend as much time around the horse room with the Daily Racing Form as they spent doing their jobs. But it was always nicer for them if things happened at times when they could legitimately claim to have been absent from the hospital with no way of knowing for certain what had gone on. They loved being able to say: "Nothing like that ever happened when I was around. I don't believe it could have happened at all. If it did, I never saw it."

So the guards ordered the patients to rearrange the oak benches in a square, for a ring, in the D-Ward dayroom that evening. Under Bulldog's supervision, of course. Then the patients gathered around the benches. They stood two and three deep. More than a hundred of them were there to watch, but even with an event as exciting as this, not all of them did. Some were prone at the base of the walls, taking trips to places only they knew existed.

Neither Garth nor Kirchoff had a position in the front row. Kirchoff had not moved from his seat quickly enough and Garth and the other kitchen workers had been brought back to the ward late. He had been given the kitchen job that Spangler had lost. Hawk had given it to him, saying he should be good at scrubbing pots and pans because "There's a little nigger in all you sharecropper types."

Garth had not bet on the fight because he didn't have any money. But he was sort of pulling for Night Train. He admired the way the bigger of the two black men had talked back to Bulldog. Garth was feeling the same way about how things were run at "this prison they call a hospital," as he had become fond of saying to other patients. The way he saw it, doing time was one thing, but doing chicken-shit time was something else. Getting your balls broken for not saying "sir" was chicken-shit, he thought.

In prison, a man who handled himself like a man, and didn't take a lot of crap, was treated like a man. He had a few rights. Damned few, but some. Not here. Only the ones with money had rights, and they only had them as long as they kissed ass or opened their own up for somebody to stick something in.

Lot of these guys, he thought, like Coda and Dureen, only had money because the guards let them have it. And the guards could —and usually did—come over and take whatever they wanted. Coda and Dureen couldn't do anything about it. All Coda was really interested in was keeping his kid, whoever it happened to be at the time, and the guards would always let him have that. More shit started with two homos fighting over a kid or two homos fighting over each other than anything else except money, yet the hospital condoned it as long as it was done kind of private. Said it occupied time and kept patients out of trouble.

He looked at Coda, standing on the opposite side of the oak bench ring, his arm dangling around the shoulder of a youngster whose face was a splotchy pink and white, the color of uncooked sausage. The older man was stroking the young man's upper arm.

Excitement mounted as the time for the fight approached. The two fighters had to crawl over the backs of the benches to enter the ring. There was not much formality. Both were barefoot and wore denims. Neither wore a shirt.

There were basically no rules. There was no time limit. The fight ended when one man could not get up and his sponsor acknowledged that he was beaten. There were no time-outs. There were no gloves. Somebody said, "Start fighting," and they did.

The two men stared into each other's eyes as they circled, feet spread, hands rotating in front of their faces, fingers loosely curled into semi-fists. First one, then the other feinted and re-acted to feint, neither taking his eyes from those of the other.

Night Train was the larger, but he appeared to be less quick, less intense than Malone. There were dark slash marks on the upper arms and shoulders of both men, indicating that they had made these kinds of circles and rotations before with something sharp in their hands.

The guards quickly tired of the circling and measuring. There were demands for action, for blood. And the racial slurs and taunts which had been such a large part of the days at Farview were poured again into the ears of the two men.

"The only thing more worthless than one scared nigger is two scared niggers," said the tall guard who had been one of the first to put the boots to Garth in the shower his first night on the ward.

"You can't beat your meat, Malone!" shouted another.

"Why don't youse guys dance?" came a third.

Some of the patients were feinting and wincing and growing nervous just watching the preliminary shuffling. Others were simpering in vicarious fear.

Visible cringing greeted the first exchange, which saw Malone fake a punch to Night Train's stomach and then get hit with a right to the point of the chin before he could cover. Malone went down to a knee and Night Train was on him. He hammered blows to Malone's back and shoulder and the back of his head while Malone struggled to get to his feet, all the while crouched almost low enough for his knees to touch his chest. His arms were wrapped around his head for protection.

He jerked away from Night Train, but the larger man pressed closer, giving him little room to use his quicker fists.

Malone went again to a knee, but this time it was to grab for Night Train's legs. He pulled as hard as he was able and the bigger man lost his balance and fell against one of the benches.

Malone followed him to the bench, faked a punch, and delivered a kick to the other man's neck. Night Train spun around from a hip to his knee and Malone kicked again, this time driving his instep into the fleshy part of his opponent's side, between the bottom rib and the point of the pelvis.

Night Train caught the foot before it could get back to the floor and he yanked Malone off his feet, then fell on top of him, trying to wrap one steel band of arm around the smaller man's neck while he used the other fist as a maul. Malone lifted his right knee hard and straight to Night Train's groin. The larger man screamed and fell away.

Malone was laboring for breath, unable for the moment to press an attack. Both men stood, not circling any more, not even measuring, but looking for an opening through which a fist could fly.

Night Train sent one to a spot between Malone's nose and cheek and Malone countered with two in almost the same place above Night Train's left eye. The skin tore jaggedly and blood spilled down the side of the big man's face.

He raised a hand to try to clear his eye and Malone shot a mortar to his stomach. Night Train jackknifed and fell to his knees gasping.

He made the mistake of lifting his unprotected head, and Malone's fist became an air hammer drilling at his mouth. Teeth broke and Malone's knuckles split and bled.

Again, Night Train rose and charged. His head hit Malone at the cheekbone and opened a gash. Blood ran into the smaller man's mouth and he began to spit red ropes while Night Train locked his arms around him and began to squeeze.

Figures behind the benches began to turn fuzzy for Malone and the light seemed to dim. He knew he could not let the bigger man use his superior strength. Fear crowded into his throat and his eyes began to see multicolored patches.

The light was fading and panic struck. He could not lose this fight. He had to get out of this place alive. He had to get one chance at Boots before he died. His eyes filled with the face of the guard and his mind with a gagging memory. His fists were flailing at Night Train's head. Blood was filling the big man's eyes and he had closed them against the flood. Malone tore at them with vicious fury until Night Train could stand the pain no longer and his vise grip loosened enough for Malone to drive one more knee to the groin and another heavy blow to the face.

Night Train was on his hands and knees, leaning as though he might fall to his side like a felled rhinoceros. Malone stood nearby, bent, his arms dangling straight from his shoulders as though his brain had forgotten they existed. His mouth was filled with his own blood. His chest hurt with every breath.

The man on his knees could not see. Blood dripped to the floor from the tip of his nose. He struggled to rise, his arms askew in search of balance, his feet shuffling in search of stability.

While his opponent groped, Malone mustered strength for one last swing and aimed an axe blow at the tottering trunk before him. It crashed into Night Train's gut and doubled him. His face hit the floor before any other part of his body, and he was out.

Malone's eyes were not focusing well and he felt he was about to succumb to a pounding darkness. He wanted somebody to say it was over before he saw more red and black than anything else. He could hardly breathe because of the pain in his ribs. He felt certain at least one was broken. His mouth was dry as a bird's nest.

He looked at the man in dreamless sleep on the floor. His face was swollen and bleeding from the nose and mouth and deep cuts above both eyes. His gasps for air contained a rattle.

Surely it was over.

"Get up, you lousy fucking nigger!" It was Boots standing over the prostrate man, who could not hear the epithets raining on his battered body. "You're losing my *money*, you black bastard! Get the fuck up and I'll show you how to fight!

Boots was screaming and the rage he felt ran from his mouth to his feet which began to slam into Night Train's back and sides.

"Get up, nigger," the screams continued. "Get up, damn you."

But Night Train did not get up. Finally, Bulldog came over the back of a bench and slapped Boots on the back.

"Hey, that's enough," he said, pulling Boots away from the man on the floor. "That fucker's out. He ain't gonna get up." He looked at another guard and said, "Toss him in the peanut and get somebody to clean up this mess."

They pushed the benches apart at one corner of the ring and a pair of blue shirts grabbed Night Train's feet. Spectators parted to open a path as they pulled him toward the small door of the peanut. Most of the patients were settling bets and walking away from the square of benches.

A few minutes later, men were putting benches back where they belonged and others were mopping blood from the floor. Some hospital employees had left the ward and Boots was sitting in the charge's office with Bulldog.

Night Train was lying twisted on the floor of the peanut, too far gone to complain or even be aware of the stench of decades of urine emanating from the wood beneath his bloody nose. He looked like a side of overaged beef that had fallen from its rack.

Malone stood swaying near the middle of the dayroom, hot and exhausted, blinking hot eyes, trying not to slip down the dark slope of pain. Nobody approached him. Nobody had offered congratulations. None of those who had bet on him had said a word. Bulldog had not even clapped him on the back.

He stood alone while a circle of morons shuffled around him.

He was the winner.

PART III

Fear is the main source of superstition, and one of the main sources of cruelty. To conquer fear is the beginning of wisdom.
—BERTRAND RUSSELL

19

DR. MCINTOSH had been to Farview before. Not exceedingly often—in fact as seldom as possible—partly because it was a long and unpleasant drive from the hospital near Philadelphia where he was superintendent, but mostly because it was a damned unpleasant place to be.

He was familiar with the place and its attitude and its reputation. He was not alone in his displeasure. It was not recognized by anyone he knew as being Pennsylvania's shining light. To some in the Department of Welfare, it was better known as the feudal estate of Dr. Dallmeyer and Walt Luker, and the bureaucrats did not make careless suggestions for change at Farview.

But pressures beyond the control of state government—or Walt Luker—were beginning to cause problems for the department. The secretary wanted the problem areas pinpointed and corrected, if possible, before they became the subject of lawsuits and a source of embarrassment to the governor.

That's why Dr. McIntosh was spending a few summer days behind the walls of what he thought was a state-run chamber of horrors. It was easily the dreariest place he had ever been. He was supposed to head up a small group of outside social workers and a few Farview staff members in a review committee to see if and where the hospital was vulnerable to action by a coterie of University of Pennsylvania law students who were using the school's Prison Research Council to challenge state laws and welfare department regulations as being unconstitutional because they denied due process to mental patients.

With the help of recent graduates of the law school who were in private practice, the council was about to go into federal court against the state. They knew better than to go into Pennsylvania's state courts. They had written to a judge near Pittsburgh who had committed a man to a mental hospital. They told the judge that two independent psychiatrists had determined that the man, who had spent more than a decade in confinement, was not insane. The judge responded: "A duck is a duck."

During the review, Dr. McIntosh was learning things about the hospital that the young lawyers already knew, and his researchers were compiling a more dismal picture with every report.

The final staff meeting was jolting to him. He sat at the head of an oval conference table, pulling at his thick beard, dark with rivers of gray. His strong hand gripped the pen tightly as he jotted notes on a yellow legal pad. He was not displaying his usual wide, toothy smile. He occasionally shook his head in sad disbelief.

"We found one man named Stadelman, who was admitted to the hospital in 1930," a member of the review team read from a sheaf of papers, "and his first psychological review came twenty-six years later. It was another twelve years, for a total of thirty-eight years since his admission, before he was given a diagnostic staff evaluation.

"We found another, named Leftwich, who was admitted in 1944, waited twenty-three years for a staff evaluation, and has yet to begin a formal treatment plan for his illness.

"We have a man named Kirchoff who was charged with disturbing the peace twenty-eight years ago, almost twenty-nine, and he finally saw an outside psychiatrist last month. He has never been to staff and never had a psychiatric or psychological examination or test or anything."

The list ran on, a litany of neglect, of men the world, and maybe God, had forgotten about.

"There's a man named Kemp who was convicted of arson in 1949 and came to the hospital that year. We asked the D.A. in the man's county if the charges could be dropped, and he said they were dropped in 1949."

"How the hell could that happen?" Dr. McIntosh asked, rhetorically. "Did anybody ever check these records or do any kind of follow-up? Who gave the state the right to put these men in cold storage? Out of sight, out of mind?"

There was no answer, except from the staff person with the list, who now began to read more in shorthand than in sentences.

"Here's one . . . man named Bissell . . . charged with contributing to the delinquency of a minor . . . admitted 1950 . . . never stood trial. D.A. says charges can be dropped, but the man's so old he may die before the paperwork can get done.

"Let's see . . . man named Darcy . . . charged with arson in '48, charges dropped in '53 . . . he's still here.

"Man named Innman . . . charged with—get this—solicitation to commit sodomy . . . probably asked a girl to blow him . . . in 1938. We asked the D.A. in that county if the charge could be dropped and he said, 'Why not?' "

She looked at her notes. "That's just a few but you get the idea."

Dr. McIntosh was visibly upset. Worried. Shaken, in fact.

"It looks like there are a number of winnable lawsuits up here," he said. "It looks like a lot of these people are here because everybody else forgot about them. Are any of them getting any treatment? I haven't seen any."

A youngish woman replied to that question.

"Many of the charts, patients' charts, indicate that they have been here twenty or thirty years without any treatment. They are termed too dangerous for anything less than maximum security, but they've never—or rarely—been tried on any medication likely to influence their supposed illness."

Dr. McIntosh interrupted. "And yet these same patients—who are dangerous enough to need maximum security but get no medication, no treatment, never go to staff, or wait years between staffings—are regarded as safe to work for ten or twenty years on the farm out there with minimal supervision."

"That's right," the woman said.

"How can they *do* that?" Again he didn't expect an answer.

"The pressures they feel here tell them to continue to hold somebody and never let them go." It was one of the lawyers working with the Prison Research Council. He was sitting in on the meeting, having participated in several patient interviews himself.

"The doctors here just recommit patients as an in-house, office procedure. These patients aren't taken before a judge to be re-committed. All it requires is the signatures of two physicians. They've got more than two there. At least more than two of them have licenses." He was trying to explain the process, trying to answer Dr. McIntosh's question. He was about to make a speech and hadn't meant to, but he was carried away, dedicated to getting a lot of patients out of Farview. Maybe as many as five or six hundred.

"You see, there is a high degree of self-preservation here. The state has entrusted these people with safeguarding society against potentially dangerous men. In essence, the state has said, 'Make sure these people never bother us.' The only way the men in charge here can make a mistake, then, is to release somebody who may go out and do something bad.

"So the doctors, and even most of the outside psychiatrists occasionally called in for independent examinations, continue to maintain that the patients are not significantly enough improved for release.

"Farview has become a place of no return. A place for forgotten individuals. For them it's like being put in a tomb."

The members of the review committee were silent. Dr. McIntosh hardly knew how to continue the meeting. He said, limply, "I think you're right. Something's got to be done about it immediately. Let's hear from you guys who surveyed the recreation and occupational therapy facilities."

A tall, earnest-looking man with a tanned, smooth face and unruly hair, cleared his throat and neatly squared the few pages of notes on the table in front of him.

"I would prefer to just read what we plan to say in our written report, if that's all right," he said, turning his head to the head of the table.

"That'll be fine," Dr. McIntosh said. "If it looks like it's running too long, I may ask you to summarize some of it."

"The problem at Farview is that the activities program appears to be for only a very few clients and what is done is done for the wrong reasons. Time and again we saw a small, well-equipped work area where a few favored inmates worked with a good staff member. By 'favored,' I mean that those allowed in the program are spared the pervasive drudgery and boredom of spending their days on the wards.

"The central damning criticism of the system, as we saw it, is this: What about the other eighty-five per cent of the patient population, who also need meaningful activities, the joy of work, and the human relationships often formed in such settings?

"In the therapeutic recreation area, little activity can be observed at the beginning of the afternoon session. The recreation staff gives the appearance of being poorly prepared for the arrival of the patients. As a result, activities are not prompt in starting and are slow to attract patients' interest. A three-lane bowling alley, a large, well-equipped gymnasium, and spacious outdoor recreation areas seem to be used on an irregular basis and are not always accessible to patients during scheduled recreation periods.

"In the occupational therapy areas, a small number of men are assigned to the workshops, without prior evaluation or testing for appropriate placement. This group remains almost stagnant, spending many hours each day repeating already familiar procedures in completing the same projects over and over. There are no clear lines of progression from these lower-level projects to more skilled vocational activity."

Again, Dr. McIntosh interrupted. "Did you see that guy in the ceramics shop? Making ashtrays? He must have had between fifty and a hundred of them, all just alike."

"Yeah," the activities specialist said. "I think the man running the department or one or two of the guards sell them for him on the outside. That's what he said."

"You know," Dr. McIntosh said, "I believe they don't use the gym because they don't want that floor to get scuffed. It shines like a lake. I don't believe it would be like that if men were playing on it regularly."

"We kind of say that in the report."

"And that library can't have five hundred books."

"It doesn't have many."

"I'm sorry I interrupted."

"No problem," the man said. He read the remainder of his report.

"I'll tell you what bothers me about what we have learned," Dr. McIntosh said near the end of the meeting. As he spoke, he ticked off his thoughts on his fingers.

"The only therapy for at least eighty-five per cent of these men is drugs. They are using drugs here as the answer to every problem. And untrained guards are administering them. I can't believe they know what they are doing.

"The scary thing about the indiscriminate use of the drugs is the easy—at least it seems to be easy—availability of contraband alcohol. And patients have access to medicine cabinets. Looks to me like that's dangerous as hell, but they don't seem to even think about it. They don't seem to give a damn.

"It seems to me we heard a lot about brutality," he went on, ticking off a third finger, "and there were several complaints of thefts.

"Within the state system, this place has a reputation for harshness and minimal treatment. It seems like the guards run the place and that everything is done for their pleasure and convenience. They unquestionably give the message to the patients that they are less than human.

"But I think the fact that some men could be here for decades and never get therapy—I mean not *any* therapy—yet be confined as crazy and just used for labor—" he was breathing through clenched teeth now "—that's almost more frightening than the misuse of drugs and the inhumane treatment."

He stroked his beard, then removed his glasses from his wide nose and a handkerchief from a hip pocket as he made a final observation.

"They should shut down this damnable place. Just close it up and put these people somewhere else. Tear it down and turn the whole place into a farm. But they have got to close it. I'm going to say just that to the secretary and the governor too."

*

While Dr. McIntosh waited for his chance to convey his assessment to the governor personally, summer wore on. Hot. One of the hottest and stickiest in easy memory. The days were scorching and the nights were heavy and steamy and thick with discomfort.

The hospital was obsessed with the weather, and tempers frayed and flared more often as the days passed with no abatement of the heat. Guards reacted more quickly, more impetuously, to the contentiousness of the patients. And some of the patients thought that pure meanness had totally replaced rational thought among some of the men in uniform. Garth and Hawk got into an argument one afternoon when the charge guard ordered Garth to put his shirt back on. The patient didn't call Hawk the names that were camped on his tongue, but there was no mistaking the venom in his eyes. The look did not escape Hawk's attention and he knew what it conveyed.

"Don't even think about doing anything, you jar-headed bastard," Hawk said. "You give me the slightest reason to, and I'll kick your fucking face around to your ear."

It wasn't long until he had his reason—or what sufficed for one.

It came on another in the series of torrid days. On the off chance that even a vague breeze might be felt outside, yard-out was offered. Not offered, actually. Nothing was offered at Farview, except possibly a chapel service. Yard-out was commanded. It was ordered for all but the bedridden, the punished, and those who were always selected to spend the time in a workshop. No matter what the review committee said, the guards still insisted that inside and outside recreation be conducted at the same time. Why allow a patient to participate in both?

So on that burning afternoon in July it was decided that everyone would go to yard-out. Movement of any kind was labored in the heat, and the patients lined up slowly for the route-step march outside.

20

WADE WAS the last man in the line from D-Ward. He had dropped
one of the largest of the kitchen vats on his foot the day before
and it still hurt badly enough to cause a limp. He was walking
slowly, falling behind the man in front of him.

"Move it faster, Wade."

Garth did not have to turn around to know it was Hawk growl-
ing behind him. He didn't turn around. He didn't say anything
and he didn't move any faster.

A few seconds later, Hawk pushed him in the middle of the
back. "I said move it, goddammit."

"Don't push me." Garth was angry at the shove, which had
made him take three or four limping skips. "I'm going as fast as I
can."

"It ain't fast enough," Hawk said. He had decided to make an
issue of this. He had been on simmer waiting for a confrontation
with the bulky Pennsylvania Dutchman, who never offered more

192

than a surly look when Hawk approached, and who seemed to think he was better than the other patients.

Garth had not asked to see the doctor after his first six or eight weeks in the hospital, although Hawk had seen him wince and rub his eyes and temple. He had never offered a favor in exchange for a chance to get medicine. Even since he went to work in the kitchen, he had never brought a sandwich or anything else back to the ward for bribe or barter. He had not gone out of his way to make a friend or a dollar. He had geared his needs to what was available to him. It was almost as if he had decided he knew how to do hard time and that he would simply bow his neck and do it. But he would not stoop or beg or even ask.

Hawk thought Garth had gotten harder after Night Train made his stand against Bulldog. And he thought he had detected a green, glacial chill in the man's eyes since Night Train and Malone took the floor. And since the incident involving the shirt, Hawk thought he should keep close watch on Garth, stay on top of him all the time. He didn't want to find himself on the defensive as Bulldog had with Night Train, or like that fool Parton had with Chamberlin.

Hawk could see light from outside glaring in the doorway to the yard. He saw two or three guards standing inside the door. He kicked at the back of Garth's legs.

"What the hell are you doing?" Garth whirled around to face the guard and could hardly see the dark eyes under the thick thatch of brows.

"I said move faster," the guard said. He pushed Garth along the hall and the patient turned around, still limping and almost losing his balance.

Hawk kicked the back of his legs again and after three or four steps, he kicked once more. He was braver now. The guards at the door were within easy range.

He kicked again and got his leg between Garth's, causing the patient to trip and fall. Hawk almost fell over him.

"Goddammit, Hawk!" Garth yelped, shoving the guard aside with the leg that was in the air. And realizing too late that his tongue—or his brain—had miscued.

"Don't kick me, you sonofabitch," Hawk shouted, looking at the same time to the other guards for assistance. He needn't have looked. They had heard Garth, and had seen the two men almost fall in a pile, and the patient kicking out. They were upon them in a matter of seconds. "And don't call me 'Hawk'!"

Hawk was now on his feet and Garth was rocking to his when the first boot struck his thigh and sent him sprawling—but not away from the barrage. His mind raced back to his first day at the hospital and the beating he received in the shower. This time he wasn't wet or naked. Nothing else seemed to be different.

When he raised his arms to protect his face, the feet found his ribs and stomach and legs. When he tried to cover his torso, open hands smacked his face, three or four at a time, like firecrackers popping on a string. He decided to roll into a tight ball and let them kick until they finished. Resistance only strung things out, he thought. He was right.

In a few moments, five men in blue shirts stood above him panting like hounds in August.

"Let's just take his ass onto J right now," Hawk said. "We can do the transferring later. Three of us can do it." He looked at the others and said. "You two go on outside."

With his arm hammerlocked behind his back, Garth was half-pulled, half-pushed to J-Ward.

"What's his problem?" asked the guard who received them on J-Ward.

"He's an uncooperative motherfucker," Hawk said. "He don't like being told what to do. Put down 'fighting.' Transferred from D-Ward to J-Ward for fighting."

"That's a goddamn lie." Garth squeezed the words out between clenched teeth. "I didn't hit nobody." He cringed as the hammer-lock yanked his hand to the hairs on his neck, which was now crimson and tingling with anger.

"Lemme get some cuffs," the J-Ward guard said. "You fellas get his clothes off."

Cuffed and stripped, Garth was pushed into a cell that had nothing except walls, floor, ceiling, door, and tiny window. His body ached from his foot to his head. He went to the floor heavily and lay on his side.

The next couple of weeks were the worst he could remember. He said something to a guard about dropping his bowl of food on the floor and the guard kicked him in the side of the face.

He was not allowed to go to the bathroom for a week and not

allowed a shower or shave. His cell began to smell like an out-house, and flies came in through the tiny window and crawled on his raw face.

His cell was hosed and for some reason, probably sadism, he was given clothes to wear in the sweltering cubicle and allowed to struggle into them before the floor was soaked. He was soaked along with it.

His hatred was building to bonfire intensity and he sensed a Night Train–like showdown coming for him. He felt there was no hope for him in the hospital, but he did not want to die in a cage.

One afternoon in August he asked a guard if he could write a letter to his sister. The guard said it would be all right and brought him a stubby pencil without an eraser and a single small sheet of paper.

Garth took the pencil in his dirty, cracked fingers and scrawled crookedly across the page:

Dere Sis

Plese come to visit me as soon as possibal. Bring some fresh peaches for me. They shuld be in season now. Come soon.

Love Garth

The guard brought an envelope and Garth addressed it. He gave both pieces of paper to the guard, who read the letter and stuffed it inside the envelope.

"You know you ain't gonna get none of them peaches," he said to Garth.

"Maybe it'll give my sister a good reason to come," Garth replied.

"Shit," the guard spat, "come all the way up here to bring you some peaches? You are crazy, ain't you?"

Garth went through another fierce couple of weeks after he sent the letter. He said something smart to a young guard who had dropped his bowl into his lap, spilling the food onto his clothes. Then the guard slapped him across the mouth. Garth kicked out and the guard kicked him in the face, laying the shoelaces diagonally across his lips, the top one of which split unevenly when it was mashed into the yellow teeth which gave way beneath it. Blood dripped from his chin and mixed with the food in his lap.

At night his eyelids stuck together while he dozed fitfully. In the daytime his stomach rebelled at the sight of what was presented in the small metal bowl, all mixed together the way his thoughts were scrambled in his hard head. He wondered if his sister had received his letter—wondered, in fact, if it had actually been mailed, and twice asked the guard who had been entrusted with it.

The guard had mailed the letter, and when Irene read it her brow knitted with concern and her lips began to tremble. When her husband came home she greeted him with bad news stamped across her face.

"Garth's in trouble," she said.

"Who said so?" her husband asked.

"He did," she said. "In this letter." She handed it to her husband, who looked at it, then up at her.

"What makes you think he's in trouble?"

"He wants me to bring him some peaches. Fresh peaches."

"So?"

"He's allergic to peaches. Especially fresh peaches. They give him a bad rash. Must be something about the peach fuzz that makes him break out in a rash. He hates peaches. He hates to be around them. Why else would he ask me to bring him fresh peaches if he wasn't trying to tell me something, give me a signal?"

She looked at the letter again. "We've got to go see him tomorrow."

The next day Irene and her husband and her two children and her sister Ruby made the trip to Farview. What should have been a five-hour drive turned into more than six when one tire went flat and the jack refused to cooperate. They did not have much money. Irene's husband had about as much luck at farming as Irene's father had enjoyed, and the car was a source of apprehension all the way to the hospital.

They arrived sometime in the early afternoon and the five of them, dirty and sweaty from the long, hot, wind-singed drive, walked through the front door of the Administration building, up the few steps to a hallway that crossed in front of them, and on through to where a guard stood at the first of the steel-barred gates in the main corridor.

Irene's heart was climbing to her throat as she got her first glimpse of the hospital.

"This don't look much like a hospital," she said to Ruby, who nodded agreement.

"What can I do for you?" asked the guard at the gate. He didn't appear to care if his question was answered, nor inclined to act on the answer should one be forthcoming.

"We're here to see her brother," Irene's husband said, looking to Irene to complete the information.

"Garth Wade," she said. "He's from Lancaster," she added, as if that would help identify him.

The guard walked from the gate into the security office and stayed there for several minutes while the visitors stood self-consciously shifting from one foot to another in the hallway.

When he came out of the office, he stood with his hands on his hips and his belly protruding defiantly in front.

"Wade can't have visitors today," he said.

"What do you mean?" Irene asked, her eyes attacking the credibility of the guard's statement.

"Just what I said, lady. The doctors say they don't think your brother is up to having visitors today."

"But we drove six hours to get up here from Lancaster and my husband took off from work, just so we could see my brother," Irene said, pleading with her eyes.

"I can't help that. Looks like you wasted a trip. Maybe next time you should call and see how he's doing before you come all this way."

"Are you telling me I've come all this way for nothing and that I should go all the way back home without seeing my brother?" Irene was fighting back the tears that were building behind her eyelids and threatening to spill over.

"I'm saying the doctors say he can't have no visitors," the guard said. "It's not my fault you drove all this way for nothing."

"But he asked me to come. He wanted us to visit. He said so in a letter he just wrote not long ago, maybe two weeks. I brought him some peaches."

"We can take the peaches and see he gets 'em," the guard said.

"No, you won't," said Irene's husband, stepping nearer the guard. "Where's the doctor that said we couldn't visit Garth?"

"He's back on the wards."

"We'd like to talk to him," Ruby said.

"I'm sorry, lady, I'm just telling you what they told me."

"Well, we want to see the doctor," Irene chimed in. "I want to talk to the person that made the decision."

"You can't do that."

"We're not leaving here 'til we do," Irene said. She was crying now and her voice was rising to the corresponding pitch. "What kind of hospital is it that won't allow you to visit your brother?"

"We're going to see her brother today if we have to go get a lawyer," Irene's husband said. "This place is run by the state and we pay taxes. This afternoon's visiting hours and we come to visit her brother if we got to go court to do it. We ain't got enough money to drive back and forth up here from Lancaster every day."

"Mister, if you want to get a lawyer, get a lawyer," the guard said. "I don't give a damn who you get, you ain't getting past these bars without I let you, and I ain't letting you until I get orders to do it."

"Where's a phone?" the husband asked.

"There's one in the superintendent's office."

"Where's that?"

"Around the corner and to the right."

Irene and her husband went to the office and asked the secretary for permission to use the telephone. When the secretary asked them who they wished to call, Irene's husband told her, "I'm calling the governor's office in Harrisburg. I'll charge it to my telephone at home."

"Why do you want to call the governor?" she asked.

"They won't let us see her brother," he said. "We come all the way from Lancaster and they say we can't see him. I think they're hiding something. Maybe somebody in Harrisburg can help us. I know some people," he lied.

She asked them to wait in the hall and she called for a doctor. A few minutes later, Dr. Zundel appeared.

"What's the problem?" he said without formality or concern.

The secretary deferred to Irene, who was squeezing a soiled white handkerchief into a wrinkled ball.

"I want to see my brother," Irene said. "I've come a long way and I aim to see him. I don't know why you won't let me see my brother." Again her voice was rising and her eyes were brimming. She was on the verge of breaking into sobbing spasms.

"Well, he's had a rough week," Dr. Zundel said, "and he's a little under the weather. Nothing serious, but I would advise against disturbing him today. Maybe some other time."

"No!" Irene stormed. "Today! Right now!"

"Okay, okay. Calm down," Dr. Zundel said, lifting his arms in mock surrender. "I don't give a damn. Go see him."

The guard at the barred gate allowed them to enter and then clanged the gate behind them. The sound sent a shudder through Irene. There was a hopelessness and a helplessness about it. It was repeated at the next gate. They were escorted to the visiting room to wait for Garth.

He came in behind one guard and in front of the one who had kicked him in the mouth earlier in the week.

Irene sprang to her feet. Her hands flew to her mouth, agape in a mixture of grief, horror, and disbelief. A weak, wailing scream came from deep within her.

"Oh . . . my . . . God . . . Garth, what have they done to you?" She stood trembling as he shuffled toward her. The others gasped. Her daughter covered her eyes and wept. Her husband turned his reddening eyes away for a moment.

Garth limped to a chair and slumped heavily into it. He looked at them.

The flesh around his muddy green eyes was swollen and the color of a pre-storm sunset. His nose was black and purple. His ears were hidden by the long, stringy, dirty, matted hair.

His lips were split and raw and protruding as though they had been stung by bees. His gums were torn and flesh hung where teeth had been.

His hands and fingers were cracked and bruised and discolored and swollen as though they had been stomped on. One thumb was double its normal size.

His clothes were soiled and torn and hung wet on him. He had lost weight since they had last seen him. He was down to about 150 or 160, so that his trousers were overlapped about five inches at the waist.

He was unshaven and dirty. He smelled like a mule's stall.

His sister could not believe what she saw before her. Her brother had always been a man who kept himself clean. He had so much pride. Now he was a shambles, a torn, battered, stinking shell of what had been. She pulled from him an account of his troubles with the guards.

He pointed to the young guard who had stayed in the visiting room to watch him.

"That's one of the sonofabitches," he grunted in a low voice. The guard was munching potato chips. Garth was unable to suck soda through a straw from the can his brother-in-law had bought at the canteen.

"Are they doing anything for you medically, Garth?" Irene asked, each word seeming to shake as it left her tear-streaked face.

"Are you kidding?" he snarled. "I'm back there in a dungeon. All I get is a little macaroni in a cup that they push through a slot in the door."

He had changed his words to the family's Germanic dialect so that the young guard could not understand.

"They don't give medicine when we get sick," he said. "They just think everybody here is crazy. And that's why they don't worry so much about what we write out in letters. But you should always watch out how you answer my letters." He was beginning to put random thoughts together, unrelated though they were. It was as if he had much to say and little time.

"And if they get mad at somebody they will kill people in here," he said, his face intense, his eyes searching their eyes for comprehension. "They want to kill me.

"I will never get out of here alive," he said. "I know that." Then he locked eyes with Irene and continued in dialect.

"Promise me one thing, Sis. If you hear that I died suddenly in here, make them do another autopsy. Get an independent autopsy. They will say I died of a heart attack or pneumonia or something normal. That's what they always say. Promise me, Sis."

"I promise," she said, "but you should just do what they say and get better and maybe you can come home. Don't fight them. That don't do you no good, Garth."

"I'll try," he said. "I'll try."

At that point the visit was terminated by the young guard. It had not been a long visit, something less than an hour. A six-hour drive for a fifty-minute visit. Garth looked at Irene one last time.

"Remember your promise," he said. Then he stared past her and through a window to the outside green hills and added softly, "God, how I wished I'd never touched that mop."

21

Yancey was enjoying the summer more than any in several years, certainly more than any previous one at Farview. He felt that things had been going his way for a long time, even if he could not go to staff and get out. And now he knew he was in good shape. He wasn't even afraid that another patient could ruin his deal by screwing him up with Pagnotti or somebody.

He was tight with Dr. Dallmeyer. Really tight. Tight enough to be the superintendent's houseboy. He might as well have been a free man. He had to come back to the bungalow at night, but other than that, he was almost on his own.

He had gotten the one big break that he needed and he seized it.

It had happened when a patient on X-Ward, who was almost as trusted as Yancey, made a serious mistake. The patient, who had some friends among the guards and supposedly was close to the chaplain, was allowed to go to staff. He thought he was on his way out.

But one of the doctors really went after him and made him angry with a lot of questions about his sex life and attitudes. The patient, who had some ability with electronics and some freedom in a workshop and in his semiprivate room, decided to plant a bug in the staffing room and record what went on so he could blackmail his way out of the hospital.

The man had put together a recorder and a wireless microphone bug that would transmit to a distance of two hundred feet. He got two identical ashtrays from the ceramics shop and got Elroy Jones to put one of them in the staffing room while he was sweeping in Center.

A couple of weeks later, when he thought the doctors and guards would be accustomed to the ashtray and pay it no attention, he brought the duplicate ashtray to Yancey and asked him to exchange it for the one on the conference table. Yancey, always suspicious and ever conscious of how something could work to his advantage, questioned the maneuver and closely inspected the new piece of ceramic. He found the bug, but he did as the patient asked anyway.

Then he went personally to see Dr. Dallmeyer and reported what he knew. Not quite all he knew. He didn't tell the superintendent who was responsible for the transmitter. He said that he saw a man leaving the staffing room with a ceramic ashtray in his hand, but that the man's back had been turned to him and he could not tell who it was.

He said that he had heard earlier that somebody was planning to bug the staff meeting and that when he saw the man leaving the room with the shiny ashtray in his hand he put things together and checked the one on the table.

It was a clumsy story, Yancey knew, but the superintendent didn't seem to notice. Yancey was one of a handful of patients who had such easy access to Dr. Dallmeyer that he could walk up to him inside the administrative section of the hospital or outside the building. And he knew how much the doctor would appreciate having such information. Yancey thought it could be converted into valuable currency. He was right.

Dr. Dallmeyer was delighted to receive Yancey's report, possibly because it was one occasion when he knew of something going on at the hospital before Pagnotti knew. He was equally pleased that the device had not been in place long enough to transmit anything.

Yancey was rewarded with the job of houseboy at the fourteen-room, tudor-style home which the state provided on the hospital grounds for the superintendent. And he was doubly rewarded by being asked to do some carpentry work on a house in Carbondale, where the superintendent planned to live when he retired. The job involved remodeling part of the house into a recreation room.

The doctor said he would pay him $750 for the job, which would probably take about a year, working the kind of hours he would have to work. He told Yancey he thought it would be good therapy for him to work on the outside.

Yancey agreed.

And it had been good therapy, of a sort. Yancey rode into Carbondale in the mornings to work on the house. He was free to walk wherever he liked in town. He bought some materials for his work and other materials seemed to simply appear. He didn't know where they came from. It looked like four or five thousand dollars' worth to Yancey.

He bought whiskey whenever he could, which was often, and brought it back to the bungalow, where he would cut it with water, about half and half, maybe a little less than half whiskey, and sell it inside the main hospital. He finally started making regular whiskey runs and would sell the whiskey for twice what he paid for it and let the buyer cut it.

He smuggled letters out of the hospital and a variety of items in. Often he was doing it for guards who didn't want to get caught doing favors for patients themselves, or didn't want to go to the trouble of having to buy things in town on which they could make a profit at the hospital. Yancey would buy the item and deliver it to the guard at the hospital, for a small profit, then the guard would sell it to a patient for more profit.

Even life in the bungalow seemed to be looser. Maybe it was because everybody knew he was Dr. Dallmeyer's favorite and they were afraid to cross him, but Yancey didn't think that was the reason. It just seemed to him that the corruption and stealing and contraband and sex were just more open and the bungalow was where a lot of it originated. Some of the guards acted like there was no chance of their getting caught doing anything and that nothing would happen to them if they did.

He wasn't in the dormitory much during the day, but a couple of times he walked in on a guard corn-holing a young man with sand-colored hair and a face like a girl, while another patient watched the action, waiting either to give or to receive. It seemed to be common knowledge that you couldn't get in a hospital truck with a couple of the staff members and ride a mile before they were reaching across the seat to grab your crotch while they drove.

All the while, Yancey was making money and the more money he made, the more freedom he seemed to gain. It culminated in a Labor Day trip to Philadelphia. Shipler, the social worker, had to attend a conference there the week after the holiday, and he decided he would go early if Yancey would go with him.

Yancey knew that Shipler was straight and figured it would be fun to spend a weekend anywhere other than Farview. Shipler arranged permission for Yancey to be placed in his custody and they drove to Philadelphia. Yancey wondered why he had been so favored.

During the trip, Shipler rambled on about people on the hospital staff and verified many of Yancey's speculations.

For one thing, everybody was afraid of crossing the guards, because everybody was afraid of the patients. The guards, through their leadership, let it be known that anybody who didn't go along with what pleased them might someday find themselves in a dangerous situation with a patient or with more than one patient, and when they looked around for help, the guards might not be looking back.

For another, Farview had compiled a history of doctors who had come and gone through the years. Some were old and incontinent with their urine. One of them was at the hospital now. Some had histories of mental problems. One of these was currently at the hospital too. Some had been drunks; some were too old to practice privately and had come there to be semi-retired on state salary. It seemed that the hospital still had some of these too.

Most of them, Shipler said, had thought the job was bullshit and had done a bullshit job.

Several foreign doctors, especially some Cubans in the wake of

Castro's takeover, had been at the hospital for short stints and then had disappeared to places unknown. There was a Cuban there now, too.

Shipler figured it was pretty much the same kind of record as most mental hospitals he knew anything about. Most of them took whatever doctors they could get, and as removed as Farview is, it didn't get much.

Many of the doctors had been afraid to walk into the ward dayrooms and counted on the guards to protect them. Those doctors were not psychiatrists, knew little if anything about psychiatry, and were totally unequipped to deal with mental patients who were more inmates than patients and more criminal than mentally ill. Those doctors did what the guards suggested.

The nurses were worse. The guards had convinced most of them that rape was as far away as the thickness of their underwear. When they came onto the wards the guards would form a kind of phalanx around them and escort them across the room. The guards did the same for doctors and visitors and social workers too, Shipler confessed. Without saying anything, by their actions the guards cemented fear in the minds of others.

Shipler gossiped about the only attractive nurse having an affair with one of the married doctors who drank a bit. He said everybody in the hospital knew about it, but he didn't know anybody who had actually seen them exchanging intimacies.

He said she was the same one who had ruined one of the few attempts at group therapy by coming to the meetings without panties and sitting spraddle-legged across from the handful of patients. He said most of the patients spent the hour jacking off inside their pants. He thought that maybe she was in need of counseling.

By the time they got to the Marriott Motor Inn on City Line Avenue in Philadelphia, Yancey had heard of one honest guard who had been transferred to outside security—in fact had asked to go outside—because of all the brutality inside; of social workers who had been threatened by guards unless they changed their story about seeing a patient beaten; of the man who came in from the outside to buy the Social Security and veterans' checks at a discount in exchange for cash; of hospital funds being placed in the bank where the superintendent was on the board of directors;

of salesmen who came to the hospital bearing cases of whiskey along with their legitimate products and found takers for both.

"Why do you stay?" Yancey asked.

"I'm from the area," Shipler said. "It's home. My wife's family's there, too."

That night and the next, Shipler brought a prostitute to Yancey's room. It cost the candy-wagon man fifty dollars for each woman.

Shipler took second turn with each one. Yancey had to pay for that too.

Then he knew why he had been asked.

22

ONE NIGHT not long after Labor Day, near the end of September, Jones was awakened by noises from beds near his in the D-Ward dormitory. It was near midnight, according to the new watch he had acquired from Coda with money he had accumulated from running numbers to the horse room from the patients on the ward.

After years of relative isolation, it took little to awaken him. He lifted his head from his pillow, and then his torso, propping himself up on his elbows. He looked toward the two beds from which sounds of discomfort and protest had been coming for the past few days.

He heard gutteral moanings and muted ragings from Night Train's bed, and tossing and thrashing and nightmarish cries from the bed beside it. The white man recently returned from J-Ward was debating with devils. The black man's gut had been hell's boiler room since he limped from the peanut. The thermostat upstairs had broken down.

Night Train had not recovered from taking the floor with Malone and the ensuing days of neglect in the peanut. He had been able to walk out of the tiny room, but in obvious pain, his face caked with dried blood, his eyes swollen almost shut.

He walked slightly bent, as though his back hurt or something inside was out of place. The irate Boots probably was responsible for that pain. Malone could be blamed for the rose color in his urine.

Jones watched Night Train lift his sheet and struggle upright. Then he saw him get to his feet and walk slowly to the toilet. A few minutes later a guard went to the door and looked in.

"You been in here long enough," the guard said.

Jones could not see Night Train look at the guard, then turn away without response. He was leaning over a commode.

"Get back to bed, boy," the guard said, the edge of aggression in his voice.

"Don't call me 'boy.' "

"I'll call you what I fucking please. Get out!" He was shouting.

"I ain't ready."

"Out, nigger." The guard took a step into the bathroom. Two other blue shirts moved quickly to the dooway.

"I ain't done."

"I don't give a damn. Move!"

"No."

The guard grabbed the nightshirt behind Night Train's neck and jerked him backward. At the same time, he planted the heel of his other hand in the small of the patient's back and roughly twisted him toward the door.

"I ain't here to play with you, jig. I say move, that's what I mean." He grunted out the last word as he shoved Night Train toward the two guards at the door. One of them aimed a low fist that struck the black man's stomach like a car bumper.

Night Train went to his knees. But he wasn't there long. The other swung a foot toward his head, missed, and caught the falling man in the chest and shoulder, lifting him over and onto his back, where he lay. The punch to the solar plexus deprived his memory of the next several minutes. He never felt the boot.

Two of the guards took him by the arms and dragged him from

the bathroom and across the dormitory to the door leading downstairs. He was in his nightshirt when Jones saw him him being dragged away. He was without it when he regained consciousness in the infirmary.

When he opened his eyes he was lying naked in a bed, spread-eagled, with leather cuffs binding his feet to one end of the bed and his hands above his head to the other end. The bed was only a few steps from the nursing office where Sullins and Dog Boy and the other ward workers sat around waiting for Costello or one of the other nurses or doctors or guards to give them a chore.

Sullins tried to feed him with a spoon the first day, a circumstance which fueled Night Train's anger.

"Why can't I eat like everybody else?" he asked.

"Some other guys are eating like this," Sullins said. "It'll just be for a day or two. Don't let it bother you."

"It does bother me. I can eat like a man. I don't want to be fed like a damn baby."

"Doctor's orders."

"Fuck the doctor. Where is he?"

"He's busy."

Costello heard the argument and walked over to the bed.

"What's the matter?" he asked with the compassion of a hyena moving from bed to bed in search of carrion.

"He don't want to be fed," Sullins said.

"Fuck him. Don't feed him."

"But, Doctor—"

"You feed him or he don't eat." He looked at Night Train. "Them cuffs ain't coming off. You want to eat, he feeds you. You don't want to be fed? Tough shit. Starve."

Night Train didn't eat that day. Or the next.

Sullins tried to persuade him.

"All you're doing is hurting yourself," he said. "They know you're pissed off and they figure if they take the leathers off, you'll knock the shit out of somebody."

"Bullshit," Night Train snapped bitterly.

"You've made a thing about not being fed, and they're gonna make you stay cuffed until you give in and let yourself be fed. That's the fact. They're gonna make you give in."

"I ain't giving in to those muthuh fuckuhs ever again." Night

Train's eyes were red-rimmed, with rivers of red running through yellowing sclera to the center that was black as hate.

About three o'clock that morning, Night Train began to thrash in his sleep. He heaved his body off the mattress and fell heavily back onto it. He bucked and tried to pull his arms and legs free.

He awakened and cursed the light that shone from the nursing office into his eyes.

He cursed his hunger.

He cursed the guards.

He cursed God.

One of the guards on duty came to his bed and told him to be quiet.

"I got things to say," Night Train roared.

"Nobody wants to hear it," the guard said.

"Listen to me-e-e-e!" Night Train wailed.

The guard had listened to too much already, from Night Train and others.

The guard grabbed the pillow from under the sable head and yanked it free. Then he put it over Night Train's face and pressed the ends to the mattress.

The scream was muffled.

The patient bucked and thrashed violently off the mattress and the guard had difficulty holding the pillow in place. Night Train twisted his head from side to side to catch an elusive breath. The guard shifted his weight to tighten the pillow over the panic-stricken head struggling for air.

Night Train lurched toward the head of the bed and found sufficient play in the leather restraints for his head to pop free of the smothering pillow for a gasp of air before the guard covered it again. Night Train slid down the bed and lurched again toward the head for breath, all the time twisting his face from side to side under the pillow to suck the tiniest pockets of air.

The guard decided he could not suffocate the stronger black patient and tossed the pillow to the floor as two other guards joined him.

"Dog Boy!" the first guard called, trying to be heard over Night Train, who was screaming obscenities and threats and pleas for help.

The three guards stood around the bed and took turns slapping and punching the trapped patient, who was twisting and squirming to avoid the blows. The one who had tried to smother Night Train finally landed a couple of stiff punches to the patient's ribs, but still Night Train fought. But now he begged. Now his screams were cries for mercy. And for his momma.

"Go get Dog Boy over here," the first guard directed one of his colleagues. The man produced the perverted ward worker at Night Train's bedside.

"Shut him the fuck up," the guard said to Dog Boy.

Dog Boy slapped Night Train repeatedly about the face and head.

"Not like that," the guard said. Then he took a handful of Night Train's wiry hair and pulled his head back with one hand, and with the other delivered a karate chop to Night Train's throat. "Like that."

Night Train could no longer scream. As he gasped for life, the three guards encouraged Dog Boy.

He took Night Train's head back and chopped twice into the throat. The neck snapped.

He wheezed and gasped for fifteen more minutes, then there was nothing to hear.

Nobody was listening anyway.

When Sullins came into the infirmary the next morning, Night Train's nude, contorted body lay lifeless and uncovered on the bed just as he had died. His feet were cuffed to one end of the bed and his hands to the other. His pillow was on the floor.

His eyes were open, staring sightlessly off at a strange angle.

The guards who quieted him had left when their shift ended and gone home to their families as they did every morning after work.

During their shift they had not called a doctor to examine the black man who had died, although more than one doctor lived within five minutes of his bed. No medical personnel were on duty at the hospital. No medical treatment was administered.

Dr. Zundel came on the ward sometime during the morning and wrote on the Physician's Record of Patient's Progress for date 9/24: "He received last hypo of sparine @ 12:30 A.M. Speech rambling, incoherent, patient was not involved in any altercation, collapsed and was pronounced dead @ 3:45 A.M. 9/24."

Below that entry, he scrawled: "Cause of death—Acute coronary occlusion with myocardial infarction."

Below that he noted that Night Train's mother had been notified, and then he felt compelled to add: "(She last visited June 12.)"

The county coroner was notified of the death about 11 P.M., some nineteen hours after it had happened, and not the most convenient time for a semi-retired physician, whose public office was part-time, to spend three hours at a hospital for the criminally insane. The hospital official said the man had a history of heart problems, so a heart attack didn't seem unusual.

No autopsy was performed. The hospital turned the body over to a guard who, conveniently enough, also operated a funeral home near the hospital. He embalmed the body and shipped it by REA Express to Night Train's mother in Philadelphia. Collect.

The State of Pennsylvania sent his mother a bill for $860 to cover what it said were some of the costs of his "care and treatment" while he was at Farview.

She paid.

*

Malone heard about Night Train's death probably before the county coroner heard. He heard it the same way people in institutions learn anything. The grapevine. There were different versions of the way it happened.

A ward worker on S-Ward, the surgical unit where no surgeon worked, told Yancey that he saw Dog Boy smother Night Train with a pillow. He said Dog Boy crawled on top of Night Train to hold the pillow against the black man's face, and that Costello stood beside the bed and watched.

Yancey didn't care whether the man was telling the truth or not. He and the ward worker did business. The ward worker had ready access to the infirmary medicine chests and he pilfered pills for sale to Yancey. The latter made a handsome middle-man's profit when he was running the candy wagon. And Yancey was the ward worker's source of booze. Or shaving lotion in a pinch.

Another version had Night Train kicking a tray of food off his bed and onto Costello while the male nurse was taking blood pressure readings on the patient in the adjoining bed. That version had the nurse hitting Night Train in the Adam's apple. About noon. Not true, but Yancey passed it along.

Malone heard those stories and another. Both Hawk and Bulldog told him that Night Train had died as a result of the beating he had administered when they took the floor. They said the doctors said Night Train had died from internal injuries. They asked him how it felt to kill a friend.

Bulldog told him that under the circumstances, he could not recommend him for staff.

"I can't say a lot good about a man that's killed somebody since he's been in here, can I?"

To the consternation of both Bulldog and Hawk, and others at the hospital, Malone was to meet staff anyway. The work his parents and their minister had done with a couple of politicians was paying off. A judge was ordering him to prison, where he would serve the balance of his time.

Malone did not know all had been arranged when he went to staff. He had not heard from his parents or from the court or from an attorney. The hospital always took care of what a patient did and didn't see or hear from outside.

At staff, he was asked very little. He was told quite a lot. Hawk told him how much he had always liked him, even though he had been a little tough on occasion. A doctor explained how stern discipline was necessary ingredient in a reorganized, reordered mind, and that things always were done at the hospital with his and other patients' best interest at heart.

Then he was told what a good record he had at the hospital, and that it was sad that the recent death of a fellow patient had marred and threatened it. They said they were prepared not to mention it to the court or to the prison to which he was being transferred. "Unless, of course, you should start spreading ugly rumors about Farview," said someone who burped in mid-sentence. He didn't see who said it. "I would suggest that you forget everything about Farview. Put it out of your mind. It would be better for you not to think about your days here."

Malone knew that would not happen. He would not say anything while he was in prison. He didn't know whether he had been responsible for Night Train's death or not. He thought he must have contributed to it. He had hit the man a lot of times. As hard as he could hit anybody. But he hadn't thrown him in the peanut and he hadn't refused to give him medical attention. Maybe that's why he died.

Still, he didn't want a murder rap. If they decided to charge him with murder and say he killed Night Train while in a crazy rage, who was going to testify otherwise? Him? And a roomful of people the whole world had decided were maniacs and morons?

He could wait to talk about Farview. He was sure there were other men in prison who had been in Farview for a while. Not many, but he had heard of some who had been transferred out to prison. He could learn from them.

But first he had to get himself educated and in decent shape for other people. When he decided to talk about Farview, he had to be believed. He had to be respectable. He had to show them that he was not a fool or a pervert or a dangerous criminal. He would need to be a man with a job. A man who was dependable. A man with some sense.

That would take time. He could not read or write. He could not add or subtract. Multiply or divide.

Who would believe an illiterate black ex-con former patient in a hospital for the criminally insane?

23

Dr. McIntosh would believe. He hadn't met Malone, but after he had prepared his report on Farview, he was ready to believe almost anything he heard about the place. And he was ready to present his case to the secretary of welfare and the governor to close the hospital.

His conversations with the secretary led him to believe he had a sympathetic listener in her.

But the governor would not meet with him.

The governor had campaigned as, and was elected as, a liberal Democrat. That meant that although he was a millionaire who lived in the posh suburbs, when he was in South Philly he loved Italians; when he was in North Philly he loved blacks; when he was in Pittsburgh he loved the Poles. He loved the poor and the heavy-laden. He said he wanted to make progressive changes in the state's penal system and mental health facilities and hospitals and schools.

He was an upgrader and a do-gooder. And a politician who wanted to be governor for another term. Dr. McIntosh hoped he would be, too. He believed in him.

The governor turned problems of other do-gooders like Dr. McIntosh and state institutions like Farview, with its five hundred state employees, over to his lieutenant governor.

Dr. McIntosh prepared for the meeting with the lieutenant governor by going back to Farview. He didn't want to see the hospital again. He wanted to see a patient he had met two or three times during the review committee work.

"How would you like to get out of here?" he asked the man. They were seated across from each other in the room in Center where patients met staff.

Yancey looked at the bearded doctor for a long minute.

"Are you on the level?" he asked.

"If you are," the doctor said.

"What do you mean?"

"I think I can get you out of here if you will go along with a deal I propose."

"What kind of deal?"

"A plan I have."

"What do I have to do?"

"Talk to the lieutenant governor."

"About what?"

"This hospital. Tell him everything you know about it."

"What happens to me?"

"I will get you transferred to another hospital. You haven't had a trial, have you?"

"No."

"Then to another hospital. A decent hospital. Probably just for a short period."

"Then what?"

"Discharge." He waited several seconds for Yancey to react.

Suspicion had built a dwelling in the canyons of Yancey's brain.

"Well, what do you say? How's that sound?" Dr. McIntosh wanted more enthusiasm. He thought the patient, any patient, would have seen it as the answer to a thousand prayers. More, if he had been in Farview more than a thousand days.

"Get me transferred first," Yancey said. "Anybody know why

you're here now? Why you're talking to me?" His voice had begun to quaver a little.

"No, I don't think so. I don't see how they could. I didn't tell anybody why."

"They have ways." He didn't know whether the man across the table had the street sense to know how mean Farview could be, what happened when they started asking questions you didn't want to answer. It didn't take much to get them started, Yancey knew.

"Look," he said, "get me transferred first and I'll do it, but I ain't about to talk to anybody about this place and then come back here and wait to be transferred. No fucking way. And get it done fast or forget it. I don't want them to start hearing things from someplace else and start asking me questions. I got it pretty good, now, and I don't want to get fucked up even a little bit."

He was pointing his finger at the doctor when he finished. He didn't want the man to get the idea that he could come in and start playing games and walk away.

Dr. McIntosh was serious and he worked fast. A couple of calls to Harrisburg worked the necessary magic and he drove Yancey away from Farview in his car a couple of days later. The patient didn't have time to tell many people goodbye. He thought it was just as well. He wouldn't have known how to explain how he got out. And he didn't want to show too much happiness around them.

He was thrilled to be leaving, but in a way the maneuver angered him terribly. He wasn't getting out because he shouldn't have been in. He was getting out because somebody wanted to use him. Because somebody had clout. Politics. He had been in that cesspool for more than seven years and nothing he could do would get him out. Not even squealing on another patient. Then a man comes along and makes two phone calls and he's sprung. Yancey knew he was no more or less dangerous or criminally insane than he had been the day before or the week before or the year or two years before.

He knew there were a lot of men inside that place because they didn't know somebody who could make the right kind of phone calls. And they would die there.

✳

Yancey and Dr. McIntosh were two of five or six people already seated in the lieutenant governor's office waiting for him to arrive and start the meeting. The secretary of welfare was not there yet, either. The door opened and Yancey looked toward it expecting to see one or the other of the executives walk into the room.

He audibly gasped and some of the coffee in the cup he was holding spilled onto his thigh. The man in the doorway was a Farview guard. Yancey didn't know his name but he knew the face.

The man stood for a moment looking about the room. When his eyes slid to Yancey's there was a flicker of recognition and the faintest trace of a smile. More like a quick horizontal slit that immediately closed. He saw an empty chair and went to it.

Yancey wanted to get out of the room. He could not look at the guard but his eyes kept returning to the ruddy face, dented with acne scars and creased with lines between the thick, unruly brown eyebrows and the neatly combed hair.

Before anything could happen, the lieutenant governor came into his office, grinning broadly and reaching for hands to shake as he introduced himself to each person. Madame Secretary did the same right behind him.

Dr. McIntosh was the first of the guests to speak. He made some introductory remarks about the review committee's work the previous summer and explained that a couple of the people in the office had participated in that survey.

He recounted some of the specific findings of the review committee, then he began to press his case in earnest.

"There simply is no treatment going on there except bad treatment. They are using drugs as the answer to every problem. They are actively popping sparine into patients regardless of their physical or mental condition and sparine is a drug that most hospitals stopped using a decade ago because it can have dangerous side effects and because there are better drugs available.

"I suspect there is unauthorized use of medications by the guard staff, which is also dangerous for the patients being given the drugs. Somebody is going to get killed up there because of an ignorant overdose or a thoughtless combination of drugs administered by guards.

"The guards basically run the place," he said.

The secretary of welfare interrupted.

"Let's hear from one of them. We have a gentleman here who just resigned his position as a guard—I think they are called psychiatric security aides—at Farview. Mr. Burack, why did you quit your job there?"

Yancey started. Burack! That was the honest guard Shipler had mentioned during the trip to Philadelphia.

Burack didn't know whether to stand or remain sitting. Dr. McIntosh had stood but was now seated. The former guard was uncomfortable enough without appearing to make a speech. He remained in his chair. He cleared his throat and pulled his shirt collar away from his neck with the tip of a finger.

"There were people there that I just would not work with any more," he said. "I knew I would spend all night pulling them off the patients."

"Pulling them off the patients?" the lieutenant governor asked, confused. "What do you mean?"

"I mean there are some guards there who just like to kick and stomp patients. I've seen guards come to work and start out the shift picking on a patient, and then put him in the peanut for punishment."

"Why?" the lieutenant governor asked.

"For no reason, except that the guard could do it."

"They kick and stomp patients? You have seen that?"

"I have seen them kick and stomp patients. Yes, sir."

"How many of the guards are involved in this kind of practice?"

"You mean kicking and stomping?"

"Yes, that, but other kinds of physical abuse too."

"Well, sir, most of the guards probably have been involved to one degree or another, but not necessarily kicking and stomping. I'd say fifteen per cent of them would be kickers and stompers."

"And the others?"

"Well, sir, there was a code among the guards that if one guard started hitting a patient you had to jump in and help him. If you didn't join in, you were branded as a coward or branded as somebody the others didn't want to work with, 'cause you wouldn't back them up. If you didn't join in, you would be pulled off that ward immediately and usually transferred to other wards. You were in trouble with the supervisors. And word got around on you."

"This code. Where was it posted? Where is it written?" It was as though he was refusing to comprehend.

"It wasn't written. But there absolutely was a code. It was an unwritten but well-understood rule among the guards."

"Did you ever report abuses to your supervisors?"

"Sir, I didn't have to report it. They all knew."

"Did you ever take part in any of these incidents?"

Burack intertwined his fingers in front of his belly as he leaned slightly forward, his elbows perched on each arm of his chair. He looked into the carpet.

"Yes, sir, I did, like a fool."

Dr. McIntosh spoke up. "You see, sir," he said, deferentially, "the guards simply cannot visualize the patients as human beings. They insist, by their words, attitudes, and actions, that the patients are animals—dogs, not people.

"There is a mind set," he continued, "shared by the staff and the community, which holds that the patients are not really people with rights but creatures to be caged . . . watched. And beaten if they do not conform.

"Minority patients, who are only barely a minority at Farview, are subjected to added derision. For the blacks and Puerto Ricans there, verbal abuse is added to the physical and psychological abuse. Racial slurs are the rule. Commonplace."

Yancey was called on to confirm or otherwise elucidate what Burack and Dr. McIntosh had said. He agreed, naturally, and then talked about the daily life inside the hospital. He told of the hustles and thefts. Gambling as a way of life. Mail censorship and opened and rifled packages. He talked about the bookmaking activities of the horse room, and the pornography rental business. The contraband whiskey. The use of patients for cheap labor, both inside and outside, himself included. He told about beatings and benchings and blow jobs and everything else he could think of.

"Almost everybody in the place has a hustle of some kind going," he said finally. "You have to have cash in order to make it, and there are guys in there who can loan you a hundred dollars as easy as a bank could. If you borrow money from a patient, you pay back one hundred per cent interest. If you borrow from a guard, you owe him a favor. If you loan money to a guard, you may have to forget it."

"Why do you need so much cash?" the lieutenant governor asked. "I thought it was not allowed."

"For cigarettes, mostly, if you want regular cigarettes in a package. But you need soap and toothpaste. Candy. A dirty picture, maybe. Cash may not be allowed, but there's a lot of it in there and a lot of it changes hands. The guards steal a lot of it."

"Do the guards bet with patients?"

"Sure. Gambling is the main pastime there. For guards too. Of course, the patients never win."

The discussion came back around to Dr. McIntosh and seemed to be limited at the end to him, the secretary, and the lieutenant governor, who mostly listened and frowned.

"If I were called to testify in a patient's lawsuit against that hospital and the state," Dr. McIntosh said, "I would have to support the basic contentions of the patients in most instances."

"What would they sue for?" the lieutenant governor asked. "I mean, on what grounds?"

"Failure to treat, inadequate treatment, and maltreatment with ridiculous combinations and uses of drugs, abuse of patients, violations of peonage regulations, and illegal commitments."

"How many are there illegally?"

"I'd estimate two hundred. Maybe more."

"And you suggest?"

"Everything considered—present staff, conditions, legal vulnerabilities—I think the only correct course is to transfer the patients to other institutions and close down the place."

"And what do we do with the more than five hundred people put out of work? That place pumps more than seven million dollars a year into that area. Unemployment up there in those coal regions is already high. That hospital is one of the biggest employers in the county."

"I agree with Dr. McIntosh that we should move the patients out of there and find another use for that property," the secretary said. "But the people in Wayne and Lackawanna counties are going to be up in arms.

"People kick and scream when we want to put a prison or mental hospital in their area and they fight it all the way," she said, "but once the institution is built, just try and take it away. The residents are the first and loudest protesters."

"Residents?" the lieutenant governor said.

"Try the union. What do you think AFSCME is going to say?"

"But that whole area up there is Republican," Dr. McIntosh said, sensing that politics was beginning to enter the considerations, as if it had ever left. "Wayne County hasn't voted for a Democrat since Lincoln, for chrissake. What do you care about it?"

"If we jerk that hospital out of there, it'll go Republican for the next hundred years," the lieutenant governor said. "And remember that the American Federation of State, County, and Municipal Employees does not limit its membership to Wayne County. Or to Farview Hospital employees."

The lieutenant governor said he believed in all the good causes and issues supported by the governor. He also believed he would like to be the next governor.

24

WORD OF the meeting in Harrisburg didn't take long to reach Farview. And Farview and Waymart and Wayne County—and AFSCME—didn't take long to react. Within days forty thousand signatures were on protest petitions that landed on the lieutenant governor's desk. They were protesting the closing of the hospital, an action that had yet to be officially proposed.

The forty thousand names represented ten thousand more people than lived in Wayne County. Including babies and probably some folks under ground.

The hospital produced "treatment plans" for visitors to read and assume would be practiced. Classes were designed to upgrade the qualifications of guards. Word seeped through the ranks of blue shirts to be careful about marking up patients too badly when they subdued them. And word was trumpeted to Harrisburg that the hospital needed more money to improve its programs, and more personnel for better patient care.

224

In addition, some of the older patients were scheduled for staffings they had been denied for decades.

Kirchoff was among those selected. He thought it was the result of his having done so well in the spring when he was interviewed by the outside psychiatrist for four minutes. He prepared for staffing as he had prepared for that meeting in May. He put on the same white shirt and tie he had worn then. Neither had been worn since. The shirt had not even been laundered. It had lain crudely folded in his small cubbyhole in the clothing room. The tie too. Both were badly creased.

Showers had been given three or four days earlier and shaves the day after that. Kirchoff's face was a scruffy gray shadow. His hair had been combed with his fingers. He had lost his comb sometime in May.

As it had before his encounter with the psychiatrist, his mind ran to fantasies of freedom. Since May he had written to the last known addresses of his wife and his brother. He also had written to two or three lawyers, a congressman, and a senator, but he had not heard from any of them. He did not hear from his former wife either. His brother said she was dead.

As he sat before the staff he was apprehensive. Frightened, actually. He wanted to do everything just right. He shivered occasionally.

"How have you been getting along, Paul?" asked Dr. Combest. His tone was not so much cold as businesslike. It sounded as if he might have continued with "since you were here last," but caught himself.

"Just fine, sir," Kirchoff responded eagerly to the younger man.

"Do you feel like you've made a lot of progress?"

"Yes, sir. I do."

"You feel like you have a grip on your emotions? Good control of yourself?"

"Yes, sir."

"You agree, I assume, that you were here because you had some problems?"

Kirchoff suppressed a keen desire to disagree as he always had with that assumption. He felt the fire starting in his chest and he doused it. But it left him shaky. "Yes," he said.

"You recognize that there was something wrong with you?" Dr.

Combest was beginning to press with a sharp probe. Intentionally.

Kirchoff was fighting within himself, but his mind was winning out over his feelings. "Yes."

"You have overcome your illogical thinking?"

"I think so," Kirchoff said. "I feel like I have."

"What do you think of Farview?" a man in a blue shirt asked. Kirchoff recognized him as Pagnotti, with whom he had almost no experience.

"It has gotten to the place it's almost like a home to me," he said. "I've been here so long." His eyes blinked back tears. "I lost my wife. . . . I never saw my children grow up. . . . I've got seven grandchildren I've never seen. The world outside has changed so much and I haven't been in it."

He was blinking furiously.

"I thought I had a good future. But my life was wasted." The dike at his eyes had held. "But I think I kept my bearings pretty well. I haven't cried at all."

Strangely, or perhaps not, there didn't seem to be a sympathetic face in the small room. Some of them were looking out the barred windows at the autumn afternoon sunlight. One or two had their eyes closed. If any of them were listening, or paying attention to what they were hearing, it was not evident.

"Are you resentful?" It was Dr. Zundel. He had an index finger in his right nostril. It looked as though he might be digging for his brain.

"Of what, sir?"

"You know what," he said callously. "What you called your wasted life."

"I guess I was at one time, sir. I think I've overcome that."

"Have you overcome your guilt feelings?" It was a young man Kirchoff had never seen. He had a clipboard in front of him, but he was staring with piercing intensity at Kirchoff. His eyebrows and eyes and the half-moons underneath them came together as two dark smudges. His beard was dark and crowded underneath his skin. His hands, in which he was rolling a pencil, were hairy and bony. He was a psychologist.

"About what?" Kirchoff was unnerved by both the question and the stranger it came from.

"Leaving your wife and children."

"I didn't leave them," Kirchoff protested. "I was taken away from them."

"How did you feel about your mother?"

"I loved her. We had our problems, I guess, but I loved her."

"Did you enjoy fucking her?"

"What?" Kirchoff was incredulous. "What did you say?" He looked back at Dr. Combest, his eyes beseeching. "Who is he?" Then back to the psychologist. "How can you ask a question like that?"

Kirchoff was quaking with anger.

"How about your sister? Did you fuck your sister?"

"I can't believe this," Kirchoff exploded. "What is going on here?" He was almost out of his chair. "What are you trying to do?"

"Can't you answer the questions?"

"Yes!" Kirchoff shouted. "But it's an insult to even be asked such a thing. What do you think I am, a cur you can kick around and laugh at?"

The psychologist seemed unmoved by Kirchoff's ranting. The others appeared to be bored by it all.

"I understand that you told the people at Norristown a long time ago that when you were very young you enjoyed fucking animals. Dogs, I believe. That true?"

Kirchoff was incensed.

"You're the one that's crazy in here," he fairly screamed. "It's not me. It's you. All of you. You should be locked in this prison instead of me."

He included them all in the sweep of his arm, just before it was caught by a guard. His other arm was pinned to his side by a second guard.

Immediately, but too late, Kirchoff realized that he had been ensnared by the psychologist's trap. He knew he had not reacted acceptably to the questions. But he didn't know how a man was supposed to react to that kind of thing. He wanted to hit the man. He supposed he might as well have. It couldn't have done any more harm. He didn't figure he would ever get out now, anyway.

As the guards guided him toward the door one of them turned back to the others: "He's shaking like a dog trying to shit a peach seed."

They all laughed.

25

ABOUT THREE minutes remained to be played in the Sugar Bowl football game on New Year's Day when Garth pulled the newspaper clipping from his pocket. He was standing near the coffee urns in K-3 dining room at the time. He was at work.

He had taken his sister Irene's advice and had decided to get along with the guards in J-Ward. About mid-September he was transferred back to D-Ward, and since then he had spent most of his days pushing the heavy floor polisher and his nights weaving cobwebs of hatred in his head. He had decided that he and all the rest of those in white nightshirts were nothing more than clutter swept into a dark corner of God's cellar and forgotten.

After leaving J-Ward, he maintained a temperate, bland, colorless exterior but a white-hot interior. He gave every appearance of just going about his tasks with no particular enthusiasm or distaste, paying little attention to the dementia around him.

He seemed not to notice how the guards would torment a mentally retarded patient they called Bonehead by picking at him and teasing him until he screamed and cried. And the hotfoot pranks they would play on patients sleeping on or under benches. He didn't seem to see how they made a brain-damaged man they called Mama's Boy so upset he would hit himself in the face. Or how they would place a pan of cigarette butts and ashes on the floor in front of the kid they called Crazy Bobby, then cuff him in leathers and watch him try to pick a butt out of the pan with his mouth.

But he saw those things and his soul was scorched.

He never complained about the headaches, although he continued to have them without knowing why and without receiving, or requesting, medication to relieve them. They were not constant, but they often were intense. He thought that they were much like Farview—maybe not all evil, but always evil.

He never complained about much of anything after he came out of J-Ward. Not the way he had complained before he went there. And he supposed that was why he had gotten a job in the kitchen again.

There, too, he was outwardly inert and inwardly aware. He watched carefully what went on around him, and had one incident not been so petty, so much like what the hospital was like every day, so indicative of the pervasive attitude, it would have been funny enough to laugh at. It happened sometime around Christmas.

A social worker put flowers in styrofoam cups, one to each, and placed them in the center of each table in the patients' dining room. A guard, who happened by later, saw the flowers and moved each cup and flower to the tables in the guards' dining room. A few minutes after he had finished, the social worker returned and moved the flowers back to the patients' dining room. When the guards brought the first patients to their meal, they complained about the patients having flowers, and transferred the flowers once again to the guards' dining room, where they stayed.

Shortly after Christmas Gaith had seen a newspaper lying around near the office in the kitchen and thumbed through it while he smoked a cigarette. A short news article caught his eye. According to the news story, the state had made a huge meat purchase for Farview State Hospital. Several thousands of dollars' worth of meat, it said. He tore out the article, folded it unevenly, and put it in his pocket.

Garth had not seen such a shipment of meat arrive, but he thought it could have been delivered when he was not working. He looked for three or four days in the meat locker and the huge walk-in freezer. He had not seen the meat and he knew it had not been served. For sure, the decent cuts of meat rarely found their way into the patients' dining room. He was certain the meat was included in the considerable portion of patients' food that was going out the back gate every week.

The more he thought about it, the angrier he became. It was time to challenge, he decided.

So, shortly before 4 P.M. on New Year's Day, Garth held out the newspaper clipping and waved it at Kronenberger, the K-3 charge guard that shift.

"Where the hell is the meat they're talking about here?" he demanded.

"I don't know what you're talking about," Kronenberger said.

"The newspaper says thousands of pounds of meat was sent here by the state. Where is it?"

"I said I don't know what the fuck you're talking about."

"Here, read it."

"I don't want to read it."

"You know where that meat is, don't you? Same as I do."

The argument was getting loud on both sides.

"Shut up and get to work," Kronenberger said.

"You stole it, that's what happened to it!" Garth shouted. He still had the newspaper clipping in the fist of his extended arm.

"I didn't steal nothing, you crazy bastard." The guard moved toward Garth.

"All of you did. The guards stole the meat. It was supposed to be for the patients and you stole it."

The noise brought guards from the nearby guards' dining room converging on K-3. They ran through the door and rushed Garth. Kronenberger stood aside as three guards grappled with the patient, jostling a pitcher of hot coffee off a serving table. The liquid spilled across the floor and footing became treacherous.

The three guards were kicking and punching from all sides. One of them made a swiping kick and cut Garth's legs from under him. He fell on the slippery floor, no longer a stack of cement blocks but more a sack of sawdust. Kronenberger joined in the fray when Garth went down. He was only afraid of patients when they were standing.

The four guards had Wade under control when other guards came, and then nothing was in control. There were six, then maybe ten men in blue shirts pushing to make contact with the sprawling, wriggling, screaming patient. They were kicking, punching, pounding, stomping Garth while he tried to evade them. They kept kicking and beating after he rolled up into a ball.

Meanwhile, Kronenberger had left the carnage to telephone for supervisory assistance. In a few minutes Bulldog and a supervisor arrived.

"That's enough, boys," the supervisor said. He and Bulldog had to pull the others away from the limp mass on the floor. A couple of them had to be pulled away twice.

"Take him to D and put him in the peanut," the supervisor said. Then he turned to the others and asked what had happened. Two guards hooked their arms under Garth's, and some of the other guards followed, intent on getting one final kick in after he had been dragged into the hallway.

"He was standing over there near the coffee urn," Kronenberger said, "and he started waving something from the newspaper, accusing me of stealing the patients' meat."

"You?" the supervisor asked.

"Well, all of us. The guards."

"And then he hit Krony, here," one of the other guards broke in, "and grabbed a pitcher of hot coffee to throw at him. We knocked the pitcher out of his hand and wrestled with him on the wet floor to get him under control. We got him subdued and Krony called you."

At that moment Garth was arriving at the D-Ward peanut. He was semiconscious and visibly injured. He was dragged into the tiny room and dropped to the floor. The same stench that had greeted Chamberlin's nostrils filled Garth's. The tiny window was open and the frost of New Year's Day was already inside.

Garth's ribs ached and his breathing was restricted. He lay with his cheek pressed into the gritty boards. He passed out.

He didn't know what time it was when the water hit him in the back and drenched his neck and head, but it seemed like a frigid eternity before he was dragged from the peanut to the dayroom. The water had frozen in his hair, and his shirt was stiff and icy.

The dayroom was vacant and it was dark inside. The other patients were upstairs in bed.

Two guards took his feet and dragged him across the dayroom and all the way to J-Ward. By the time he reached there, the trail of water and blood behind him indicated that the ice had thawed in his hair and shirt. At J-Ward his shirt was removed, along with all his other clothing except his undershorts.

He was still vaguely conscious, but apparently still a threat. He was cuffed with leathers all around and dragged into a cold, damp cell. Like the others, it was devoid of anything except peeling paint and a concrete history of man's inhumanity to man.

The next morning Garth lay motionless on the floor of his cell and did not respond to inquiries spoken through the small rectangular opening in the door. Though he exhibited clear signs of injury, if blood is a sign, no medical attention was given to him.

As the morning wore on, semiconsciousness, then consciousness, reclaimed his brain and he twisted to a sitting position against the wall. He complained to a guard that he was in terrible pain and he was walked to R-Ward for X-rays.

Sullins saw him coming in. He flashed a signal to another ward worker he knew only as Sly, telling him that guards were coming. Sly was standing in the doorway of an examining room as a lookout for Costello and Dog Boy. Costello was sitting on the examining table with his trousers and underwear bunched down on his ankles. Dog Boy had his face in Costello's crotch and his hand on his own genitalia, moving rhythmically.

Costello couldn't afford to get in trouble with guards. He already was suspected of smuggling a .22-caliber pistol in to Dog Boy. Pagnotti found it under the mattress of the bed that belonged to another patient, but he believed that the patient was being framed by both Dog Boy and Costello. He sent the patient to J-Ward for one week anyway.

When Sullins saw Garth come onto the ward he could see that the cuffed patient was hurting. He was walking slowly and carefully, yet he winced with each step. His face was swollen and the pasty skin was splotched with scrapes of red.

The X-ray disclosed a fractured rib on the right side. The area around the fracture was discolored, and Garth seemed to be unaware of his red and stiff left hand frequently rising to shield and stroke the bruise.

A few minutes later he was taken back to his cell on J-Ward to remain in seclusion and bondage.

He ate little of his supper, but he asked for water. He was ignored. He asked a number of times during the night and each time was ignored.

The next morning his requests were louder and more frequent.

Finally he was pulled from his cell and dragged to the bathroom. On the way, he was kicked a couple of times by someone he did not see. Inside the bathroom he was thrown to the floor and brutally stomped. Then he was doused with water and returned to his cell to greet the gusts of piercing polar air.

He slipped in and out of consciousness during most of the day, awakening with pleas for water, then gone again. At some point the guards closed the window, probably for their own comfort, and he awoke realizing that it was warm and the pain seemed worse. He was lying in a puddle of his own making.

During the course of the next two days he ate little, cursed often, and shouted when he could. He called hundreds of times for guards and almost as often for doctors. And over and over again he asked for water.

Each time the aggravation reached a point of intolerability for the guards, regardless of shift or hour, some guards would come to his cell and pound him into senselessness and silence. Occasionally he was taken to the bathroom, kicked going and coming, and pummeled and doused while there.

As the days wore by, Garth became weaker. He struggled to stand but could not wobble across his cell. When the barber came to J-Ward to give shaves and haircuts, Garth tried to say something but he couldn't. His face was puffed and disfigured and his jaws were stiff as a marionette's.

He seemed to be having trouble breathing and he was favoring his left arm and side. He was dazed and dirty and stinking.

The barber said he couldn't shave Garth. He didn't try to give him a haircut.

The next afternoon late, while making a rather impromptu

check on patients in J-Ward, Dr. Minoso, a Cuban who had been at the hospital only a few months, looked into Garth's cell. What he saw startled him and he ordered Garth to R-Ward.

"If we no do sometheeng soon, I theenk maybe he in trouble," the doctor said in the lilting accent of the Caribbean.

By that evening Garth was in a steadily deteriorating condition. He complained of pain in his ribs, his kidneys, and his spine.

The guards paid him no attention. Their interest was confined to watching two Siamese fighting fish in their battle to the death. Costello had brought the fish in separate containers. The guards viewed in cheering fascination as the two fish tried to destroy each other.

Garth finally asked Duhamel and Sullins to help him to the bathroom.

"I don't feel anything in my legs," he said.

"Starting where?" Duhamel asked.

"All up and down," Garth said. "I can't feel nothing from my waist on down. It's numb."

Sullins told Dr. Minoso what Garth said, and the doctor had the ward workers take him for X-rays of his spine. They disclosed nothing that would assist the doctor in prescribing aid. He gave morphine and streptomycin.

By 6 A.M., Garth was obviously and critically ill. Dr. Minoso concluded that he was hemorrhaging internally. He thought that the organs inside Garth's body had been too badly battered to continue their fight, unless surgery were performed quite soon.

Dr. Combest came to R-Ward later in the morning and took over the case. Another X-ray was taken of the lumbar region of Garth's spine and at 10:20 A.M., more morphine was ordered. Then Levophed too.

Dr. Minoso was urging emergency surgery.

Dr. Combest was ordering Levophed.

At 11 A.M. Dr. Minoso wanted to operate.

At 11:26 Dr. Combest ordered adrenaline.

A minute before, the pain behind Garth's eye had stopped. So had his heart.

At 3:12 that afternoon, Garth's sister Irene was read a telegram from Farview which said that her brother was SERIOUSLY ILL THIS HOSPITAL MAY REQUIRE EMERGENCY SURGERY MAY VISIT AT YOUR CONVENIENCE. It was from the superintendent.

At 9:43 A.M. the next day she was read another telegram from Farview which said, REGRET TO ADVISE GARTH WADE DIED AT THIS HOSPITAL PLEASE ADVISE AS TO DISPOSITION OF BODY.

Irene thought things could have been handled differently.

By the time the county coroner was performing an autopsy on Garth Wade's body, she was calling state officials in Harrisburg and hospital administrators at Farview. She was asking questions about the nature of her brother's death. She was living with a promise to keep and she was bent on keeping it.

The state referred her to the hospital and the hospital said Garth had died of "acute coronary occlusion due to coronary atherosclerosis and embolism anterior descending coronary artery." She did not know what that meant. Basically, a heart failure.

She wanted to know all about the autopsy and the superintendent assured her in a letter that a full and complete autopsy was done by the county coroner, who had made the ruling of death by natural causes, and that the "remarkable finding was the marked and extensive generalized atherosclerosis."

He did not tell her about the three broken ribs the coroner found on her brother's left side, in addition to the one broken rib already disclosed by hospital X-rays. He did not tell her about abrasions or bruises, both of which the coroner noted.

But she remembered how her brother had looked the last time she saw him. And she remembered his prediction of death. And she remembered her last promise of a second autopsy.

She was tormented by the promise. She could not afford to pay for an autopsy. She and her sister and their mother had been forced to sell household possessions, even blankets and dishes, just to pay for Garth's funeral.

So she wrote letters to state officials. She asked for exhumation of Garth's body and another autopsy. She wrote the governor and legislators. She called preachers and politicians. Until one day she received a letter.

It was from her brother Leonard at Western State Penitentiary.

"Last week I was called into the warden's office and told that you was nervous about things," the letter read, "and that you was making other people nervous and they want me to tell you to lay off. They made it clear to me that if you did not lay off, I was headed for Farview myself. I'm begging you to lay off like they say."

She did.

But when she went to the cemetery, she had a hard time telling Garth why she couldn't keep her promise.

26

IT WAS a bitterly cold February evening when the young mechanic walked out of his apartment, leaving his wife to commiserate with the squalling, lonely blues album on the stereo phonograph.

He ducked into his 1976 Plymouth and drove slowly through the night. Snow was beginning to feather down a little faster, and in the glare of his headlights it seemed to burst before the car like summer fireworks that never faded.

He finally located what he was looking for and stopped the car. He got out into the snow and listened to the quiet for a moment before he walked into the tiny cubicle and pulled the folding door shut behind him. The smell reminded him of another tiny cubicle. He put the heavy paper bag of coins on the narrow shelf and picked up the telephone receiver. He took a small, dog-eared notebook from his shirt pocket and flipped the pages.

He dialed some numbers he had dialed before. He listened to

the falling coins gong as they had gonged before. He said the things he had said before—and so did the people who answered.

He was discouraged. More. He was becoming disillusioned now. He had worked like hell and had done what he had set out to do, and it hadn't mattered at all. He had spent a couple of nights every week for the past year trying to complete his plan, achieve his goal, and he was failing. He had driven from North Philadelphia to South Jersey, to Delaware, to Maryland, to New York, so that the calls couldn't be traced. He had talked to the Pennsylvania State Police, the F.B.I., the state attorney general, a couple of county coroners, a few mothers and fathers, a couple of preachers, and nine newspapers.

Nobody believed him. Not after they found out that he had been there. Man, oh, man, when they send you away to that place, they never let you return, he thought, as he hung up the telephone and decided to call it a night.

The next morning, during a break in his work at a garage, he picked up the morning newspaper and began thumbing through it. A short item caught his eye, and as he read, his pulse raced. He discovered that his plan was working. Or at least it was not dead. The article said the coroner in Wayne County, Pennsylvania, was planning to ask the court for permission to exhume the body of a former patient at Farview State Hospital. He said he had received permission from the family to do so. He said he was acting on the basis of an anonymous tip he had received by telephone.

The body to be exhumed was Venance "Night Train" Lane's.

The mechanic ran across North Broad street to a fast-food restaurant that had a pay telephone inside. He had to look up the number. For some reason, he had not called this newspaper before. He had called the other two in town. They had said they weren't interested in his story. Maybe one of them said they didn't believe him. That didn't seem to matter now. He put a dime in the slot and dialed LO3-1600. After six rings a tinny, nasal voice answered, "*Inquirer* city desk."

"Can I speak to Acel Moore?" he asked, looking at the name at the top of the news story he had read.

A moment later a male voice came on the line. "This is Acel Moore."

"You the one that wrote the story about Farview and the coroner digging up a body in this morning's paper?"

"Yes."

"Well, Night Train Lane didn't die of no heart attack. He was murdered. I was there and I saw it."

"You saw it?"

"Yeah, man, and a lot more too."

"Like what?"

"They kill people up there, man."

"Who does?"

"The guards, man. They stomp them to death. Kick 'em and stomp 'em. They steal from the patients. Take their money and take their food. And they make 'em like zombies. It's a awful place, man. You oughta write a story about that place."

"How do you know so much about it?"

"I was there, man."

"What were you doing there?"

"I was a patient there, but I wasn't crazy."

"How long were you there?"

"Couple of years. I can tell you all about Farview, man. You interested?"

"Sure, I'm interested," Moore said. "Sounds like a helluva story."

Epilogue

AFTER THE newspaper series was published, a special investigating committee of the Pennsylvania State Senate looked into the alleged abuses and corroborated the newspaper's findings with sworn testimony. In addition, Farview's highest-ranking physician, who had been on the staff for twenty-one years, resigned abruptly after he was criticized by a coroner's jury for failing to help a patient who had died untreated in the hospital.

Every patient in the hospital at the time of the newspaper articles was given a psychiatric examination, and fifty-eight of them were ordered transferred out of the hospital. A state government task force subsequently recommended that half the remaining patients (then numbering about 250) be transferred to five medium-security mental hospitals around Pennsylvania.

A number of judges ceased committing patients to Farview, and some ordered the transfer of patients committed earlier.

The hospital hired a full-time lawyer to handle patients' legal questions, and then hired several full-time psychologists and psychiatrists. The administration installed pay telephones for patient use and placed emergency life-saving equipment on the wards. A statewide bill of rights for mental patients was put into effect on an accelerated basis and the Farview trustees adopted a policy of notifying the coroner whenever a patient dies.

The federal government cut off its $600,000 annual payment to the state for the care of aged patients at Farview, and the special State Senate committee recommended that the hospital be closed down. Former Governor Shapp finally recommended that the facility not be used as a mental hospital, that roughly half the early structure be razed, and that the remaining, more recently built portions be used as a maximum-security prison. Nothing has come of that plan.

Not long after the newspaper series was published, a special investigating grand jury was impaneled in Wayne County, where the hospital is located. A special prosecutor and a special judge, both from the Philadelphia area, were selected to conduct and supervise the investigations.

The prosecutor determined that twenty-one deaths over the course of two decades at Farview were of a suspicious nature. The grand jury eventually handed down murder indictments in four of the cases, and said that homicide was the cause of another eight deaths for which the jurors didn't recommend prosecution, because the defendants were deceased or for other reasons.

In all, the grand jury deliberated for about nineteen months and indicted thirty-six people in twenty cases, including the four murders. The other cases primarily involved assault. From the outset the investigation was a pitched battle, with the grand jurors and the prosecutors on one side and the local community and the presiding judge on the other.

Judge John E. Lavelle was from nearby Schuylkill County and had sat on the Governor's Justice Commission, which had initially refused to fund the special grand jury investigation, then decided to do so over the judge's objections. A copy of handwritten notes the judge made during discussions about the funding reflected his opinion that "The *Inquirer* should fund the investigation," since it had started the commotion about Farview.

Judge Lavelle refused to excuse himself from hearing the cases brought before him and refused to grant the special prosecutor's request for change of venue from the small town of Honesdale and from Wayne County, where the hospital was the second largest employer, edged out by the Katz Underwear factory, which had 540 employees to Farview's 500.

Many of the county's 30,000 residents know or are related to people who work at Farview, and the grand jurors maintained that there was no way the prosecution would get a fair trial in Honesdale.

Nevertheless, Judge Lavelle refused to transfer the cases, and the Pennsylvania State Supreme Court, politically appointed and often accused of being politically motivated, upheld him.

After the first four trials of guards accused of assaulting patients, seven jurors said publicly that they believed the remaining cases should be moved from Honesdale. Two of the jurors said they had voted for acquittals only because of pressure from fellow jurors and fear of community reaction.

"I have to live here," one of the jurors, a woman, said. "If I had said guilty, I'd probably be dead the next day. You don't know what Honesdale's like."

But much of Pennsylvania found out. The *Inquirer* printed the story about the jurors' feelings, as well as extensive interviews with townspeople who acknowledged no doubt of the guilt of some hospital guards, but ventured the "honest opinion that they'll never convict a one of them in Wayne County."

In one of the cases, a patient testified that after he had thrown a cup of urine on a guard two guards forced him into a bathroom and severely beat him on his head and face, cutting a cornea and causing heavy bleeding from his eyes. A nurse and a doctor testified that he had been injured, and another guard testified that the three men had been in the bathroom alone and that he had heard the sound of blows being struck.

Then the two guards' immediate superior testified that after the incident the two guards had told him, "We fixed that nigger."

The two guards were acquitted.

"Why put somebody in jail for doing something to a crazy?" asked a mechanic who was a member of the jury. "If the guards were lying about the beating of some man on the street, that's something else, but lying about that bullshit in Farview, why waste all that money for that?"

A barber on Main Street perhaps best summed up the community's attitude: "How do I feel? Just the way everybody feels. It's going to zilch, a big farce, big expense for nothing. They're going back so far . . . into things that happened so damn long ago."

Again the special prosecutor, Elliott D. Goldberg, moved for change of venue in light of unrebutted testimony which showed that jurors who sat in the trials were biased against the prosecution and felt pressured to return not-guilty verdicts. Again he was refused. Again the State Supreme Court upheld the judge.

Then the prosecutors faced a bigger problem. The first year's funding of the investigation was at an end and it was necessary for the county commissioners to make a pro forma application for funds to complete the special prosecution. The money had been allocated by the Governor's Justice Commission, but the county commissioners were required to make application in order to receive it.

The commissioners refused to apply for the funds.

For a while some of Goldberg's assistants served without pay, but one by one they were forced to seek gainful employment. Finally the commissioners agreed to fund the trials through District Attorney Nicholas Barna's office. The job of district attorney in Wayne County is only part-time, mixing burglary prosecutions between private-property closings, for the most part.

Barna decided to drop the charges in six cases, including two alleged murders and a cover-up charge against a former superintendent, "because we simply didn't have the evidence for conviction," he said. "You can bring indictments, but the standard of proof is stricter for a conviction. Witnesses—the guards, especially the guards—would testify in low, even tones, not the emotional statements they may have made before the trials."

But the district attorney said that the attitude of the Wayne County people who made up the Farview trial juries was the main reason for the acquittal or dropping of charges against all but one former guard, who was convicted of assault.

"The truest test of what happened here was one case where the defendant [a guard] was tape-recorded and he admitted on tape to 'taking that fucking nigger [a patient] and hitting him up against the wall,' " the district attorney said. "Even after the jury heard that tape and the defendant's admission, they acquitted him."

*

At last count there were between 150 and 200 patients remaining in the hospital. Men like Elton Jones and Paul Kirchoff were released by constitutional means, as were some 550 others, through the work of attorney Richard Bazilon and the University of Pennsylvania Law School's Prison Research Council.

*

In the course of the newspaper's investigation, the body of the man identified in this book as Garth Wade was exhumed. The second autopsy, promised him by his sister, disclosed multiple fractures. The doctor who had performed the first autopsy reconsidered his finding and acknowledged that death was not due to a heart attack as he had said initially, but that the patient had died from "acute blunt force." A guard who had been in the dining room during the altercation that resulted in Wade's death admitted to state police investigators, after he had retired, that he had seen other guards "knock the patient down on the floor. . . . I didn't see any one person kick him, but there was a flurry and none of the guards was down. . . . I never saw him again."

Nobody was convicted of the murder of Garth Wade and nobody knows what happened to his Bible—or to its promise of a higher court.

Appendix 1

DISTRICT ATTORNEY'S OFFICE

NICHOLAS A. BARNA
DISTRICT ATTORNEY
_____
SPECIAL ASSISTANTS
ELLIOTT D. GOLDBERG
THOMAS E. BUTLER, JR.
CHARLES A. HADDAD
ALEXANDER BRATIC
JAMES E. DELBELLO
DAVID RICHMAN
JOHN J. O'KEEFE
AIMEE A. TOTH
PIERRE B. PIE, II
DOLORES M. TROIANI

WAYNE COUNTY
600 MAIN STREET
HONESDALE, PENNSYLVANIA
18431
_____
(717) 253-4000

GRAND JURY INVESTIGATION
OF
FARVIEW STATE HOSPITAL

October 12, 1978

Mr. Wendell Rawls
New York Times
Washington Bureau
Washington, D.C.

        Re: Special Investigating Grand Jury
              Farview State Hospital

Dear Wendell:

      I thought that you would appreciate a copy of
the Final Report of the Grand Jury. The same was presented
in open court on October 9, 1978. I also enclose a copy
of the public statement of the Grand Jury criticizing the
Department of Welfare. Further, on the same date, the Grand
Jury issued a Presentment charging various employees with
covering up the true circumstances surrounding the death
of _____.

      In fact everything that you and Acel reported was
confirmed through the Grand Jury investigation. Note that
the Grand Jury categorized eight of the suspicious deaths as
homicide, four of which it recommended prosecution. Note
that in the case of _____ the defendant (a patient)
confessed to the crime. Unfortunately, he was found to be stone
crazy at the time of the incident and consequently was not guilty.

      I hope the Final Report might be of some assistance to
you in your continuing efforts on this matter. If I can be
of any further service, please do not hesitate to contact me
personally.

      Best personal regards.

                    Sincerely yours,

                    ELLIOTT D. GOLDBERG
                    Assistant District Attorney

EDG:kg
Enclosures

Appendix 2

Having spent nearly 18 months hearing and reviewing evidence from hundreds of witnesses who appeared before us, we have had an opportunity to examine Farview State Hospital as perhaps no other investigative body before us.

Mindful that our only inquiry was specifically focused and directed to matters criminal in nature, nevertheless we feel compelled to make the following observations.

First, for a great many years Farview was a prison operating in the guise of a hospital. Patient care was minimal in light of the poor training and limited staff. To a great extent the fault for these conditions and the climate which allowed these crimes to flourish lies with the Department of Welfare, which for years continued to ignore allegations of criminality and poor conditions at Farview.

Second, local law enforcement officials were lax and not vigilant in performing their duties. Up until the last several years, local officials too often dismissed allegations of criminality and brutality as rumors and tales from crazy patients. Former County Commissioners too often refused to provide the District Attorney and Coroner's Office with the proper resources to conduct thorough investigations of these crimes.

Finally, the recent conduct of the present Wayne County Commissioners must be recognized for what it really is:

1. Their repeated refusal to apply for funding, which only they can do, from the Governor's Justice Commission despite assurance that nearly $250,000 had been set aside for the cost of prosecution and only awaited the execution of an application for its release to Wayne County.

2. Their action in setting unrealistic salaries for two full-time prosecutors resulted in the resignation of two members of the prosecuting staff.

3. Their refusal to pay even the most minimal expenses, such as room and board, for prosecutors who live over 150 miles away.

4. Their recent release to the local newspapers of a two-page letter indicating a refusal to fund the prosecutions could only add

246

fuel to the already hostile feelings among the citizenry over the costs of prosecution.

Their actions have seriously hampered and jeopardized the continuing prosecutions and can only be viewed as part of an ongoing effort to hinder and frustrate the criminal justice system in Wayne County.

Appendix 3

IN THE COURT OF COMMON PLEAS OF WAYNE COUNTY
TRIAL DIVISION, CRIMINAL SECTION
IN RE: The Amended Petition of :   JANUARY TERM, 1977

NICHOLAS A. BARNA   :
District Attorney of   :
Wayne County   :

ELLIOTT D. GOLDBERG   :
Assistant District Attorney :

REQUESTING A GRAND JURY
INVESTIGATION   :   NO. 122

FINAL REPORT

TO THE HONORABLE HARRY A. TAKIFF, PRESIDING JUDGE:

We, the Special Investigating Grand Jury of April Term 1977, and thereafter, duly charged by the Court to investigate allegations of criminal conduct at Farview State Hospital involving public officials, public employees and others within the County of Wayne, having obtained knowledge from witnesses sworn by the Court and testifying before us and finding thereon reasonable grounds to believe, and so believing, upon our respective oaths not fewer than twelve concurring do hereby make this Final Report to the Court:

INTRODUCTION

When we embarked on our task last February 1, 1977, we were specifically instructed by the Court, that as an arm of the Court, our sole function was to investigate the allegations of criminality at Farview State Hospital and to determine if crimes had been committed and whether prosecution was warranted. Our objective was not to close Farview State Hospital or to lend support to those who would close this institution.

One of the primary bases of this Special Grand Jury Investigation was the persistent presence of allegations of murder of patients at

Farview State Hospital, Waymart, Wayne County, Pennsylvania. *We find that for the most part the apprehensions of the general public were justified and that there were in fact murders of patients by guards at the said institution.*

When we embarked upon our investigation we heard various characterizations of Farview—these allegations coming primarily from present and former patients. We heard horror stories of continuous beatings of patients with implements such as blackjacks and brass knuckles, as well as guards hitting and punching them unmercifully; oftentimes after a beating, patients were thrown into small cells ("peanuts") where their injuries went unattended. And we heard of secret burials, unmarked graves, fraudulent record keeping and falsification of death certificates.

We further noted that previous investigations by various governmental agencies encountered a "stone wall" of silence on the part of guards and supervisory employees concerning these serious allegations of abuse. The "stone walling" on the part of employees at Farview State Hospital has its roots deeply embedded in the history of the institution. An example was set at the highest levels of the administration in an effort to "cover up" the true causes of death of various patients, to ignore factors which clearly indicated beatings and to fail to properly investigate internally all such circumstances.

This Grand Jury summoned before it literally hundreds of witnesses in its quest for the truth concerning the murders, including present and former patients as well as present and former employees. While the employees for the most part attempted to thwart our investigation by "stone walling," breaching their oath of secrecy (in terms of keeping secret the nature of their interrogation before the Grand Jury) and on many occasions perjuring themselves, we were able to overcome these obstacles. Through our subpoena power, we were able to secure many records which were previously unavailable to the investigative agencies for the Commonwealth. And since witnesses were compelled to appear before the Grand Jury and give testimony, we were able to elucidate the records or determine the lack thereof.

With regards to the record keeping at Farview State Hospital, we find the allegations of the Petition to Empanel a Grand Jury to be too often true. During the period from the 1950's to the early 1970's, the *patient records were seriously deficient* in charting a patient's progress. And, as has been testified to by physicians, *outright false.* For example, in one case the patient (who was being treated for severe internal injuries and terminally ill) was listed on his medication chart as receiving medication for tuberculosis, and sleeping pills, on the verbal orders of the attending physician. The physician testified that such entries were a lie and "covered up" the true nature of the treatment. *Further, in some instances patients were mostly listed as dying from some physical malady in the hospital ward when in fact they were beaten to death on a regular ward and brought to the hospital ward after death.* And the cause of death was usually listed as heart attack when the real causation was manifest abuse.

While the record keeping tended to improve in the 1970's, the presence of serious falsification failed to subside. In 1976, [a] patient . . . died of an overdose of drugs. His medication charts and the postmortem toxicological examination of his body were at serious variance. The toxicology report revealed the presence of drugs which he did not allegedly receive, drugs in far greater quantity than listed and drugs which he had not supposedly received for many months prior. The physical evidence overwhelmingly indicated the falsification of his medical records by employees of the institution.

These records that were present and intact indicated a "cover-up" of the precise nature of the injuries in communications between the Superintendent of the "hospital" and the Department of Public Welfare. They demonstrated a course of treatment which many times constituted gross negligence on the part of the attending physician in not transporting the patient to a facility that was equipped to deal with terminal illnesses such as cancer. And even the engaging of the coroner when they were concerned with a death but not properly disclosing the precise circumstances surrounding death. . . .

In terms of the actual beatings, there were many. *Typically, in those cases where we have found homicide, the patients were severely and unmercifully kicked, beaten and punched by groups of guards of five or more. Usually, the patient was left thereafter in his injured condition with no medical attention, to die a painful death. We have continuously found evidence of torn livers, punctured lungs, broken ribs, ruptured spleens and the like.* On the other hand, the guards involved have testified that the patient "must have fallen" or had a "heart attack." With the exception of a small number of guards willing to tell truthfully the events which brought about the injury to the patients, the guards have denied any knowledge of beatings. Those who testified candidly before the Grand Jury expressed extreme fear regarding their exposure.

The necessity for empanelling this Grand Jury cannot be denied. Were it not for the invocation of this extraordinary investigative power, the truth would never be known. Too often, the allegations of abuse met with unresponsive bureaucratic red tape, and/or lack of concern. They were most often passed off as the tales of deranged minds, since Farview is ostensibly an institution for the criminally insane. *However, we were impressed with the lucid testimony of present and former patients which has for the most part been corroborated by medical records and the testimony of guards. . . .*

In summary, we determine that the rumors concerning Farview were true. Patients were killed there and their deaths covered up. We sincerely believe that notwithstanding the extreme obstruction of our investigation, we have determined the truth. Including the deaths that were not reported to the Coroner.

Of course, in everybody's minds the murders were the most dramatic revelation of this investigation. However, as indicated further on in this Final Report, the investigation concerned itself to a substantial degree with relation to assaults on patients. *There were literally hundreds of assaults on patients which our investigators brought to our attention.* A certain portion as indicated were the result of Presentments. Scores of others were found to be in fact true, but due to lack of corroborating evidence we elected not to recommend prosecution. In fact, one of the most difficult jobs was to categorize and itemize all of the assaults. *Without fail, every former patient who appeared before us spoke of the beatings given to themselves and their fellow patients.* While the guards at first refused to acknowledge that *beatings did in fact occur, eventually many guards confirmed the happening of beatings. We find as a fact that beatings and assaults of patients were a way of life at Farview.* While many of them constituted a legitimate subduing of the patient to protect others, *the majority constituted excessive brutality.*

Finally, this Grand Jury must mention perjury and obstruction of justice. As indicated many, many guards appeared before the Grand Jury. We were able to observe their demeanor in the full course of questioning. And we had the advantage of hearing other testimony prior to theirs which indicated a particular crime. *We find that a majority of the guards and former guards perjured themselves to cover up the true circumstances of crimes under investigation.* They continuously tried to hamper the Grand Jury investigation and obstruct justice by failure to be fully and completely candid with this Grand Jury. We find this sequence to be deplorable. Our findings are reflected in the various Presentments issued wherein the people were charged with perjury and obstruction of justice in addition to the principal crime.

ASSAULTS

Beatings and assaults of patients by guards were the most wide-spread of all crimes committed at Farview. This practice had its origin in the use of physical force to control patients prior to the advent of drug therapy. It became ingrained as an accepted pattern of conduct by Farview guards and perceived by the citizens of surrounding communities as a necessary practice.

There existed an unwritten or tacit rule among the guards that if a patient was to be beaten, all the guards present on a given ward would join in the beating. One of the primary reasons for this rule was a feeling that if all the guards joined, it would be difficult if not impossible to identify the actual culprits as well as reducing the chances of injury to any one guard.

Oftentimes these assaults and beatings had their origin in the most trifling or petty circumstances. Patients were routinely beaten for playing radios too loud, disturbing a guard who was trying to sleep and even for being victorious in a game of cards.

This is not to say that all guards at Farview engaged in these practices. But of the handful that did, a popular phrase was "giving them the boots." This was a reference to savage kicking and stomping of patients. On the old maximum security ward, "J" Ward, and the new maximum security ward, "CC" Ward, this was a popular form of punishment. Patients' ankles were stomped and kicked, causing injury to the legs and feet and thereby immobilizing the patient for days and even weeks. Guards would then explain that the swelling and pain was caused by prolonged standing or walking.

We have investigated well over one hundred cases of alleged assault at Farview State Hospital. Scores were determined to be true but for one reason or another prosecutions could not be commenced. In fact, so many people reported so many assaults that it was impossible to identify all of the victims. We were hampered in our inquiry by poor record keeping, continuous lack of memory by many guard witnesses and sometimes by the sheer number of assaults against a particular patient. . . .

THEFTS

We investigated numerous allegations of thefts of personal property of patients. In addition we uncovered a form of theft from patient accounts that was practiced for a number of years.

All patients at Farview had their various sources of income credited to their patient accounts. With the balance in their accounts patients could purchase sundry items such as candy and cigarettes from the commissary as well as more expensive items by mail order such as clothes and tape recorders.

Various patient workers who worked in the commissary or held other jobs around the hospital would make "phantom" purchases from the accounts of patients who were unaware of the transactions. Most frequently the victims were patients with no capacity to comprehend even the most basic of financial transactions.

Guards on various wards were aware of these "phantom" purchases and took no affirmative action to stop them. They sanctioned [them] and would frequently demand "payoffs" from these enterprising patients. The "payoffs" most often took the form of cigarettes although occasionally they would have the patients order clothes and small appliances from the victim's account.

The hundreds of instances of unexplained disappearances of personal items and money belonging to patients cannot be dismissed as the wild allegations of disturbed patients. Many of these allegations were legitimate, but identifying the culprit or culprits proved to be difficult.

Our ability to identify perpetrators was hampered by poor record keeping, fragmented assistance from the victims and their families, as well as the redundant denials and lapses in memory by guard witnesses. . . .

The instances of theft include the actual theft by guards of patients' goods.

COCKFIGHTS

Throughout the many years of its existence and well into the last few years, there existed a practice among the guards of engaging patients in "cockfights," or sanctioned combat between two patients. With the exception of the brutal and senseless murders of patients, no single aspect of Farview exemplified more man's inhumanity to man.

These fights were arranged and sanctioned by charge guards of the various wards. They served to provide live entertainment to the guards as well as an opportunity to wager on the outcome. Often patients who engaged in these cockfights were seriously injured or maimed.

There was also a despicable practice closely akin to cockfights. This was known as "taking the floor." In practice, one patient would go to the charge guard and ask to "take the floor." Once the charge guard gave the permission, and after all guards and patients arranged themselves in a circle, the two patients would commence the fight. Oftentimes, the guards would beat the loser.

Guards testified to witnessing and having heard reports of various cockfights throughout the institution. Their testimony is corroborated by that we received from numerous former patients who told of watching and participating in such depravity. Winners were rewarded special privileges while losers often were subjected to punishment.

SEXUAL CRIMES

As in most institutions where men are confined for long periods of time, homosexuality occurred at Farview State Hospital. However, as with other aspects, homosexuality at Farview assumed a bizarre status.

We have determined that at Farview homosexuality was widespread and rampant, including in its participants a number of guards and hospital personnel who have worked at Farview through the years. Witnesses appeared before us and repeatedly told of having to engage in sodomy and perverse homosexual acts in order to amuse and entertain guards.

Guard witnesses testified that homosexual practices were condoned by the professional staff, who felt that it was a constructive way to keep patients "occupied." Patients were allowed to dress in female clothing and one patient was even allowed to maintain a small room which he used as a dressing room.

This rampant homosexuality, while it was condoned by the supervisory staff and guards, served to cause tension among patients often leading to fights, and causing further psychological distortions and stresses among patients who did not wish to engage in homosexuality.

Much of the homosexuality we have uncovered, although criminal in nature, is unprosecutable because of the statute of limitations. Of those few more recent acts, we feel no constructive results could be achieved by revealing the names of those patients and guards involved or recommending prosecutions.

GAMBLING AND ALCOHOLIC BEVERAGES

Gambling appears to have been the most prevalent of the nonviolent pastimes of Farview patients and guards. Although in recent years the hospital administrators have permitted guards to engage in card games with patients, we have determined that for many years prior guards and supervisory personnel engaged in illegal card games with patients.

Wagering on the outcome of these games was done with currency, even though hospital policy prohibited patients from carrying money. Enterprising patients were allowed to conduct widespread gambling operations provided they "shared" the proceeds with various charge guards and supervisors. . . .

We have also uncovered several occasions where individual guards, in direct violation of hospital policy and criminal statutes, have surreptitiously supplied patients with liquor. Whiskey was the drink most often in demand and guards would charge as much as $25 a pint for supplying a particular patient.

Guards testified to occasionally finding empty whiskey bottles on wards and encountering patients who were inebriated and smelled of whiskey. . . .

ACKNOWLEDGMENTS

In addition to the four men to whom this book is dedicated, an expression of gratitude must be directed to others who assisted, encouraged or supported my efforts. Dr. Michael McGuire and his wife, Judy, were enormously helpful and generous with their time. They provided technical and medical expertise as well as firsthand accounts and documentary evidence of what happened to them and others during their brief tenure trying to make Farview a better place for patients and staff. Wayne County Coroner Robert Jennings and Special Prosecutor Elliott Goldberg both made useful contributions of time and information, for which I am deeply grateful. Attorneys Richard Bazilon and David Ferleger provided special ideas, leads and contacts which were immensely helpful in the early stages of the newspaper series. Former Pennsylvania State Senator Henry J. Cianfrani and his successor, Vincent Fumo, were ever ready to intercede in my behalf and did so. Robert Hammel, the present superintendent at Farview, and John Baldino, chief of the guards there, were kind enough to allow me additional access to the hospital and provide needed historical facts and accounts. Also to the patients and staff, who provided covert help, this book owes a great deal.

Some special friends merit special mention. Jack Hurst, a wonderful writer for the *Chicago Tribune* and my good and dear friend and soul brother, was, and is, a source of constant encouragement. Jim Wooten, an especially gifted journalist, was always an unselfish friend who, when asked, provided honest, helpful guidance that somewhat shaped the structure of this book. I am grateful to Roland Page, now associated with Pennsylvania Governor Richard Thornburgh, for his objective and constructive criticism as well as for his friendship.

I would like to thank Joan Sanger, a fine, patient editor who allowed me great freedom, but deftly maintained newspaperlike deadlines to assure completion of this book. Her assistant, Jill Freeman, was likewise knowledgeable, helpful, prompt and equipped with kind words which I appreciated. I also am indebted to Morton Janklow and Arthur Klebanoff, agents of tremendous skill and honesty; and to William Safire, columnist for *The New York Times*, who sponsored me to them. A special thanks goes to Laura Foreman, a marvelously talented journalist who first interested Joan Sanger and Simon & Schuster in me and my idea for a book.

Finally, there is no adequate way to express my gratitude to my wife and best friend, Katie. She and Mandy and Matt made the sacrifices so that writing this book could be easier for me. I am profoundly grateful.

And to the late John Hemphill, who started it all, thanks.

Wendell Rawls, Jr.